AF361366

SOFT POWER
BEYOND
THE NATION

SOFT POWER BEYOND THE NATION

SYLVIA DUMMER SCHEEL,
CHARLOTTE FAUCHER, AND
CAMILA GATICA MIZALA, EDITORS

GEORGETOWN UNIVERSITY PRESS / WASHINGTON, DC

The publisher is not responsible for third-party websites or their content. URL links were active at time of publication.

Library of Congress Cataloging-in-Publication Data

Names: Dümmer Scheel, Sylvia, 1979- editor. | Faucher, Charlotte, 1988- editor. | Gatica Mizala, Camila, editor.
Title: Soft power beyond the nation / Sylvia Dümmer Scheel, Charlotte Faucher, and Camila Gatica Mizala, editors.
Description: Washington, DC : Georgetown University Press, 2024. | Includes bibliographical references and index.
Identifiers: LCCN 2023049294 (print) | LCCN 2023049295 (ebook) | ISBN 9781647124991 (paperback) | ISBN 9781647124984 (hardcover) | ISBN 9781647125004 (ebook)
Subjects: LCSH: Soft power (Political science) | International relations. | Cultural relations.
Classification: LCC JC330 .S633 2024 (print) | LCC JC330 (ebook) | DDC 327.1/1—dc23/eng/20240414

LC record available at https://lccn.loc.gov/2023049294
LC ebook record available at https://lccn.loc.gov/2023049295

∞ This paper meets the requirements of ANSI/NISO Z39.48-1992 (Permanence of Paper).

25 24   9 8 7 6 5 4 3 2   First printing

Printed in the United States of America

Cover design by Jeremy John Parker
Interior design by Westchester Publishing Services

CONTENTS

FOREWORD

I warmly welcome this collection of essays as part of a growing body of literature in the humanities engaging with the concept of "soft power." This book adds to our understanding in new and exciting ways. The papers are global and transnational in their sweep, adopt a distinctly historical perspective—which the editors rightly assert is relatively understudied—and seek to utilize not simply a top-down, power-centric approach but underline the importance of circulation, networks, and collaboration across national boundaries and over time. The case studies cover the *longue durée* from the eighteenth century onward and reveal how the widely held assumption that soft power became a global phenomenon only in contemporary times stands in need of correction. There is a consistent attempt to move away from a predominantly nation-state or national approach in understanding soft power strategies. The concept itself and its operation is shown to be flexible, subject to varying interpretations and adopted by a range of groups, not simply powerful or wealthy elites. Nor was its use limited to, or exclusively in, the realms of foreign policy that formed the context of Joseph S. Nye's original and landmark work. Chapters also explore the relationship between soft and hard power and soft power and propaganda, as well as concepts such as cultural diplomacy, and identify the Global South as a major site for the use and exploitation of such strategies. This collection should serve to encourage more detailed studies in this important field.

—Professor Chandrika Kaul
School of History
University of St Andrews

ACKNOWLEDGMENTS

We would like to thank our editor at Georgetown University Press, Donald Jacobs, and the two anonymous reviewers for their thoughtful comments and suggestions on the manuscript. This volume was born out of a series of workshops organized in 2020 and 2021, and we would like to thank the Pontificia Universidad Católica de Chile, the Universidad de Chile, and the University of Manchester for supporting these events. We are particularly thankful to the Agencia Nacional de Investigación y Desarrollo (ANID, Chile) for the funding that facilitated the live interpretation that allowed us to organize bilingual panels (projects Fondecyt 3200615 and 3190267). We would also like to thank the authors of the different chapters that make *Soft Power beyond the Nation* the book that it is.

None of the editors are native English speakers, so we are thankful for the time Chapman-Joy, James E. Connolly, Elspeth Dow, Craig Griffiths, Laure Humbert, Harry Stopes, and Andrea Yáñez Knaack took reading and commenting on various drafts of the project.

Sylvia Dummer Scheel acknowledges funding from the ANID-Fondecyt project number 3200615. Charlotte Faucher acknowledges funding from the European Commission's Horizon 2020 program (project INVCUL-TURALDIPLO–101022204). Camila Gatica Mizala is grateful to ANID-Fondecyt project number 3190267 and ANID-Fondecyt Iniciación project number 11241340 for its support.

Rethinking Soft Power in History

Transnational Circulation, Collaboration, and Identities

*Sylvia Dummer Scheel, Charlotte Faucher,
and Camila Gatica Mizala*

In June and July 1530 the sultan of the Ottoman Empire, Süleyman I (1520–66), held a twenty-day celebration to mark the circumcision of three Ottoman princes: Selīm, Meḥmed, and Muṣṭafā. The festivities in the Hippodrome brought together a cross-section of Constantinople society: ordinary citizens, as well as the sultan and political elites. The celebrations afforded Süleyman an opportunity to assert the power and prestige of his empire within the Ottoman world and beyond, in a context marked by fierce Habsburg-Ottoman rivalries. Both Ottoman and Venetian observers published lengthy, widely read accounts of the scenes.[1]

In 1832 Eugénie Allix, a schoolteacher, left her husband and daughter behind in rural France and set off for Algeria. At first, she barely made ends meet in Algiers, working as a laundress and giving private tuition, but by 1845 she had opened her own school aimed at Muslim girls. Allix hoped to "change native morals," introducing students to European culture so that they would "become our guarantee of the country's submission to our authority, as well as the unimpeachable pledge of its future assimilation." In mid-nineteenth-century Algiers, Allix (now Madame Luce) became a forceful champion of the French "civilizing mission" that targeted colonial subjects and served to assert French colonial power along racist lines.[2]

In 2012 the Indian government launched the Development Partnership Administration within its Ministry of External Affairs. Today India's humanitarian budget, averaging $40 million annually, is close to that of Luxembourg's. Thus, New Delhi has sought to show the rest of the world that India should not be perceived as a recipient of aid on the international stage—indeed it has been able to offer aid to neighboring South Asian countries and beyond. By projecting an image of the country as a humanitarian donor, the Indian government seeks to support its long-standing bid for permanent membership on the United Nations Security Council.[3]

In all three of these cases, states, rulers, or individuals sought to exert power in the international arena through attraction and persuasion rather than force. Even if they did not use the term, and indeed even if it is absent from the scholarship on these three cases, they were all seeking to exercise what we will call "soft power." As Nancy Snow points out, soft power is a new name for old habits.[4]

In this book we take a historical approach to soft power, while acknowledging that the term also matters in other disciplines. Here, we use it as a broad label to refer to the processes through which persuasion, the search for influence and power, and public opinion as an actor in foreign affairs converge in the international arena. The phrase was originally coined by American political scientist Joseph S. Nye in 1990 and refers to the ability of political, social, and intellectual actors to exert power abroad through attraction rather than coercion. In the conceptual framework that Nye developed, soft power is the counterpart of the more familiar "hard power," which encompasses military and economic power.[5] The relative absence of the term in historical studies, compared to its wide use in political science and international relations,[6] does not mean that these types of processes have been ignored by historians. Instead, they have explored soft power through other concepts, including public diplomacy,[7] cultural diplomacy,[8] propaganda,[9] and, for the medieval and early modern periods, under terms such as honor, reputation, and image.[10]

As this book shows, a historical approach to ideas and practices of soft power invites us to pay attention to aspects that international relations and political science scholarship has left aside. Insofar as these disciplines are overwhelmingly focused on the idea of power and the measurement of the phenomenon, the concept has been widely questioned.[11] Some scholars agree that it is difficult to establish causality between soft power policies and their results and even suggest that the very existence of soft power is debatable.[12] In contrast, historians consider that even if they cannot always determine the impact of soft power in the international arena, the mere *search for soft power* is a subject worthy of investigation. Historical actors across time have been deeply convinced that it is possible, and desirable, to influence the attitudes, beliefs, and values of foreign audiences in order to position their interests in the world; studying their efforts can help us to comprehend the ways in which individuals and groups have understood and implemented the different mechanisms to obtain power (successfully or not). A historical approach also enriches the understanding of the dynamics of soft power by providing a detailed study of particular cases instead of looking for universal patterns as other disciplines are more inclined to do. Historians understand that these cases are inseparable from their specific contexts and that the quest for soft power cannot be observed as an isolated element but instead one that intersects with other large historical social, political, and cultural processes. Colonization, decolonization, racial struggle, and the emergence of modern public opinion are examples of the latter. Historians also pay particular attention to the agency of groups and individuals who have their own needs, motivations, and skills. Certainly, historical studies of soft power are also enriched by the debates currently being held in political science and international relations, such as the relationship between soft and hard power and the unidirectional or bidirectional nature of soft power. These points of discussion inspire historical analysis and lead to richer and more complex understandings of the past.

Soft Power beyond the Nation continues to deepen the study of soft power in history by taking a distinct approach that enriches the ways in which both historical and international relations / political science scholars have looked at the concept. We move beyond the perspective from which soft power has often been approached: that of the nation-state. It is not only a matter of recognizing the role of nonstate actors seeking and using soft power but of understanding that even "national" soft power is mediated by actors, models, and identities that fall outside this framework. We propose that soft power ought to be studied through a transnational lens, looking at the flows and exchanges that occur across the porous borders of nations.[13] To this end, the book is based on three interconnected thematic lines of argument. First, it discusses the circulation of knowledge and strategies across borders in order to understand how various soft power models and narratives were transferred and appropriated from one country to another. Second, this edited collection pays attention to various forms of transnational collaboration. In particular, its contributors concentrate on intermediate agents of soft power who operated in national, transnational, and supranational contexts but also had their own interests and agendas. Third, the book argues for an assessment of the role of interests and loyalties that are motivated by belongings such as gender and the idea of race,[14] which do not necessarily align with the nation-state and yet play a role in the making of soft power strategies.

The book's key arguments invite us to go beyond a chronological and spatial frame that has been limited. Much of the work on soft power has focused on the Cold War period. Historians who began working on the "cultural Cold War" at the turn of the millennium found soft power to be a fruitful concept with which to study the ambitions of, and tensions between, both the Western and Eastern blocs as well as their satellite states.[15] This period of world history witnessed the extraordinary rise of institutions, organizations, and governmental offices in charge of developing a cultural or public diplomacy. However, a growing number of historians warn against a chronologically narrow approach to soft power,[16] with some cautioning that it has led the conversation to take place "in something of a historical vacuum."[17] Thus, some of the chapters delve into periods that have only been minimally considered to date through the lens of soft power. In doing so, they establish a dialogue with scholars who have turned their attention to early modernity,[18] the Age of Revolutions,[19] the nineteenth century,[20] and the first half of the twentieth century,[21] for example. While historical research on soft power is ongoing, it is important to fully appreciate how strategies of influence were used and changed over a longer *and* earlier period.

PERICENTRIC SOFT POWER

Soft Power beyond the Nation argues that the pursuit of soft power was a global phenomenon in which a far wider range of nations and groups were early participants than the US and European models tend to present. To explore this theme, some chapters in the book delve into the experiences of groups and countries that scholars have tended to dismiss as minor players of international relations. In particular, we are interested in so-called peripheral countries—with the understanding that ideas of periphery change over time and according to different contexts. We open up the geographical scope of studies in soft power to escape US- and Eurocentrism, which looks toward models of ideas and political constructions (such as the nation-state) that reflect only a limited experience.[22] Thus, the book makes visible the uses of public diplomacy and propaganda by regions that have been neglected in the general debates on the subject, such as Africa, Asia, and Latin America.

Historical studies of soft power have largely been limited in terms of geographical coverage, in part because of the aforementioned focus on the cultural Cold War and the US-USSR rivalry. By the 2010s several authors had noted how this focus on the United States had narrowed the analysis of global soft power.[23] Since then, studies have diversified in time and space. In the past ten years, the rest of Europe and the countries of Asia—especially China—have received much attention.[24]

In spite of this welcome development, scholars still shy away from discussing peripheral countries as agents (rather than recipients or targets) of soft power.[25] Not only have these regions been less studied, but the case studies that emerge are also often relegated to the realm of local historiographies or "area studies." Separating these strands of scholarship can lead to limited understandings of soft power. First, it wrongly suggests that the search for soft power is a practice that has only become globalized in recent years. Indeed, many scholars of current public diplomacy judge that countries in Africa, Asia, and Latin America have only been considering what soft power might bring to their international relations since the beginning of the new millennium. Philip Fiske de Gouveia, for example, talks of "newcomers to public diplomacy" in reference to China—which today is a powerful player of soft power but once a peripheral actor in the field—and other, small countries.[26] Jan Melissen, meanwhile, refers to the "slowly growing interest in the Global South" in public diplomacy and argues that during the Cold War this field of foreign affairs was not a central concern in the "poverty-stricken parts of the world."[27] All these assertions overlook a much longer history of soft power practices in this large part of the world—for example, the cultural diplomacy work exercised by China in the 1960s and the intense public diplomacy that countries such as Mexico, Iran, and Hungary were already developing in the 1920s.[28]

Second, geographical narrowness also obscures the understanding of soft power models. Jessica C. E. Gienow-Hecht and Mark C. Donfried have shown, citing Freeman M. Touvell's analysis,[29] that European countries' practices of cultural diplomacy differed not only from the US model but also from each other in terms of their motivations, agents, resources, techniques, and contents. In their volume they explain why it is necessary to move away from the US model of cultural diplomacy in order to make space for a wider range of understanding.[30] Thus, our definition of soft power becomes broader and more nuanced when we also take into account the history and contemporary situation of soft power in peripheral countries, integrating diverse cultural paradigms of public diplomacy into our research.[31]

Third, a narrow geographic focus has also affected the discussion about the concept of soft power itself. One of the most interesting debates within the soft power framework concerns its relationship with hard power as well as other intermediate concepts such as "smart" and "sticky power."[32] Although in his initial definition Nye posited soft power as a strategy distinct—albeit complementary—from hard power, other scholars suggest that the two are interdependent. They consider that the very success of soft power depends on the resources deployed in support (including infrastructure and communication technologies), which rely on economic power and even on the coercive use of international communication channels.[33] For this reason, Ludovic Tournès argues there is nothing "soft" about soft power.[34] While these conclusions are significant in highlighting the complex nature of power in international relations, they tend to be based only on the case of hegemonic countries. However, there are several examples of countries that use the techniques of public diplomacy not to sweeten the pill of their militarily, politically, and economically coercive behavior but to survive and assert themselves in an unequal power relationship.[35] For such countries, but also for many sub- and transnational groups, soft power was the only available form of power in the international arena. Gaining support among foreign public opinion protected them—to some extent—from the coercive or interventionist policies of those who possessed hard power, or it allowed them to enhance their situation by attracting tourists, investors, and collaborators.[36] Thus, counting these nations among those who sought, and sometimes exerted, soft power allows us to suggest that soft power can also be an act of empowerment in asymmetrical contexts or even an act of resistance. Several chapters in this book address the topic from this perspective. The authors look at soft power carried out by the governments of Ghana, Senegal, and Mexico and analyze the efforts implemented by Afro-American groups against racism in the United States. The public diplomacy of China and Japan, which were once peripheral countries in the field of soft power, are analyzed as key players in this area of foreign affairs.

Thus, we call for a geographically decentered approach to the study of soft power. We propose to incorporate into this field the notion of pericentrism, a term coined by Tony Smith to understand the global processes of the Cold War, which focuses on the agency of small countries in influencing global dynamics.[37] In the book, we not only observe the active participation of these countries as agents of soft power but also in their creation of alliances and links that remained outside the ascendency of the great centers of power. In the period that we consider, public diplomacy strategies circulated and networks operated within what some call the "Global South."[38] These structures had their own dynamics and objectives, such as empowering regional leaderships, forming regional alliances, and influencing local conflicts.[39] In short, in order to grasp the complex patterns and dynamics of soft power in modern history, it is essential to study it as a global transnational phenomenon that necessarily connects all nations, not only those that have received the most attention in the dominant historiography. To understand these processes, some chapters of this book observe the configuration of soft power in South-South relationships, such as Pan-African or Sino-Latin American networks.

CIRCULATIONS

This book invites us to understand soft power beyond national allegiances and does so by delving into three central themes discussed in the present and following sections: "circulation," "collaboration and intermediate agents," and "identities." Each chapter of the volume discusses one or more of these themes.

The first theme is the transnational circulation of knowledge and soft power models.[40] At different times, soft power strategies have circulated rapidly across borders, allowing propaganda and public diplomacy techniques to be learned, replicated, and adapted by the countries that receive them. For example, during World War I, Mexico was one of the main propaganda targets of the Committee on Public Information (CPI), the US propaganda agency, which opened offices and implemented many of its strategies in Mexico City. After the war the US government put an end to propaganda policies toward Mexico, but by this time the Mexican governments of the interwar period had learned to use the techniques of the CPI to position their interests before US public opinion.[41]

The transnational circulation of strategies and instruments for exercising soft power and their consequent implementation by various countries have sometimes led to the emergence of standardized models. Already in seventeenth-century Europe, a certain type of multilingual pamphlet became a genre of public diplomacy with its own rules and language, after being used repeatedly by representatives of various countries who drew inspiration from each other.[42] Strategies and tools developed in the following centuries continued to rapidly expand globally. In the first decades of the twentieth century, the USSR, China, the United States, France, Mexico, and Germany relied on similar soft power instruments, such as media management, student diplomacy, and invitations bestowed upon foreign intellectuals.[43]

However, all appropriation implies transformation.[44] Public diplomacy models were adapted to the needs and resources of each country or organization that promoted them, and they were also influenced by different cultural paradigms. Therefore, it is relevant to explore how the transnational circulation of soft power techniques has operated in the past and to analyze the limits and possibilities of the transferability of such models in diverse scenarios in terms of culture, resources, and power. In her chapter, Rui Kohi-yama explores the circulation of soft power techniques toward and within Japan. She examines the influence of late-nineteenth-century foreign Christian missions on practices that were then incorporated by Japanese state and nonstate actors into part of the nation's soft power. The central case study is an analysis of the origins of Karuizawa, a well-known summer resort in Japan that was first developed by Protestant missionaries from the United States in the 1880s. This site of missionary soft power was important for helping missionaries introduce "innocent" entertainment and leisure practices such as tennis, music, and concerts to the Japanese population. This "civilizing" mission aimed to replace traditional and popular Japanese equivalents such as bathing in hot springs, drinking parties, and consorting with geishas. The chapter argues that the Japanese gender- and leisure-based approach to soft power progressively shifted in the early twentieth century toward embracing moral elements of entertainment first introduced by Protestant missions. It examines how the Japanese nation created a new pattern of soft power that served as a blueprint for contemporary practices. This transnational analysis shows that foreign missionary activities in Japan contributed to a new con-struction of *omotenashi* (hospitality) that gradually became a central tenet of Japanese culture and soft power during the twentieth century. The chapter is an example of how a tradition promoted to foreigners as "national" can draw from foreign sources. A similar process is observed in Kelly R. Colvin's con-tribution (later discussed in detail) where the conversion of Brigitte Bardot into an icon of French femininity was initially propitiated by American film critics and publicists and then appropriated by the French state.

Drew Flanagan, for his part, analyzes the circulation of colonial ideology and soft power practices from one context to the other by focusing on the writings and cultural activities of French folklorist, orientalist, and propa-gandist Robert Boutet in the protectorate of Morocco (1931–45) and the French zone of occupation in defeated Germany (1945–55). In both sce-narios, Boutet used folklore as a vector of soft power. Two of his stories, "Le voleur de lumière" (1942) and "Der Seezwerg" (1947), reveal how he adapted "civilizing" practices developed in North Africa to the problem of democratic reeducation in postwar Germany. Central to these publications was Boutet's ambition to employ an ethnographic knowledge of both indig-enous cultures to influence the thinking of young readers about France. In his work, Boutet identified Frenchness with rationality, "a sense of progress," and the light of a "revealed religion"—antidotes to the Moroccan and Ger-man cultures' "superstition," "irrationality," and "backwardness." Thus, Bou-tet's stories demonstrate how postwar and Cold War soft power practices were rooted in nineteenth-century French colonial thinking about its "civilizing" mission. Ultimately, in dialogue with recent scholarship, this prompts the reader to consider the entanglement between the categories of "colonial history" and "European history."[45]

Coline Desportes's chapter also addresses the appropriation of foreign soft power models, by looking at how recently independent Senegal sought to use the arts and exhibitions to assert its place in the world. Part of Senegalese cultural diplomacy replicated France's model of using major art exhibitions to promote the nation overseas, which the French government had institutionalized through the Association Française d'Action Artistique, created in 1922.[46] Racist and imperialist ideas meant that many French officials considered that countries such as Senegal should receive and host exhibitions of reproductions rather than original works of art, as was French policy in most of the world. As Desportes shows, the first Senegalese president, the poet and politician Léopold Sédar Senghor, had other, loftier plans for his new nation. While he welcomed French plans to organize exhibitions in Senegal, he influenced the model of soft power designed from Paris, demanding to host exhibitions of original pieces from the School of Paris, based on the model of those France usually reserved for the Global North. Thus, Desportes suggests that "Senghor wanted to project abroad the image of a modern country, capable of digesting and appropriating the modernist discourse."

COLLABORATION AND INTERMEDIATE AGENTS

A second theme of this book is transnational collaboration. "National" soft power is often defined in essentially competitive terms as countries act in their national interest and compete with each other for trade, tourism, political influence, and goodwill.[47] Meanwhile, researchers who approach collaboration linked to soft power do so by looking at multilateral or supranational alliances—in organizations such as the European Union and the United Nations—where different nations pursue similar objectives.[48] However, these analyses look at collaboration only at the level of soft power sponsors, ignoring other forms of collaboration that permeate the dynamics of public diplomacy. In fact, soft power relies to a large extent on the collaboration of a series of intermediate agents such as ambassadors, advertising commissioners, movie stars, artists, migrants, tourists, and exchange students, who stand between the sponsor and the final recipient. Aware or not of their role, paid or voluntary, nationals or foreigners, these individuals move in this transnational space and convey the message of public diplomacy in what Maria Montt Strabucchi has called in this book "nonlinear cultural diplomacy."[49]

To understand the scope and shape of these dynamics of collaboration, it is necessary to examine the motivations of people who participated in soft power initiatives. Such motivations ranged from a convergence of objectives to win-win alliances in which each party satisfied different interests.[50] In fulfilling their role, intermediate agents responded not only to the interests of soft power agents but also to their own motivations and personal perceptions, which were not always aligned with the principal sponsor(s). Thus, the message sent by the sponsors can be reinterpreted, modified, or even resisted in this intermediate space, affecting the way it was received by the final recipients. Although the state-centric model of soft power is often seen as hierarchical and top-down, it is important to recognize that governments did not have complete control over intermediate agents, who also have agency in the implementation of soft power strategies.

Different chapters of this book delve into the role and interests of these intermediate agents. Cyril Cordoba discusses the central part played by Chinese friendship associations scattered throughout the world in upholding Beijing's soft power strategies from 1949 to 1989. His chapter focuses on these intermediaries between the source and the target of Chinese soft power, arguing that the "people-to-people" diplomacy that Beijing deployed was in fact the expression of a transnational clientelist system in which friendship associations obtained numerous benefits from the Chinese state that resulted in an absolute fidelity to the Chinese Communist Party.

Maria Montt Strabucchi explores the agency of Latin American intellectuals who were invited to visit the People's Republic of China (PRC) during the Cold War. She analyzes the case of Tomás Lago, a Chilean national who, upon his return from China in the early 1960s, projected images of "revolutionary" and "essentialist" China while simultaneously challenging stereotypes about the country. By focusing on what Latin American visitors were allowed to see of Maoist China and how they behaved after they returned to the Americas, the chapter suggests that foreign visitors were part of a "nonlinear cultural diplomacy" set up by the PRC, whereby soft power was articulated through reflections and in fragments rather than through a top-down approach. Visitors, this chapter argues, were not passive recipients of the PRC's policies.

Claire Nicolas explores Ghanaian table tennis policies in the 1960s to understand sports diplomacy as it stood at the crossroads of government-sponsored diplomacy and unofficial agents such as sportsmen and sportswomen. Through table tennis, benevolent images of Third Worldism and Pan-Africanist cooperation were designed by the newly independent Ghanaian government and were directed toward Ghanaian citizens as well as allied countries through dedicated institutions, tours, and international championships. Nicolas shows that Ghana framed athletes as informal ambassadors, in which role they were carefully monitored by politicians, journalists, and sports administrators who supervised not only their achievements but also their behavior and the impression they gave of the country to foreign audiences.

The chapter by Sylvia Dummer Scheel analyzes the dual role of diasporic publics both as recipients and potential collaborators of public diplomacy in the context of Mexico's foreign propaganda in the 1930s. She argues that although emigrants are often seen as agents of soft power toward the host country, they are not always equally useful to the governments of their country of origin. In the case studied, the low educational level of most Mexican immigrants in the United States and their poor assimilation into local culture limited their possibilities for exerting influence in that country, while educated and influential Mexicans in the US were generally opposed to the postrevolutionary government of Lázaro Cárdenas. Faced with this situation, the Mexican government did not approach diasporic communities as transnational actors that could mediate between the two cultures but as domestic audiences on foreign soil. The public diplomacy that the Mexican State directed toward these communities reproduced the contents of domestic propaganda, causing tensions with the soft power that the Ministry of Foreign Affairs was simultaneously directing toward US public opinion. Thus, she concludes that public diplomacy toward diasporas not only has the potential to strengthen soft power but also to weaken it.

Collaboration is also a theme adjacent to some chapters of the book that are discussed in the other thematic sections. For example, Meredith Roman analyzes the convergence of two soft power strategies—those of the USSR and African American groups—beginning with the so-called Scottsboro campaign of 1931–32. Through it, the USSR sought to win the support of Black Americans for communism, while African American groups took advantage of this backing to denounce internationally the racist violence that existed in the United States. Roman argues that such collaboration reveals the "circular nature" of soft power politics. The author also analyzes the role of African Americans such as Langston Hughes and Ada Wright, who traveled to the USSR as "intermediary agents" of Soviet soft power and who later wrote articles or gave statements about the country. The chapter concludes powerfully that their collaboration was not homogeneous, especially when divergences with USSR politics arose: while some African Americans chose to continue with the alliance where they saw it serving their own interests, others were not willing to defend the Soviet Union unconditionally. Coline Desportes, meanwhile, discusses how the Senegalese government in the 1960s and 1970s sought to rely on the French government for its cultural diplomacy. The author acknowledges that there was a lack of commitment on the part of the French authorities, which was balanced by the collaboration of nongovernmental actors such as French artists and gallery owners. This did not, however, prevent tensions and mistrust from arising between the two sides due to differing national interests. Finally, Michael L. Krenn explores the transnational collaboration that various actors in the Western academic world sustained in order to reaffirm the supranational hegemony of an entire conglomerate of countries based on racial prejudice.

IDENTITIES

A third theme explored in this volume is the role of nonnational identities in shaping and implementing soft power strategies. This approach sharpens our understanding of the workings of soft power because it allows us to consider the role in soft power of belongings linked to class, race, ethnicity, and intellectual or political ideas, which emerged beyond and below the nation-state in both imperial and nonimperial contexts.

The volume concentrates on a period that witnessed the expansion of soft power alongside fundamental changes in gender and race relations, together with the rise of new politics of identities. Discourses and practices of soft power were profoundly affected by identity norms, hierarchies, and representation. For postmodernist theorists such as Judith Butler and Paul Ricoeur, identity is constructed through language and representation, whether material, visual, or symbolic. It is also within the public sphere that much diplomatic strategy takes form, through newspapers, films, and posters, for example.[51] In this volume, some authors thus consider how and why some agents utilized gendered and racialized identities in the international arena.

Academic publications on identities in international relations are growing in number and have so far largely focused on gender and race.[52] They have allowed historians to challenge essentialist approaches to diplomacy and to examine how identities operate in the policymaking process (production of policy, its content, and its target audiences). Despite the growing attention to identities in international relations, the field of soft power has yet to integrate these discussions. Certainly, some important groundwork has been done in relation to gender,[53] and there are even proposals that invite us to rethink the very notion of soft power from a feminist perspective.[54] Historians, meanwhile, have paid attention to the role of women in developing and carrying out policies of soft power, through the example of female missionaries in the European "civilizing" missions and in the making of French and Latin American cultural diplomacy.[55] There are also historical studies that examine the visions of gender roles underlying certain soft power strategies.[56] Others, more along the lines of what this book proposes, have addressed the intersection between gender and the projection of national identities—for example, with the construction of a sexualized image of Brazil in the 1930s and 1940s based on the triumph of the actress Carmen Miranda in Hollywood and the international publicity about the extension of women's rights in Turkey in the 1930s, part of the effort of the government in Ankara to present Turkey as a modern nation.[57] Gender has also been important to the intersectional ways scholars have begun thinking about race and soft power. They have done this through an examination of white feminine beauty as an element of soft power. In the context of East Asian cinema, whiteness and the Western build of actors and actresses have left their marks on the capacity of films to serve as elements of soft power.[58] In the French context too, the whiteness and beauty of icons shaped the cinema industry in the postwar period, as Kelly R. Colvin shows in her chapter. Race was also pivotal in shaping scientific discussions in the Western world, as outlined in Michael L. Krenn's chapter. Beyond this volume, Krenn has played a key role in thinking about race in the scholarship of US soft power.[59]

The central arguments formulated in these chapters are twofold. First, communities that united through nonnational affiliations, including those of race, politics, and intellectual belief, were also at the origin of strategies of soft power. For example, in the 1930s African Americans sought to use communication strategies and media to make their views heard on the international stage. Second, governments also used gender and racial identities when reinforcing national soft power. The chapters in this volume include the study of remarkable individuals (such as actresses) as well as transnational communities and their broader networks (such as antiracist activists from the US). These groups' identities rarely aligned with those of the nations or empires in which they found themselves, and yet they were instrumentalized by supposedly "national" discourses. As the contributors argue, these communities' constructions and narrations of identities shaped and were shaped by soft power politics, with significant political ramifications throughout the world.

Some chapters focus mainly on the relationship between soft power and racial identities, such as the chapter by Michael L. Krenn, which examines a striking network of scientists in the United States and Europe during the nineteenth century. These men led a multination campaign to define humanity that served their personal prestige and the interests of their nations but also the larger collective interests of the nations of Western Europe and the United States in pursuing their goals of colonialism, territorial expansion, and slavery. The aforementioned chapter by Meredith L. Roman also explores the role of racial and political affiliations in public diplomacy by showing how a community that was oppressed in its national context exercised agency by resorting to soft power techniques. In the 1930s a number of African Americans used their alliance with the USSR not only to advance their own political and civil rights goals in the face of intransigence on the part of their own country's government but also to encourage fellow Blacks to imagine a world beyond racial apartheid, thus bolstering the African American community. At the same time, by delving into the USSR's political use of racism, the chapter shows how national soft power strategies deployed or responded to racialized discourses. For the USSR, portraying itself as a champion of antiracism was also a means of undermining the democratic image that the US sought to promote abroad and at home. Race plays an important role as well in how Colline Desportes approaches postindependence Senegalese soft power. Her chapter focuses on Senghor and his project of *Négritude*, which called for the exaltation of "the values of the black world" and which served as his framework for cultural policy. Desportes also links policies of soft power with domestic aims, including Senghor's ambition to uphold a "Pan-Africanist and afrocentric vision providing evidence of the unity and long history of 'Black civilization.'"

Other chapters delve into the crossover between soft power and gender. In "The Soft Power of Brigitte Bardot," Kelly R. Colvin, exposes how gender operated in the service of a national soft power. She writes about the French actress Brigitte Bardot, whose body and persona became a cultural ambassador for a purported superior French femininity and was even transformed by French authorities into a representation of the republican symbol Marianne. Innovatively, this chapter argues that in postwar France the cultural joined with the political and economic in the physical form of Bardot, who formed a crucial component of France's soft power–based campaign to combat perceptions that France was economically and imperially weak at the end of the war. Meanwhile, in her exploration of hybrid Japanese soft power, Rui Kohiyama reflects on how both missionaries and Japanese actors sought to police entertainment of a sexual nature (with the presence of geishas common in

many Japanese resorts), understanding that conforming to Christian morality could boost Japan's reputation in the eyes of foreigners and support the
development of the tourist economy.

The chapters of *Soft Power beyond the Nation* follow a chronological order rather
than a thematic one because, as shown in this introduction, most of them do not
fit into just one of the proposed axes but are in dialogue with more than one.
These contributions deal with soft power tools as varied as folklore and legends,
art, sports, the press, the construction of "scientific" knowledge, leisure practices, and female figures. Together they help to construct a global and pericentric
approach to soft power in the history of the past two centuries. They demystify
the ideas of soft power as something recent and as a resource associated only
with powerful countries by showing an early globalization in which nations and
groups that lacked hard power also made particular use of these tools to empower
themselves internationally. Moreover, the studies presented here account for an
intermediate space between sponsors of soft power and its recipients, where
diverse transnational actors conveyed their messages but also resisted, altered, or
subverted them. Finally, the chapters in this volume recognize the transnational
transfer of models and the crossover with nonnational identities, contributing to
an understanding of soft power that goes beyond national loyalties and frontiers.
In doing so, they offer a productive road map for future work in the study of soft
power.

NOTES

The authors would like to thank the two anonymous reviewers for their thoughtful
comments and suggestions. Sylvia Dummer Scheel acknowledges funding from the
ANID-Fondecyt project number 3200615. Charlotte Faucher acknowledges funding
from Horizon 2020 for the INVCULTURALDIPLO—101022204. Camila Gatica
Mizala is grateful to ANID-Fondecyt project number 3190267 for their support.

1. Kaya Şahin, "Staging an Empire: An Ottoman Circumcision Ceremony as Cultural Performance," *American Historical Review* 123, no. 2 (April 1, 2018): 463–92.
2. Rebecca Rogers, *A Frenchwoman's Imperial Story: Madame Luce in Nineteenth-Century
   Algeria* (Stanford, CA: Stanford University Press, 2013), 66.
3. "From Aid to Partnerships: India's Humanitarian Assistance," International Committee of the Red Cross, November 24, 2014, https://www.icrc.org/en/document/aid
   -partnerships-indias-humanitarian-assistance; "India as a Humanitarian Donor in the
   21st Century: The Seeds of a More Ambitious Role," Active Learning Network for
   Accountability and Performance, April 5, 2013, https://www.alnap.org/help-library
   /india-as-a-humanitarian-donor-in-the-21st-century-the-seeds-of-a-more-ambitious
   -role.

4. Nancy Snow, "Rethinking Public Diplomacy," in *Routledge Handbook of Public Diplomacy*, ed. Nancy Snow and Phillip M. Taylor (New York: Routledge, 2008), 4.

5. Joseph S. Nye, *Soft Power: The Means to Success in World Politics* (New York: Public Affairs, 2004), x.

6. Naren Chitty, Lilian Ji, and Gary D Rawnsley, eds., *The Routledge Handbook of Soft Power* (Abingdon, UK: Routledge, 2020); Hendrik W. Ohnesorge, *Soft Power: The Forces of Attraction in International Relations* (Cham, Switz.: Springer International, 2020).

7. Olga Lebedeva, "Russia Public Diplomacy: Historical Aspects," in *Russia's Public Diplomacy Evolution and Practice*, ed. Anna A. Velikaya and Greg Simon (Cham, Switz.: Palgrave Macmillan, 2020), 27–44; Bahar Rumelili, Senem Aydın-Düzgit, and Seçkin Barış Gülmez, "Gendering Public Diplomacy: Turkey and Europe in the 1930s," *Journal of Balkan and Near Eastern Studies* 25, no. 2 (March 4, 2023): 239–56, https://doi.org/10.1080/19448953.2022.2143778; Sylvia Dummer Scheel, "¿De quién es la diplomacia pública? El rol del Departamento Autónomo de Prensa y Publicidad (DAPP) en la propaganda exterior cardenista," *Estudios de Historia Moderna y Contemporánea de México*, no. 55 (2018): 279–312; Kenneth Alan Osgood and Brian Craig Etheridge, eds., *The United States and Public Diplomacy: New Directions in Cultural and International History*, Diplomatic Studies (Leiden: Brill, 2010); Sarah Ellen Graham, *Culture and Propaganda: The Progressive Origins of American Public Diplomacy, 1936–1953* (Farnham, UK: Ashgate, 2015).

8. Jessica C. E. Gienow-Hecht, "What Are We Searching For? Culture, Diplomacy, Agents and the State," in *Searching for a Cultural Diplomacy*, ed. Jessica C. E. Gienow-Hecht and Mark C. Donfried (New York; Oxford: Berghahn Books, 2010), 3–12; Benjamin G. Martin and Elisabeth Marie Piller, "Cultural Diplomacy and Europe's Twenty Years' Crisis, 1919–1939: Introduction," *Contemporary European History* 30, no. 2 (May 2021): 149–63; Michael David-Fox, *Showcasing the Great Experiment: Cultural Diplomacy and Western Visitors to Soviet Union, 1921–1941* (Oxford: Oxford University Press, 2012); Mary Niles Maack, "Books and Libraries as Instruments of Cultural Diplomacy in Francophone Africa during the Cold War," *Libraries and Culture* 36, no. 1 (February 1, 2001): 58–86; Juliette Dumont, *Diplomaties culturelles et fabrique des identités: Argentine, Brésil, Chili (1919–1946)* (Rennes: Presses Universitaires de Rennes, 2018); Dafne Cruz Porchini, *Arte, propaganda y diplomacia cultural a finales del cardenismo, 1937–1940* (Mexico City: Secretaría de Relaciones Exteriores, Dirección General del Acervo Histórico Diplomatico, 2016); Joseph Mayi, *La diplomatie culturelle de la France au cœur des enjeux de coopération en Afrique: Le cas du Cameroun* (Paris: Les Éditions du NET, 2021).

9. Philip M. Taylor, *Munitions of the Mind: A History of Propaganda from the Ancient World to the Present Era*, 3rd ed. (Manchester: Manchester University Press, 2013); John A. Britton, "Propaganda, Property, and the Image of Stability: The Mexican Government and the US Print Media, 1921–1929," *Secolas Annals* 19 (March 1988); Kátia Falcão, *A propaganda na Era Vargas: A propaganda oficial (1930–1945) de um regime que saiu da vida e entrou para história* (Niterói, Brazil: Editora Itapuca, 2018); Sandrine Lemaire, Pascal Blanchard, Nicolas Bancel, Alain Mabanckou, and Dominic Thomas, *Colonisation et propagande: Le pouvoir de l'image* (Paris: Cherche Midi, 2022); David Brandenberger, *Propaganda State in Crisis: Soviet Ideology, Indoctrination, and Terror under Stalin, 1927–1941* (New Haven, CT: Yale University Press, 2011).

10. Helmer Helmers, "Public Diplomacy in Early Modern Europe: Towards a New History of News," *Media History* 22, nos. 3–4 (October 2016): 401–20.

11. The concept has been criticized for being a term that brings nothing new to the table, for being irrelevant and inconsistent, for lacking a solid theoretical framework, and for not defining the notion of power on which he bases his concept, as well as for being constructed solely on the basis of the United States' case. See Ilan Manor and Guy J. Golan, "The Irrelevance of Soft Power," *E-International Relations* (blog), October 19, 2020, https://www.e-ir.info/2020/10/19/the-irrelevance-of-soft-power/; Margaret Seymour, "The Problem with Soft Power," *Foreign Policy Research Institute* (blog), September 14, 2020, https://www.fpri.org/article/2020/09/the-problem-with-soft-power/; Melissa Nisbett, "Who Holds the Power in Soft Power?," *Arts and International Affairs* 1, no. 1 (2016); and Ien Ang, Yudhishthir Raj Isar, and Phillip Mar, "Cultural Diplomacy: Beyond the National Interest?," *International Journal of Cultural Policy* 21, no. 4 (August 8, 2015): 365–81.

12. Christopher Layne, "The Unbearable Lightness of Soft Power," in *Soft Power and US Foreign Policy: Theoretical, Historical, and Contemporary Perspectives*, ed. Inderjeet Parmar and Michael Cox (London; New York: Routledge, 2010): 51–82; Nisbett, "Who Holds the Power in Soft Power?"; Ang, Isar, and Mar, "Cultural Diplomacy."

13. In recent years there has been an increase in soft power studies that take a transnational approach, such as Martin and Piller, "Cultural Diplomacy and Europe's Twenty Years' Crisis." The work by Elisabet Carbó-Catalan and Diana Roig-Sanz has also opened up the scope by looking at soft power and the role of culture from an interdisciplinary approach that allows us to understand the intersection of culture, politics, and international relations from a more integrated perspective. Elisabet Carbó-Catalan and Diana Roig Sanz, eds., *Culture as Soft Power: Bridging Cultural Relations, Intellectual Cooperation, and Cultural Diplomacy* (Berlin: De Gruyter, 2022).

14. We understand the term "race" as a social and politically constructed category.

15. See, e.g., Jennifer Louise Anderson, *Propaganda and Persuasion in the Cold War: The Canadian Soviet Friendship Society, 1949–1960* (Winnipeg: University of Manitoba Press, 2017); Greg Barnhisel, *Cold War Modernists: Art, Literature, and American Cultural Diplomacy* (New York: Columbia University Press, 2015); Stéphanie Gonçalves, "Dance as a Tool for Cultural Diplomacy in the Cold War: Bolshoï and Kirov Ballets in Paris and London, 1954–1968," in *East-West Cultural Relations Exchanges in the Cold War*, ed. Simo Mikkonnen (Farnham, UK: Ashgate, 2014).

16. Jessica C. E. Gienow-Hecht, "'How Good Are We?' Culture and the Cold War," in *The Cultural Cold War in Western Europe, 1945–60*, ed. Hans Krabbendam and Giles Scott-Smith, (London: Frank Cass, 2003), 269–82; Charlotte Faucher, "Cultural Diplomacy and International Cultural Relations in Twentieth-Century Europe," in special issue "Agents of Internationalism," *Contemporary European History* 25, no. 2 (May 2016): 373–85; Martin and Piller, "Cultural Diplomacy and Europe's Twenty Years' Crisis"; Chandrika Kaul, *Reporting the Raj* (Manchester: Manchester University Press, 2017), 119–34.

17. Kenneth A. Osgood and Brian C. Etheridge, "Introduction: The New International History Meets the New Cultural History; Public Diplomacy and U.S. Foreign Relations," in Osgood and Etheridge, *United States and Public Diplomacy*, 6.

18. Helmers, "Public Diplomacy in Early Modern Europe."

19. Rahul Markovits, *Civiliser l'Europe: Politiques du théâtre français au XVIIIe siècle* (Paris: Fayard, 2014).

20. See, e.g., Frank Lorenz Müller and Heidi Mehrkens, *Royal Heirs and the Uses of Soft Power in Nineteenth-Century Europe* (London: Palgrave Macmillan, 2016).

21. Stephen G. Gross, *Export Empire: German Soft Power in Southeastern Europe, 1890–1945* (Cambridge: Cambridge University Press, 2015); Martin and Piller, "Cultural Diplomacy and Europe's Twenty Years' Crisis."

22. Dipesh Chakrabarty, *Provincializing Europe: Postcolonial Thought and Historical Difference* (Princeton, NJ: Princeton University Press, 2008), 38–42.

23. Osgood and Etheridge, "Introduction: The New International History Meets the New Cultural History," 5; Gienow-Hecht, "'How Good Are We?'"; Faucher, "Cultural Diplomacy and International Cultural Relations"; Martin and Piller, "Cultural Diplomacy and Europe's Twenty Years' Crisis."

24. Kenneth King, *China's Aid and Soft Power in Africa: The Case of Education and Training*, African Issues (Woodbridge, UK: Boydell & Brewer, 2013); Guozuo Zhang, *Research Outline for China's Cultural Soft Power* (Singapore: Springer Singapore, 2016); Chandrika Kaul, "'The Meek Ass between Two Burdens?'": The BBC and India during the Second World War," in *Allied Communication to the Public during the Second World War: National and Transnational Networks*, ed. Simon Eliot and Marc Wiggam (London: Bloomsbury Academic, 2020), 203–22.

25. Some interesting exceptions are S. J. Timothy-Asobele, *Nigerian Cultural Diplomacy in the Twentieth Century* (Lagos: Promocomms, 2001); Héctor Perla Jr., "Transnational Public Diplomacy: Assessing Salvadoran Revolutionary Efforts to Build U.S. Public Opposition to Reagan's Central American Policy," in Osgood and Etheridge, *United States and Public Diplomacy*.

26. Philip Fiske de Gouveia, "The Future of Public Diplomacy," in *The Present and Future of the Public Diplomacy: A European Perspective; The 2006 Madrid Conference on Public Democracy* (Madrid: Real Instituto El Cano, November 2006), 6–8.

27. Jan Melissen, "The New Public Diplomacy: Between Theory and Practice," in *The New Public Diplomacy: Soft Power in International Relations*, ed. Jan Melissen (New York: Palgrave Macmillan, 2005), 10.

28. Jeremy Scott Friedman, *Shadow Cold War: The Sino-Soviet Competition for the Third World* (Chapel Hill: University of North Carolina Press, 2015); Alejandro Ugalde, "Las exposiciones de arte mexicano y las campañas pro México en Estados Unidos, 1922–1940," in *La mirada mirada: Transculturalidad e imaginarios del México revolucionario, 1910–1945*, ed. Alicia Azuela and Guillermo Palacios (Mexico City: El Colegio de México; Universidad Nacional Autónoma de México, 2009), 267–97; Pablo Yankelevich, "En la retaguardia de la Revolución Mexicana: Propaganda y propagandistas mexicanos en América Latina; 1914–1920," *Boletín Americanista* no. 49 (January 1999): 245–78. (http://www.raco.cat/index.php/BoletinAmericanista /article/view/98828); Martha Strauss Neuman, *El reconocimiento de Alvaro Obregón: Opinión americana y propaganda mexicana* (Mexico City: Universidad Nacional Autónoma de México, 1983); Sylvia Dummer Scheel, 'En defensa de la Revolución: Diplomacia pública de México hacia Estados Unidos bajo el gobierno de Lázaro Cárdenas (1934–1940)" (PhD diss., Freie Universität Berlin, 2015); Camron Michael Amin, "The Press and Public Diplomacy in Iran, 1820–1940," *Iranian Studies* 48, no. 2 (March 2015): 269–87; Zsolt Nagy, *Great Expectations and Interwar Realities: Hungarian Cultural Diplomacy, 1918–1941* (Budapest: Central European University Press, 2017).

29. Freeman M. Tovell, "A Comparison of Canadian, French, British, and German International Cultural Policies," in *Canadian Culture: International Dimensions*, ed. Andrew Fenton Cooper (Toronto/Waterloo: Canadian Institute of International Affairs and Centre on Foreign Policy and Federalism, University of Waterloo / Wilfrid Laurier University, 1985), 69–82.

30. Jessica C. E. Gienow-Hecht and Mark C. Donfried, "The Model of Cultural Diplomacy: Power, Distance and the Promise of Civil Society," in Gienow-Hecht and Donfried, *Searching for a Cultural Diplomacy*, 20.

31. R. S. Zaharna, *The Cultural Awakening in Public Diplomacy* (Los Angeles: Figueroa Press, 2012).

32. See Ernest J. Wilson, "Hard Power, Soft Power, Smart Power," *Annals of the American Academy of Political and Social Science* 616, no. 1 (March 1, 2008): 110–24, and Joseph S. Nye, "Hard, Soft, and Smart Power," in *The Oxford Handbook of Modern Diplomacy*, ed. Andrew Fenton Cooper, Jorge Heine, and Ramesh Thakur (Oxford: Oxford University Press, 2013).

33. Ludovic Tournès, *Américanisation: Une histoire mondiale, XVIIIe–XXIe siècle* (Paris: Fayard, 2020); Nisbett, "Who Holds the Power in Soft Power?"; Charlotte Faucher, "Restoring the Image of France in Britain 1944–1947," *Historical Journal* 64, no. 5 (February 2021): 1428–48.

34. Tournès, *Américanisation*, 8–10. Nisbett concludes that rich countries will always have a monopoly on soft power. See Nisbett, "Who Holds the Power in Soft Power?"

35. David J. Snyder has studied the relationship between hard and soft power, focusing on the asymmetrical relation between the Netherlands and the United States during World War II. See David J. Snyder, "The Problem of Power in Modern Public Diplomacy: The Netherlands Information Bureau in World War II and the Early Cold War," in Osgood and Etheridge, *United States and Public Diplomacy*. See also Asri Salleh and Asmady Idris, eds., *Malaysia's United Nations Peacekeeping Operations (1960–2010)* (Singapore: Springer Singapore, 2021).

36. Seth Center, "Supranational Public Diplomacy: The Evolution of the UN Department of Public Information and the Rise of Third World Advocacy," in Osgood and Etheridge, *United States and Public Diplomacy*; Perla, "Transnational Public Diplomacy."

37. Tony Smith, "New Bottles for New Wine: A Pericentric Framework for the Study of the Cold War," *Diplomatic History* 24, no. 4 (October 2000): 567–91.

38. We are using the term "Global South," from which the idea of "South-South relations" is derived, to allude to the empowerment of social actors who have been disadvantaged by global networks of power. However, we recognize that the term is geographically and conceptually imprecise and tends to homogenize different realities. For a critical discussion of the concept, see Arif Dirlik, "Global South: Predicament and Promise," *Global South* 1, no. 1 (2007): 12–23; Nina Schneider, "Between Promise and Skepticism: The Global South and Our Role as Engaged Intellectuals," *Global South* 11, no. 2 (2017): 18; Pablo Palomino, "On the Disadvantages of 'Global South' for Latin American Studies," *Journal of World Philosophies* 4, no. 2 (December 2019): 22–39; Marlea Clarke, "Global South: What Does It Mean and Why Use the Term? Global South Political Commentaries," University of Victoria, August 8, 2018, https://onlineacademiccommunity.uvic.ca/globalsouthpolitics/2018/08/08/global-south-what-does-it-mean-and-why-use-the-term/; "What's Wrong with the Global North and the Global South?," *Engaging with the World*, May 4, 2015, https://www.hyllanderiksen.net/blog/2018/12/13

/whats-wrong-with-the-global-north-and-the-global-south; and "The 'Global South' Is a Terrible Term. Don't Use It!," *RE-DESIGN* (blog), November 6, 2018, http://re -design.dimiter.eu/?p=969.

39. See, e.g., David Bénazéraf, ed., "Soft power chinois en Afrique: Renforcer les intérêts de la Chine au nom de l'amitié sino-africaine," special issue, *Asie.Visions* 71 (September 2014), https://www.ifri.org/sites/default/files/atoms/files/ifri_av71 _softpowerchinoisenafrique_benazeraf.pdf, and Kenneth King, *China's Aid and Soft Power in Africa: The Case of Education and Training* (Woodbridge, UK: James Currey, 2013).

40. For a critical discussion of the concept of "circulation" in global history, see Stefanie Gänger, "Circulation: Reflections on Circularity, Entity, and Liquidity in the Language of Global History," *Journal of Global History* 12, no. 3 (November 2017): 303–18.

41. Dummer Scheel, "En defensa de la Revolución."

42. Helmers, "Public Diplomacy in Early Modern Europe," 406.

43. David-Fox, *Showcasing the Great Experiment*; Elisabeth Piller, *Selling Weimar: German Public Diplomacy and the United States, 1918–1933* (Stuttgart: Franz Steiner Verlag, 2020); Graham, *Culture and Propaganda*; Dummer Scheel, "En defensa de la Revolución"; Cyril Cordoba, *China-Swiss Relations during the Cold War, 1949–1989: Between Soft Power and Propaganda* (London: Routledge, 2022).

44. Christine Eisenberg, "Cultural Transfer as a Historical Process: Research Questions, Steps of Analysis, Methods," in *Metamorphosis: Structures of Cultural Transformations*, ed. Jürgen Schlaeger (Tübingen, Ger.: Gunter Narr Verlag, 2005), 99

45. See, e.g., Janet Horne, "'To Spread the French Language Is to Extend the *Patrie*': The Colonial Mission of the Alliance Française," *French Historical Studies* 40, no. 1 (February 2017), 95–127, and Megan Brown, *The Seventh Member State: Algeria, France and the European Community* (Cambridge, MA: Harvard University Press, 2022).

46. Bernard Piniau, *L'action artistique de la France dans le monde: Histoire de l'Association française d'action artistique (AFAA) de 1922 à nos jours* (Paris: L'Harmattan, 1998).

47. Fiske de Gouveia, "Future of Public Diplomacy," 6–7; Ang, Isar, and Mar, "Cultural Diplomacy," 373; Melissen, "New Public Diplomacy," 14; Nisbett, "Who Holds the Power in Soft Power?"; Mark Leonard, Catherine Stead, and Conrad Smewing, *Public Diplomacy* (London: Foreign Policy Centre 2002), chap 3.

48. E.g., Seth Center studies the way "third world" countries collaborated between themselves in the 1970s, using the United Nations' propaganda platform to put forward a decolonial agenda. See Center, "Supranational Public Diplomacy."

49. This approach is in line with the "new public diplomacy" theory, which highlights the contribution of actors who have not traditionally occupied a central place in the history of international relations, paying attention to members of civil society and to individuals who often operate on the margins or completely separate from foreign ministries. Giacomo Giudici, "From New Diplomatic History to New Political History: The Rise of the Holistic Approach," *European History Quarterly* 48, no. 2 (April 2018): 314–24; Giles Scott-Smith, "Introduction: Private Diplomacy, Making the Citizen Visible," *New Global Studies* 8, no. 1 (2014): 1–7; Brian Hocking, "Rethinking the 'New' Public Diplomacy," in Melissen, *New Public Diplomacy*.

50. Neal M. Rosendorf, "Hollywood, Dictatorship and Propaganda: Samuel Bronston's Special Relationship with the Franco Regime, 1957–1973," in Osgood and Etheridge, *United States and Public Diplomacy*.

51. Paul Ricœur, "L'identité narrative," *Esprit* 7/8, nos. 140/141 (July/August 1988): 295–304; Judith Butler, "Performative Acts and Gender Constitution: An Essay in Phenomenology and Feminist Theory," *Theatre Journal* 40, no. 4 (1988): 519–31. Jean-François Bayart, *L'illusion identitaire* (Paris: Fayard, 1996); Rogers Brubaker and Frederick Cooper "Beyond 'Identity,'" *Theory and Society* 29, no. 1 (2000): 1–47. We work with the concept of identities while remaining aware of the criticism it has faced. In particular, the concept of identity is an extremely difficult analytical category to define, and it was strongly criticized in the 2000s in part because of the risks of essentialism and reification. Scholars have expressed fears that the notion of "identity" might lead to projecting a motif of unity onto a very diverse group.

52. Focusing on gender: Helen McCarthy, "Gendering Diplomatic History: Women in the British Diplomatic Service, c. 1919–1972," in *Women, Diplomacy and International Politics since 1500*, ed. Glenda Sluga and Carolyn James (London: Routledge, 2015): 167–81; Glenda Sluga and Carolyn James, eds., *Women, Diplomacy and International Politics since 1500* (London: Routledge, 2015); J. Ann Tickner, *Gender in International Relations: Feminist Perspectives on Achieving Global Security* (New York: Columbia University Press, 1992); Cynthia H. Enloe, *The Curious Feminist: Searching for Women in a New Age of Empire* (Berkeley: University of California Press, 2004); Yves Denéchère, "La place et le rôle des femmes dans la politique étrangère de la France contemporaine," *Vingtieme Siècle: Revue d'histoire* 78, no. 2 (2003): 89–98; Carol Miller, "'Geneva—the Key to Equality': Inter-War Feminists and the League of Nations," *Women's History Review* 3, no. 2 (June 1, 1994): 219–45. Focusing on race: Alexander Anievas, Nivi Manchanda, and Robbie Shilliam, eds., *Race and Racism in International Relations: Confronting the Global Colour Line* (London: Routledge, 2015); Duncan Bell, *Dreamworlds of Race: Empire and the Utopian Destiny of Anglo-America* (Princeton, NJ: Princeton University Press, 2020); Michael L. Krenn, ed., *Race and U.S. Foreign Policy from 1900 through World War II* (London: Routledge, 2020); Michael L. Krenn, *Black Diplomacy: African Americans and the State Department, 1945–1969* (Armonk, NY: M. E. Sharpe, 1999).

53. Damaris Seleina Parsitau, "Soft Tongue, Powerful Voice, Huge Influence: The Dynamics of Gender, Soft Power, and Political Influence in Faith Evangelistic Ministries in Kenya," in *Pentecostalism and Politics in Africa*, ed. Adeshina Afolayan, Olajumoke Yacob-Haliso, and Toyin Falola (Cham, Switz.: Springer International, 2018), 159–80; Min Suk Kim, "Hallyu Fandom in Mexico City and Lima: Soft Power, Gender, and New Media Self-Fashioning of Transcultural Youth" (PhD thesis, University of Texas at Austin, 2021); Andrea Stanton, "Sober Masculinity and Nurturing Femininity: A Gendered Analysis of the Syrian Presidency Instagram Account," *Place Branding and Public Diplomacy* 18, no. 4 (December 2022): 346–56; Willow F. Williamson, "Claiming Change and Tradition in the United Arab Emirates: Women's Empowerment as a Public Diplomacy Strategy," *Place Branding and Public Diplomacy* 18, no. 4 (December 2022): 335–45; Isabelle Karlsson, "'We Try to Be Nuanced Everywhere All the Time': Sweden's Feminist Foreign Policy and Discursive Closure in Public Diplomacy," *Place Branding and Public Diplomacy* 18, no. 4 (December 2022): 325–34.

54. Nadia Kaneva and Cecilia Cassinger, "Centering Gender in Public Diplomacy and Nation Branding: An Invitation to Reimagine the Future of the Field," *Place Branding and Public Diplomacy* 18, no. 4 (December 2022): 305–13.

55. Sarah Ann Curtis, *Civilizing Habits: Women Missionaries and the Revival of French Empire* (Oxford: Oxford University Press, 2010); Rogers, *Frenchwoman's Imperial*

Story; Rebecca Rogers and Myriam Boussahba-Bravard, eds., *Women in International and Universal Exhibitions, 1876–1937* (London: Routledge, 2017); Christian Birebent, "Militantes pro-SDN en France et au Royaume-Uni dans les années 1920: Quelle influence?," in *Femmes et relations internationales au XXe siècle,* ed. Jean-Marc Delaunay and Yves Denéchère (Paris: Presses Sorbonne Nouvelle, 2006), 255–65; Charlotte Faucher, *Propaganda, Gender, and Cultural Power: Projections and Perceptions of France in Britain c. 1880–1944* (Oxford: Oxford University Press, 2022); Charlotte Faucher, "Women, Gender and the Professionalisation of French Cultural Diplomacy in Britain, 1900–1940," *English Historical Review* 136, no. 583 (December 1, 2021): 1513–41; Paula Bruno, Alexandra Pita, and Marina Alvarado, *Embajadoras culturales: Mujeres latino-americanas y vida diplomática, 1860–1960* (Rosario, Arg.: Prohistoria, 2022).

56. Greg Castillo, *Cold War on the Home Front: The Soft Power of Midcentury Design* (Minneapolis: University of Minnesota Press, 2010).

57. Mary Elizabeth Eiland, "'Look at Me and Tell Me If I Don't Have Brazil in Every Curve of My Body': Women, Propaganda, and Nation during the Estado Nôvo, 1937–1945" (MA thesis, Vanderbilt University, 2012); Rumelili, Aydın-Düzgit, and Gülmez, "Gendering Public Diplomacy."

58. Adrian Athique, "Soft Power, Culture and Modernity: Responses to Bollywood Films in Thailand and the Philippines," *International Communication Gazette* 81, no. 5: 470–89.

59. Michael L. Krenn "'The Low Key Mulatto Coverage': Race, Civil Rights, and American Public Diplomacy, 1965–1974," in *Reasserting America in the 1970s: U.S. Public Diplomacy and the Rebuilding of America's Image Abroad,* ed. Hallvard Notaker, Giles Scott-Smith, and David Snyder (Manchester: Manchester University Press, 2016): 95–110; Michael L. Krenn, "Carl Rowan and the Dilemma of Civil Rights, Propaganda, and the Cold War," in *African Americans in U.S. Foreign Policy: From the Era of Frederick Douglass to the Age of Obama,* ed. Linda Heywood, Allison Blakely, Charles Stith, and Joshua C. Yesnowitz (Urbana: University of Illinois Press, 2015): 58–80.

CHAPTER 1

Race for Power

Science and the Creation of White Supremacy in the Nineteenth Century

Michael L. Krenn

In the early and mid-nineteenth century, scientists from the United States and throughout Western Europe increasingly turned their attention to the study of their fellow human beings. Because they understood humankind to be divided into separate races, they sought to understand this ordering's scientific origins. Led by the American scientist Samuel George Morton, these men focused much of their attention on human skulls and other remains and sought to explain how and why the races were supposedly different. Yet their scientific work also resulted in repulsive theories about how those differences translated into the "superiority" of the white race and the varying levels of "inferiority" of people of color. In this essay, we will explore how these theories were developed and how they became the foundation for the ideology of white supremacy and the cornerstone of policies of territorial expansion, annihilation of native peoples, and chattel slavery utilized by government officials in the United States and elsewhere. And although the United States will be a focal point for this study, it will also reveal the very deep and significant international webs of intellectual cooperation and dissemination of their pseudoscientific findings through-out the "white world."[1] This science diplomacy became, in short, an early and powerful example of what would become known in the twentieth century as soft power.

SOFT DIPLOMACY AND SCIENCE

It has now been over three decades since Joseph S. Nye introduced the phrase "soft power" into the lexicon of diplomatic history and the study of international relations. The result was an outpouring of scholarly books and articles analyzing such diverse topics as tourism, the use of advertising models, the many and varied forms of cultural diplomacy, international exchanges, educational programs, and myriad other examples of diplomatic interactions that sought to convince rather than coerce. These studies were enlightening but also came with their own set of limitations: an overwhelming focus on the twentieth century, most particularly the Cold War decades, and on individual nations (often the United States or the Soviet Union) in an effort to determine how these states utilized soft power initiatives to help shape international perceptions of, and willingness to work with, the home nation.

One enticing possibility for breaking through these limitations lies in the study of science as soft power. The work of scientists in a variety of different fields spans decades, generations, and even centuries. Although these men and women come from distinctly national backgrounds, their research and findings are not contained by national borders. By its very nature, science seems a perfect fit for the purposes of soft power. In general, it has been viewed as completely objective and apolitical. It relies on the power of logic and reason rather than intimidation and brute force to sway the minds of people and nations. The term "science diplomacy" has been developed in recent years to describe the ways in which science can serve as a tool in international relations. According to Marga Gual Soler,

> science, technology, and innovation are taking center stage in international affairs and increasingly influencing the geopolitical dynamics and a country's standing on the global stage. New scientific and technological advancements are acquiring greater strategic relevance to ensure competitive advantages in the twenty-first century global order. At the same time, international scientific collaboration contributes to generating and democratizing knowledge and improving relations between countries as a "soft power" tool to coordinate science-based solutions to transboundary problems, and to build bridges between countries with tense diplomatic relations.[2]

The American Association for the Advancement of Science (AAAS), working with the United Kingdom's Royal Society, defined "science diplomacy" as composed of three relatively distinct components: "informing foreign policy objectives with scientific advice (science in diplomacy); facilitating international science cooperation (diplomacy for science); using science cooperation to improve international relations between countries (science for diplomacy)."[3]

Some fascinating recent scholarship suggests the ways in which science diplomacy as soft power can be utilized in the study of international relations. Some of this research pushes against the earlier chronological boundaries that have been imposed. Audra Wolfe's 2018 work suggests that while science became embroiled in the Cold War, even after it ended the role of science in US diplomacy continued: "Shortly after taking office in 2009, President Barack Obama appointed a series of 'science envoys' to strengthen the United States' relationship with Muslim countries." Other works encourage us to look to the years before the Cold War, including an important piece of work by Emily J. Levine that asks us to consider earlier (and broader) manifestations of the international exchange of knowledge by focusing on the interactions and competition between American and German universities in the early twentieth century. Tamson Pietsch examines the "empire of scholars" created by British universities and academics stretching back to the mid-nineteenth century.[4] Another group of scholars has expanded the breadth of the study of science diplomacy through examinations of the ways in which race and science coalesced to support European imperialism in the nineteenth century. Ricardo Roque, for example, focuses on how "French race science, known as *anthropologie*, was adopted and adapted across the European Latin world as a type of 'stranger-science'" that proved extremely useful in constructing colonial empires in the late 1800s. Fenneke Sysling's fascinating examination of Dutch imperialism in Indonesia catalogs the ways in which various sciences were put to work in the colonial mission.[5]

Other research presses us to comprehend both the official and unofficial uses of science as a form of soft power and the ways in which those uses sometimes lead to cooperation and sometimes to conflict. David H. Price's fascinating work on the interactions between anthropologists and the US government in the decades after World War II reveals the complex nature of "dual use anthropology," in which the supposedly apolitical research of academicians found itself transformed into "militarized applications" by US officials and agencies (who also provided much of the financial backing for the supposedly neutral scientific research). This dynamic could lead to conflict, as academicians decried the "weaponization" of their work.[6]

Yet the vast majority of the literature on science as a form of soft power still tends to concentrate on the years of the Cold War: Price's book is titled *Cold War Anthropology*; the subtitle of Wolfe's work is *The Cold War Struggle for the Soul of Science*. Hence, the *national* science of one nation is squared off against the *national* science of an opposing country. And even those studies that have escaped the confines of the Cold War years still tend to emphasize the role of governments and government-supported institutions in pushing science and education as a weapon in their diplomatic arsenals.

This essay examines the use of the soft power of science in the early nineteenth century in helping to shape the development of the ideology of white racial superiority among American and Western European societies and governments. In the absence of official government bureaucracies to carry out these efforts, the focus will be on individual scientists from a number of different nations who used their power, prestige, and access to nineteenth-century forms of mass communication to reach the general public and, most important, government officials. Although much of the focus will be on the work of a particular American scientist of that period, this is not primarily a study of US soft power. Instead of looking at just one nation as the creator of soft power productions and other nations as simply receivers and interpreters of the message, this study suggests that what occurred was a transnational campaign to define humanity in ways that served both the national interests of the particular scientists and the larger interests of the "white nations" of Western Europe and the United States. Together they formed a powerful international information machine that functioned much like the propaganda bureaucracies utilized by governments in the twentieth century. The fact that they spoke as men of knowledge, not official mouthpieces of their respective nations, allowed them to use the supposedly neutral language of science to promulgate their opinions on how the different races of humankind came into existence and how and why those physical differences translated into distinct moral and intellectual characteristics that not only placed "Caucasians" at the top of humanity and the other races in varying degrees of inferiority below them but also suggested that these differences were unchanging. Armed with these rationales, the "white nations" tried to explain the slaughter, displacement, and/or enslavement of millions of people of color as simply the unbending result of science in action.

SCIENCE, RACE, AND EXPANSION

The central character in this early exercise in soft power was a somewhat unassuming physician from Philadelphia, Samuel George Morton. Born in 1799, Morton took up medical studies at the University of Pennsylvania and then traveled abroad to the University of Edinburgh. As with a number of his contemporaries, he took an interest in the natural sciences, joined the Academy of Natural Sciences in Philadelphia, and presented his own research on geology and fossils. In the 1830s, however, he turned his attention to human beings, specifically their skulls. He began to amass a collection of human crania that eventually numbered nearly one thousand, most of them collected and sent to Morton (who rarely traveled outside Philadelphia) by a willing group of fellow scientists, explorers, military men, and diplomats from around the United States and the world. Morton came to believe that through careful measurements of these remains, he could determine the alleged differences among the races of mankind. In particular, he focused on measuring the "cranial capacity" (brain size) of his numerous skulls and then using his findings to hypothesize about the moral, cultural, and intellectual differences between the races rather than merely the physical characteristics. From his detailed drawings and massive tables of data, Morton spun more speculative notions regarding the intelligence and moral characteristics of those peoples whose brains were smaller. He interpreted that people of color—Native Americans and Africans, in particular—were at the bottom of his racial hierarchy.[7]

During the 1830s and 1840s Morton published numerous works on his research into what he considered human differences, but his two most important books are clear evidence of how his supposedly objective scientific work came to serve as an early example of the use of soft power in America's international relations. In 1839 he published *Crania Americana*, in which he focused his attention on the skulls of the indigenous people of North and South America. It was hardly coincidental that this work appeared just as the national fervor for westward expansion was reaching its peak and only a few years before the phrase "Manifest Destiny" came to be used by politicians and journalists alike to whip up support for expanding the United States to the shores of the Pacific Ocean.[8] Yet, as the historian Frederick Merk notes, that phrase had a somewhat hollow ring to it at first. Some Americans worried that territorial conquest would lead to an empire, not a democracy. Others were concerned that Manifest Destiny would simply mean more regions into which slavery might expand. As Merk argues, the term did not evoke national support because "it did not reflect the national spirit."[9] Where political and economic arguments failed to provide the ideological glue that might bring the nation together in a push toward the West, Morton supplied what was not only viewed as a scientifically objective outlook on the matter but also one that combined American nationalism with the powerful argument that westward expansion and the displacement of the indigenous people inhabiting that region was not only inevitable but also absolutely necessary.

Crania Americana was filled with tables, charts, and, most strikingly, hundreds of detailed drawings of human skulls representing various tribes from both North and South America. The precise measurements of these skulls, particularly their cranial capacity, provided rather dry numerical data for the average reader. However, when Morton turned to his interpretation of what these numbers meant, the real intent of his findings became apparent. The shapes of skulls and the sizes of brains were, in Morton's view, directly related to intelligence and the "moral peculiarities" of these native peoples. Morton concluded that "in their mental character the [Native] Americans are averse to cultivation, and slow in acquiring knowledge; restless, revengeful, and fond of war." This led Morton to offer his thoughts about the comparative characteristics of Native Americans and whites. He argued that the "Caucasian Family" had "peopled the finest portions of the earth, and given birth to its fairest inhabitants." It did not take long for Morton to explain the supposed consequences of the meeting of these races. For civilization to flourish in the West, he reasoned, the indigenous peoples would have to give way: "However much the benevolent mind may regret the inaptitude of the Indian for civilization," the two races could not "harmonise in their social relations except on the most limited scale." Speaking before students at the Pennsylvania Medical College just a few years later, Morton painted an even more powerful picture of the racial component of Manifest Destiny. Starting from his now well-publicized view that the various races were the result of "a primeval difference among men; not an accidental occurrence," he concluded that these "primeval attributes" had "given our race a decided and unquestionable superiority over all of the nations of the earth." Indeed, were it not for this "same mental superiority, these happy climes which we now inhabit would yet be possessed by the wild and untutored Indian, and that soil which now rejoices the hearts of millions of freemen, would be yet overrun by lawless tribes of contending Barbarians. Thus it is that the white race has been able to plant and to sustain its colonies in every region of the habitable earth."[10]

While the term "soft power" was not yet in the English language's lexicon, Morton quickly realized that his theories could provide valuable ammunition for US officials who were attempting to encourage public support for westward expansion and what he argued was the unfortunately necessary, yet inevitable, displacement or annihilation of the Native Americans. Indeed, for Morton it could be a useful reciprocal relationship. As he began his preparations for *Crania Americana*, he quickly realized that he needed more skulls. When he learned that the US government was preparing to send an exploratory mission into the western regions of North America,

Morton jumped at the opportunity to write to Secretary of War Lewis Cass about the scientific work that could be an important part of the expedition and suggested that one of his close colleagues tag along to collect "specimens." Cass, a strong proponent for the removal of Natives Americans who, to his understanding, stood in the way of US expansion, was thrilled and promised Morton that he could "be assured of his desire to promote the views of the Academy [of Natural Sciences]" through the collection of useful materials. Morton immediately made clear his objectives when he wrote to his colleague that he wanted "any skulls of animals, from *Homo sapiens* to the lowest links. . . . You may possibly meet with some Indian Crania."[11]

Morton's work could also be seen as an effort to curb international criticisms of the destruction of indigenous peoples who found themselves in the path of white expansionism. Just as *Crania Americana* made its way to bookstores and libraries, he received a letter from a colleague in England, Thomas Hodgkin. Hodgkin included a printed pamphlet describing the work of the recently established Aborigines' Protection Society. The society's goal was to preserve "from utter ruin and extermination, many whole tribes and families of men." If current trends continued, "more than one half or than three fourths of the great families of mankind, if we count their races, will have vanished from before our view in no long space of time if we do not interfere to protect them from the daily encroachments of this one more powerful tribe."[12] The group included supporters in Parliament and representatives from various British holdings, including Canada, New Zealand, and various African colonies. Morton's book argued that given what he viewed as the deep and permanent racial "inferiority" of the aborigines, "interference" with their displacement and destruction was not only impossible but counterproductive to the spread of the much more "civilized" and progressive white. America's Manifest Destiny was not simply a heartless land grab by greedy settlers. It was to him the entirely natural and logical expression of the "racial superiority" of the white race.

SCIENCE, RACE, AND SLAVERY

Having concluded his study of Native Americans, Morton then turned his attention to Africans, which resulted in the publication of *Crania Egyptiaca* (1844). Working with hundreds of "ancient Egyptian" skulls and "research" acquired from sometimes less-than-reliable sources, Morton started his study with the same conclusion he had reached in *Crania Americana*: the racial characteristics among humans were not by chance but rather due to the "primeval differences" that existed from the beginning of mankind's existence.[13] Focusing on the history of Egypt, Morton now applied his thinking about the immutability of the races to ancient Egyptian culture and society. The ruling class, he declared, had always been white, and they were in turn served by Black slaves: "Negroes were numerous in Egypt, but their social position in ancient times was the same that it now is, that of servants and slaves."[14] To Morton, neither the passage of time nor the impact of climate and environment made any difference in either the racial differences between whites and Blacks or their respective places in the hierarchy of human society. Masters had always been masters (and white); slaves had always been slaves (and Black).

Appearing just one year before the publication of *Narrative of the Life of Frederick Douglass, an American Slave*, Morton's latest foray into the science of humanity landed directly in the boiling cauldron of the national (and international) debate over slavery. This, again, was not coincidental. Much of his "research" for *Crania Egyptiaca* was conducted in absentia. Morton relied on a motley crew of skull collectors for his Egyptian crania and was also assisted by a more than willing group of southerners who provided him with their firsthand experience with Black Africans. Not that he particularly needed to be told about African slaves. During one of his few trips outside the United States, in 1834 Morton made several stops at the Caribbean island colonies of the European powers. In Barbados he came upon a society that had just declared an end to slavery, but this did little to assuage Morton's views of the recently freed slaves. Based on just a few days on the island (and no direct contact with the Black population), Morton gave his racism free reign, describing Barbadians as "repulsive," "listless," "stupid," "uncouth," "squalid," and "degenerate."[15]

US officials were quick to grasp the usefulness of Morton's research. Almost as soon as *Crania Egyptiaca* was published, one of Morton's southern admirers (and a former diplomat) sent a copy of the book to Secretary of State John C. Calhoun, informing Morton that "this gentleman will appreciate the powerful support which may be deduced from it, of our peculiar institution, here." Supporters of American slavery would "not be so much frightened hereafter by the voices of Europe or of North America" who wished to abolish the practice. Secretary Calhoun certainly recognized the value of Morton's work. Just a month after receiving a copy of *Crania Egyptiaca*, he addressed a letter to the British minister to the United States, Richard Pakenham, discussing the recent US annexation of Texas. He condemned what he perceived as the British intention to abolish slavery "throughout the world." Calhoun noted, as Morton had during his visit to Barbados a decade before, that in all instances in which the states have changed the former relation between the two races, the condition of the African, instead of being improved, has become worse. They have been invariably sunk into vice and pauperism, accompanied by the bodily and mental inflictions incident thereto—deafness, blindness, insanity, and idiocy—to a degree without example; while, in all other states which have retained the ancient relation between them, they have improved greatly in every respect—in number, comfort, intelligence, and morals—as the following facts, taken from such sources, will serve to illustrate.

Calhoun felt that abolishing slavery in the United States, which now included Texas, where the numbers of slaves were so great, would be a disaster: "[The] two races differing so greatly, and in so many respects, cannot possibly exist together in the same country, where their numbers are nearly equal, without the one being subjected to the other. Experience has proved that the existing relation, in which the one is subjected to the other, in the slaveholding states, is consistent with the peace and safety of both, with great improvement to the inferior."[16] The stamp of Morton's "science" was all over Calhoun's letter. As in ancient Egypt, slavery in the United States was portrayed as both natural and necessary because of the allegedly immense (and permanent) racial differences between whites and Blacks.

THE NINETEENTH-CENTURY ORIGINS
OF SCIENCE DIPLOMACY

To understand Morton's work as simply a tool utilized by US officials to defend American actions and institutions against international criticisms misses a vital point. There is little doubt that Morton's research served as an early example of soft power for it provided a benign patina of scientific objectivity and authority to portray America's ruthless and deadly territorial expansion and enslavement of millions of African slaves. His contemporaries in America certainly recognized the power of his publications. Writing just a few years after Morton's death in 1851, a colleague, Henry S. Patterson, summarized his significance for national greatness and power:

There are reasons why Ethnology should be eminently a science for American culture. Here, three of the five races . . . are brought together to determine the problem of their destiny as they best may,

while Chinese immigration to California and the proposed importa-
tion of Coolie laborers threaten to bring us into equally intimate contact with a fourth. It is manifest that our relation to and management
of these people must depend, in a great measure, upon their intrinsic
race-character. While the contact of the white man seems fatal to the
Red American, whose tribes fade away before the onward march of
the frontier-man like the snow in spring (threatening ultimate extinc-
tion), the Negro thrives under the shadow of his white master, falls
readily into the position assigned him, and exists and multiplies in
increased physical well-being.[17]

According to Patterson, it was not God or any particular dedication to an
economic or political ideology upon which America's power rested. Instead,
power flowed from a more easily discernible foundation—race.

Scientific racism's role as an early example of soft power is more complicated and, ultimately, more destructive than this, however. A closer examination reveals that Morton was merely a part, albeit a central part, of what can
only be classified as a transnational application of soft power that involved
men of learning from numerous nations in an effort to construct an unas-
sailable philosophical, ideological, and, most important, scientific basis for
the white assault on peoples and nations of color. There is little doubt that
Morton was a leading voice for this soft power in the service of empire in the
United States. His list of correspondents, many of whom provided him with
advice and insights; research materials (usually in the form of human skulls);
and outlets for his work via scientific societies, publications, and reviews in
newspapers and journals, is replete with the names of some of the leading
American figures in science, the military, politics, and diplomacy.[18] Of even
more importance in terms of our global understanding of this particular
example of nineteenth-century soft power is the fact that Morton's work was
not simply absorbed by American society and politics and then broadcast
to a waiting world where it worked to improve US prestige and influence.
The theories he espoused through his numerous published works were not
entirely unique or particularly singular to the American experience. The scientific racism he helped to promote could not be contained within national
boundaries.

Morton worked within a constellation of natural scientists around the
"white world." If his prestige and influence in America was notable, so too
was his reputation among his international peers. Yet, while Morton occupied a prominent position among these men of science, he was by no means
the sole creator of their growing interest in theories of white supremacy or

the only intellectual voice seeking a wider audience among the general public and national officials. This group of scientists saw themselves as working together toward the common goal of not only explaining the differences between the various races of man but also how and why these differences led to progress, civilization, and power for the white race and ignorance, decadence, and eventual destruction or slavery for people of color. Indeed, it was only by working together as an international network for the dissemination of their views that they could ensure that their theories would be heard and utilized by the public outside of their small academic circles.

A very good example of this transnational alliance can be found through an examination of the Swedish scientist Anders Retzius, who was appointed the supervisor of the prestigious Karolinska Institute in 1840. Born just a few years before Morton, Retzius also practiced medicine and developed an intense interest in the anatomy of humans. And, like Morton, this interest led him to collect numerous human skulls for his research, "using methods that are today considered unethical or illegal." Retzius, and later his son Gustaf, became fascinated with the issue of race, and "their research on human variation was premised on the widespread belief that there exist distinct human 'races.' The Retziuses measured human skulls in the hope of coming up with quantitative methods for determining national and ethnic differences."[19] It was little wonder, then, that the elder Retzius was immediately drawn to Morton's work. Writing to his American colleague in 1845, the Swedish anatomist congratulated him on his "excellent work on the Crania Americana" and assured him that a copy would be delivered to the Royal Library in Stockholm. He then got straight to the point: the study of ethnography was gaining interest in Sweden, and Retzius needed skulls because he "found that the best basis of classification of the human tribes is the form of the Skulls." His own preliminary work in this regard led him to identify "four principal classes." And so he wrote to ask Morton for some skulls (or plaster copies) and even offered "in future to furnish you with others from our collection as you may desire." Two years later, after receiving some reading materials from Morton, Retzius could barely contain his admiration, informing the American, "You have done more for Ethnography than any living physiologist." Certainly, he felt that Europe lagged behind in this important science, having just "two or three Ethnographic Societys [*sic*], but our own races are not explored." He soon remedied that situation by using his own massive collection of skulls to construct "a hegemonic anthropological narrative of blond, long-skulled Aryan metal-users displacing or conquering Europe's broad-headed Stone-Age 'aborigines.'"[20] As in the United States, Retzius theorized that a "superior race" supplanted an "inferior race" of "aborigines."

And, as had Morton, he explained this action as the logical and inevitable working out of scientific principles of human development and interactions.

The relationship between Morton and Retzius also highlighted their commitment to the transnational transmission of their ideas about race and power of these international connections through the only means available in the mid-nineteenth century. Morton, often portrayed as a rather retiring figure who simply went about his scientific work, was, in fact, a fairly tireless self-promoter. He worked to ensure that his books, articles, and reviews were placed into the hands of his colleagues both at home and abroad. As Retzius's letters suggest, Morton kept him well stocked with his research, including sending him copies of his books, which, for the time, were quite expensive. For his part, the Swedish scientist made sure to promote Morton's work by sharing it with his colleagues in Stockholm and placing the books in nationally recognized libraries. And the information circle continued as Morton would then cite Retzius and thank him for his contributions in the form of useful skulls.

Retzius was not the only notable man of science lavishing praise on Morton, engaging in collaboration on research efforts, and/or helping to spread the ideology of the "natural superiority" of the white race. There were numerous German intellectuals, including the greatest of them all, Alexander von Humboldt. Having just received a copy of Morton's *Crania Americana* (likely provided by Morton himself), Humboldt could barely contain his admiration:

> Works of this class, which extend by very different means the sphere of our knowledge, serve to add to the glory of one's country. . . . The craniological treasures which you have been so fortunate as to unite in your collection, have in you found a worthy interpreter. Your work is equally remarkable for the profundity of its anatomical views, the numerical detail of the relations of organic conformation, the absence of those poetical reveries which are as the myths of modern physiology.

Noting that he was currently working on what would be his colossal study of natural history, *Cosmos*, Humboldt informed Morton, "I shall know how to profit by so many excellent views upon the distribution of the races of mankind that are scattered throughout your beautiful volume. One cannot, indeed, but be surprised to see in it such evidences of artistic perfection, and that you could produce a work that is a fitting rival of whatever most beautiful has been produced either in France or in England." Although

Humboldt disagreed with some of Morton's conclusions on race, he found it fitting to include a tribute to the American scientist's work in the pages of *Cosmos*: "On the American race generally, see the magnificent work of Samuel George Morton."[21]

Other Germans also worked with Morton. Prince Alexander Philipp Maximilian zu Wied-Neuwied, who conducted explorations in Brazil and the American West in the early 1800s, became aware of Morton's forthcoming *Crania Americana* on "American man," which he said would be of "great interest to me." He regretted that he could provide but a single drawing of one of the skulls he collected on his explorations in Brazil. Morton thanked the German diplomat Baron Friedrich von Gerolt (who served as his nation's minister and then ambassador to the United States) for his help in procuring an "Ancient Mexican skull from the cemetery of Santiago de Tlatilolco."[22] Peter S. DuPonceau, a French immigrant to America, introduced Morton to the work of Marie Jean Pierre Flourens, a scientist who was also extremely interested in the size and shape of the human brain and was eager to get his hands on some of Morton's precious skulls. But simply securing crania was not the only reason for the introduction from DuPonceau: "As Dr. Flourens & yourself are pursuing the same object with the same eagerness, it appears to me that it would be a great advantage to Science, & to the learned institutions of both countries, if you could be made more particularly known to each other." Certainly, their ideas meshed together concerning the immutability of the human races. Flourens, like Morton, concluded that these differences were "primeval" and permanent. These findings were then used by the Frenchman to lead the assault against Charles Darwin's theory of evolution. Antoine Barthelemy Clot, who served as the surgeon-in-chief of the French army during the occupation of Egypt (where he acquired the name M. Clot Bey), worked with Morton's collaborator on *Crania Aegyptiaca*, George Gliddon, to collect ancient Egyptian skulls. He "obligingly presented" Morton with at least thirty-two skulls taken from burial sites.[23] British scholars, despite their nation's recent abolition of the slave trade, still found much of interest in Morton's description of the supposedly inferior races. James Cowles Prichard, whose own study of humankind, *The Natural History of Man*, appeared in 1848, advised the readers of his massive book to take note of Morton's research on Egypt: "A most interesting and really important addition has lately been made to our knowledge of the physical character of the ancient Egyptians." He went on to shame his fellow European scientists for not picking up the pace of their studies of man and race, rather abashedly noting that "it is in the United States of America that a remarkable advancement of this part of physical science has been at length achieved." And the giant of the science of geology, Charles Lyell, was a frequent promoter of Morton's work, corresponding often with Morton and paying a call to see his skull collection during a visit to America in 1842. A review of Morton's *Crania Americana* in an 1840 British science journal explained why the work was so important. The book was "an exquisite treasury of facts, well adapted, in all respects, to establish permanent organic principles in the natural history of man. . . . We rejoice in ranking his 'Crania Americana' in the highest class of transatlantic literature, foreseeing distinctly that the book will ensure for its author the well-earned meed of a Caucasian reputation."[24]

Perhaps the most notable of all of these scientists working across borders to create the foundations for white supremacy was Louis Agassiz. Agassiz moved from Switzerland to the United States just a few years before Morton's death in 1851, but he had already visited America in 1846 and had a lengthy visit with Morton, declaring that his collection of skulls "had been worth the visit to America." Writing to his mother, Agassiz further expressed his amazement with Morton's crania: "Imagine a series of six hundred skulls, mostly Indian, of all the tribes who now inhabit or formerly inhabited America. Nothing like it exists elsewhere. . . . Dr. Morton has had the kindness to give me a copy of his great illustrated work representing all the types of his collection." In another letter from America, he continued to fawn over Morton, already well known for his "great work upon the indigenous races of America. He is a man of science in the best sense; admirable both as regards his knowledge and his activity."[25] Just three years after Morton's death, Agassiz contributed an essay to the racist screed *Types of Mankind*, written as a sort of "memorial" to the fallen scientist, in which he declared, "I am prepared to show that the differences existing between the races of men are of the same kind as the differences observed between the different families, genera, and species of monkeys or animals, and that these different species of animals differ in the same degree one from the other as the races of men— nay, the differences between distinct races are often greater than those distinguishing species of animals one from the other."[26]

Agassiz was also a perfect example of how men of science on both sides of the Atlantic assiduously worked to not only spread their views on race and mankind but also ensure that their theories gained authority and influence beyond their fairly small coterie of intellectuals and skull collectors. As we have already seen, Morton and his contacts around the world were busily engaged in sharing books, articles, research specimens, and memberships in national and local scientific societies. Agassiz proved even more adept at making sure that his pseudoscientific findings about race were kept in front of the American and world audiences. As James Costa notes, even "measured by the standards of his time, his racial views were extreme mostly because he talked about them so frequently, so vehemently, and so publicly. As a whole, they reflect . . . his fervent desire for science, *his* science, to be taken seriously and to be considered socially and politically relevant."[27] As Agassiz's gushing comments about Morton's work suggest, however, he was well aware those views were not his alone. Through his numerous publications, editorials, and letters in American newspapers and magazines and his well-attended lectures around the country, Agassiz served as nothing less than a one-man broadcasting machine for the theories of white supremacy.

The work of Morton and his fellow scientists, while seemingly beyond the normal definitions of what constitutes soft power, was, in fact, an early example of what would later come to be known as science diplomacy. Morton used his writings about the alleged natural inferiority of Native Americans and Black Africans to reach out to US officials such as Cass and Calhoun, who eagerly incorporated his views into their defenses of the displacement of the former and the continued enslavement of the latter. In so doing, Morton's work thus fulfilled the first component of what the AAAS and the Royal Society defined as science diplomacy—"informing foreign policy objectives with scientific advice." The constellation of scientists from America and abroad in which Morton functioned soon led to important connections as these men avidly traded ideas (and human remains) in their shared quest to determine the nature of humanity. They exchanged papers and books, facilitated memberships in national and international scientific organizations, and, whenever possible, visited their fellow scientists throughout the United States and Western Europe. All of this activity helped to meet the second component for science diplomacy, which was "facilitating international science cooperation." Finally, while Morton and his compatriots from across the Atlantic were most certainly representatives of their particular nations, they also eagerly shaped their theories into an international language of race and "human progress," thereby constructing a common racial basis of whiteness that brought their respective countries into a sense of a shared mission that served to justify the exploitation, enslavement, and annihilation of people of color. Thus, the final component of science diplomacy was put into practice: "using science cooperation to improve international relations between countries."

CONCLUSION: SCIENCE, RACE, AND SOFT POWER

In 2003 the historian Gerald Horne argued that during much of the latter nineteenth and early twentieth centuries, British and American officials and intellectuals often shared their thoughts about race. Focusing on the "quint-essential westerner" and "Indian fighter" Frederick Russell Burnham, Horne recounted his trip to Southern Africa in the 1890s: "An avowed advocate of what he called 'white supremacy,' he was quick to compare the wars that led to the expropriation of Native Americans to the war that led to the dispossession of the Africans. For Burnham, the defeat of darker peoples, be they in North America or Africa, was an inevitable process." Along with British imperialists such as Cecil Rhodes and Winston Churchill, Burnham, in an effort to defend their imperialism and the "benefits" that resulted from their colonizing efforts among people of color, fell back upon ideas of white superiority. These interactions, according to Horne, highlighted "the cosmopolitanism embedded in the civilizing mission of white supremacy. Empire builders compared notes across continents and people."[28] While Horne's analysis is correct, it is also somewhat incomplete. The origins of that "civilizing mission"—indeed, its very foundation—are to be found decades earlier in the first half of the nineteenth century when a multinational group of scientists worked to define humanity in terms that served the interests of "white nations" by providing a patina of "scientific" objectivity in defense of expansionism, imperialism, and racial hierarchy.

This brief review touches on only a handful of the many scientists in America and in Europe who were working *together* on the issue of race. That their ideas and publications so nicely meshed with their nations' imperialism and/or slavery was hardly coincidental. The key issue here is that these men recognized the cultural power of science to sustain and support the national missions of conquest and subjugation, particularly if they could use their findings to reach and influence a larger public. Their use of the soft power of science diplomacy was a multinational effort to both create a mythology of white racial superiority and ensure that it was propagated among the literate leaders of the dominant "white nations." As Morton concluded in an 1842 lecture, the message should be clear: "In Asia, in Africa, in America, in the torrid and in the frigid zones, have not all the other races of men yielded and given place to this one? . . . The Anglo-Saxon race to which we ourselves belong, has marched onwards from one degree of cultivation and refinement to another, which the other races have never approached, nor are likely, in the ordinary course of events, ever to realise." And then, with the hubris that only a deeply held sense of racial superiority can provide, he concluded with a quote from a "poet": "The noblest study of mankind is Man."[29] Nearly twenty years later, and a decade after his death, Morton would have taken comfort in the fact that the written media of that time continued to grasp the meaning of his message. In 1861 the physician and newspaper editor Sanford B. Hunt reminded his readers that Morton's findings "lead to the grave conclusion, that the events of history and of national conquests have, from the creation of the world, rested as much upon the relative superiority or inferiority of the cranial capacity of nations, as upon those other causes of climate, education, or warlike character, which have heretofore been supposed to govern and control the progress of human events." Morton's studies of crania led him to believe that "there existed broad national differences. . . . And so on through other races, he traced a permanent, unchangeable type of form, which dated back to the earliest historic periods . . . not only variety in form, but actual difference in cranial capacity, in the size of the brain itself, was one of the conditions of national greatness."[30]

And, as Morton and his colleagues in America and Europe argued, those differences were the clear and significant preconditions for the use of theories of white superiority in their respective nations' interactions with people of color around the world. The history of their work and impact suggests the power of science diplomacy as part of international soft power relations by demonstrating the ways in which the pseudoscientific theorizing of Morton and others could be utilized as "objective," "scientific," and seemingly incontrovertible support for policies that had horrendous and deadly consequences. The millions of people of color who were brutally enslaved, coerced into serving their colonial masters, or simply slaughtered would find little comfort in the twisted logic of Morton and his compatriots who employed science as a shield for murderous racism.

NOTES

1. Although the men who studied race during this period presented their work as the results of objective and through scientific methodologies and experiments, the term "pseudoscience" seems a more appropriate description, for two reasons. First, as will become apparent in the discussion of their work, racism and the desire to provide support for slavery, colonialism, and the annihilation of indigenous peoples pushed their "scientific" research to conclusions that were, to a large extent, predetermined. Second, the work of these men, particularly Samuel George Morton, was judged by later scholars to be fatally flawed.

2. Marga Gual Soler, "Science Diplomacy in Latin America and the Caribbean: Current Landscape, Challenges, and Future Perspectives," *Frontiers*, June 17, 2021, https://doi.org/10.3389/frma.2021.670001.

3. American Association for the Advancement of Science and the Royal Society, *New Frontiers in Science and Diplomacy: Navigating the Changing Balance of Power* (London: Royal Society Science Policy Centre, 2010), v–vi.

4. Audra J. Wolfe, *Freedom's Laboratory: The Cold War Struggle for the Soul of Science* (Baltimore: Johns Hopkins University Press, 2018), 8, 199; Emily J. Levine, "Baltimore Teaches, Gottingen Learns: Cooperation, Competition and the Research University," *American Historical Review* 121, no. 3 (June 2016), 780–823; Tamson Pietsch, *Empire of Scholars: Universities, Networks and the British Academic World, 1850–1939* (Manchester: Manchester University Press, 2013).

5. Ricardo Roque, "The Latin Stranger-Science, or *l'Anthropologie* among the Lusitanians," *History of Science* 60, no. 1 (2022): 69–95; Ricardo Roque, "Transnational Isolates: Portuguese Colonial Race Science and the Foreign World," *Perspectives on Science* 30, no. 1 (2022): 108–36; Fenneke Sysling, *Racial Science and Human Diversity in Colonial Indonesia* (Singapore: National University Press, 2016).

6. David H. Price, *Cold War Anthropology: The CIA, the Pentagon, and the Growth of Dual Use Anthropology* (Durham, NC: Duke University Press, 2016), xiv–xv.

7. For more on Morton, see Ann Fabian, *The Skull Collectors: Race, Science, and America's Unburied Dead* (Chicago: University of Chicago Press, 2010); William Stanton, *The Leopard's Spots: Scientific Attitudes toward Race in America, 1815–59* (Chicago: University of Chicago Press, 1960); and Stephen J. Gould, *The Mismeasure of Man* (New York: W. W. Norton, 1981).

8. The term "Manifest Destiny" first appeared in the 1840s, and the journalist John L. O'Sullivan is generally credited with creating the phrase. While it was defined in different ways by different people, its basic thrust was that the United States was "destined" to expand across the North American continent, bringing its unique institutions and ideologies with it.

9. Frederick Merk, *Manifest Destiny and Mission in American History: A Reinterpretation* (Cambridge, MA: Harvard University Press, 1995), 216. Later scholars would disavow Morton's "science" of cranial measurements. The famous British-American scientist Ashley Montagu argued that "physical anthropology as practiced in Morton's day was a pretty idiotic activity. . . . It consisted in measuring and in describing skulls under the benign impression that this extraordinary activity would somehow lead to the ultimate solution of the relationships of man to one another. . . . Morton had thousands of skulls but apparently no brains at all, and . . . had the complete courage of his confusion." Letter from M. F. Ashley Montagu, Assoc. Prof. of Anatomy at the Hahnemann Medical Center and Hospital of Philadelphia, to Mr. J. Percy Moore, Academy of Natural Sciences of Philadelphia, January 30, 1945, J. Percy Moore Papers, box 18, folder 4, Archives of the Academy of National Sciences, Drexel University.

10. Samuel George Morton, *Crania Americana; or, a Comparative View of the Skulls of Various Aboriginal Nations of North and South America: To Which Is Prefixed an Essay on the Varieties of the Human Species* (Philadelphia: John Penington, 1839), iii, 1, 5–7, 82; Samuel George Morton, *Brief Remarks on the Diversities of the Human Species, and on Some Kindred Subjects: Being an Introductory Lecture Delivered before the Class of Pennsylvania Medical College, in Philadelphia, November 1, 1842* (Philadelphia: Merrihew & Thompson, 1842), 6, 21.

11. Morton to T. A. Conrad, April 19, 1833; "Note to T. A. Conrad on His Leaving Philadelphia for Alabama, Dec. 17, 1832," in "Letter Book: Philadelphia, PA, 1832–1837," Rare Books and Special Collections, Manuscript Division, Princeton University Library.

12. James Cowles Prichard to Thomas Hodgkin, May 20, 1839 (pamphlet), and Thomas Hodgkin to Morton, December 11, 1839, box 5, Morton Papers, Series I: Correspondence, American Philosophical Society Library (hereafter APSL), Philadelphia.

13. Morton's primary source for both the Egyptian skulls and the "history" of ancient Egypt was George Gliddon, a self-proclaimed Egyptologist who would go on to perform "mummy unwrappings" in front of American audiences during the 1840s.

14. Samuel George Morton, "Observations on Egyptian Ethnography, Derived from Anatomy, History, and the Monuments," *Transactions of the American Philosophical Society* 9, no. 1 (1846): 158.

15. Samuel George Morton, "Diary of Trip to the West Indies, and Notebook," Series II, Journal, 1833–ca. 1837, Papers of Samuel George Morton, APSL, Philadelphia.

16. W. B. Hodgson to Morton, March 29, 1844, Series I: Correspondence, box 1, Morton Papers, Library Company of Philadelphia; John C. Calhoun to Richard Pakenham, April 18, 1844, in *The Works of John C. Calhoun, Vol. 5: Reports and Public Letters of John C. Calhoun*, ed. Richard K. Cralle (New York: D. Appleton, 1859), 333–39.

17. Henry S. Patterson, "Memoir of the Life and Scientific Labors of Samuel George Morton, M.D." (Philadelphia: Lippincott, Grambo, 1854), xxxii–xxxiii.

18. In their study of Morton's cranial collection, Emily S. Renschler and Janet Monge claim that "his worldwide connections included as many as 138 contacts, from scientific colleagues to merchants, military figures, and missionaries." Renschler and Monge, "The Samuel George Morton Cranial Collection: Historical Significance and New Research," *Expedition* 50, no. 3 (2008): 31.

19. "KI and the Legacy of Anders and Gustaf Retzius," Karolinska Institutet, November 13, 2021, https://ki.se/en/about/ki-and-the-legacy-of-anders-and-gustaf-retzius. As the Karolinska Institutet summary of Retzius's work explains, the scientist's collection of human skulls was amassed without much regard to the cultures from which the skulls were taken: "Today, the collection of human remains are [*sic*] stored and managed in accordance with international law and ethical rules." The "top priority is to repatriate remains to indigenous peoples." This was not a priority shared by Morton, Retzius, and their contemporaries.

20. Anders Retzius to Morton, July 12, 1845, Morton Family Papers, box 1, Historical Society of Pennsylvania (hereafter HSP), Philadelphia; Retzius to Morton, April 3, 1847, Morton Family Papers, box 3, HSP; O. Larsell, "Anders Adolf Retzius (1796–1860)," *Annals of Medical History* 6, no. 1 (Spring 1924): 19; Richard McMahon, "Anthropological Race Psychology, 1820–1945: A Common European System of Ethnic Identity Narratives," *Nations and Nationalism* (September 21, 2009), https://doi.org/10.1111/j.1469-8129.2009.00393.x. See also Jeff Werner, "Curman's Skull: Scientific Racism and Art," *Journal of Art History* 87, no. 3 (2018): 154–72, for an interesting look at the contributions made to scientific racism by Anders Retzius and his son Gustav.

21. Alexander von Humboldt to Morton, January 27, 1844, in Charles D. Meigs, *Memoir of Samuel George Morton, M.D., Late President of the Academy of Natural Sciences of Philadelphia* (Philadelphia: T. K. and P. G. Collins, 1851), 48; Alexander von Humboldt, *Cosmos: Sketch of a Physical Description of the Universe*, 3rd ed., vol. 1 (London: Longman, Brown, Green & Longmans, 1847–58), cxiii, note 431. In his letter to Morton, Humboldt was most likely referring to the earlier works of Carl Linnaeus, Georges-Louis Leclerc, Comte de Buffon, Johann Friedrich Blumenbach, and Georges Cuvier

and the more recent study by James Cowles Prichard, *Researches into the Physical History of Man* (London: J. and A. Arch, 1813).

22. Prince Alexander Philipp Maximilian zu Wied-Neuwied to Morton, May 2, 1837, box 4, Series I: Correspondence, Morton Papers, APSL; Samuel George Morton, *Catalogue of Skulls of Man and the Inferior Animals, in the Collection of Samuel George Morton*, 3rd ed. (Philadelphia: Merrihew & Thompson, 1849), entry 1226.

23. Peter S. DuPonceau to Morton, October 28 1833, Samuel George Morton Manuscript, Series I: Correspondence, box 2, APSL. For Flourens's views on Darwin and evolution, see Freeman G. Henry, "Anti-Darwinism in France: Science and the Myth of Nation," *Nineteenth-Century French Studies* 27, nos. 3/4 (Spring/Summer 1999), 290–304, and Linda L. Clark, *Social Darwinism in France* (Tuscaloosa: University of Alabama Press, 1984), 15. Clot's contributions are mentioned in Morton, *Catalogue of Skulls*, entries 759 and 846.

24. Prichard's statement is found in Patterson, "Memoir," xlii. See also Lyell to Morton, February 21, 1842, Morton Papers, Series IV: Microfilm, 1838–1844, APSL. Morton wrote in an 1849 article, "I sent my specimens [in this case some fossil remains of what he thought might be a new species of hippopotamus] to London by the hands of Mr. (now Sir Charles) Lyell." "Additional Observations on a New Living Species of Hippopotamus, of Western Africa (Hippopotamus Liberiensis)," in *From the Journal of the Academy of Natural Sciences of Philadelphia*, vol. 1, second series (Philadelphia: Merrihew & Thompson, 1849), 10. The review from the October 1840 edition of the *London Medico-Chirurgical Review* is cited in Patterson, "Memoir," xxxiv. Not every scientist from Europe found Morton's ideas so appealing. Charles Darwin, upon reviewing some of Morton's recent work on hybrids, wrote to Charles Lyell in 1847, "My opinion, of it, as you ask for it, is that it is in main part, a merely tabulated compilation from Griffith's Cuvier, with a few other facts interpolated. He is, I think, too credulous; but it is a pretty good compilation: his worse fault is that he has not gone to his original source. . . . There is a want of exactness in the manner Morton gives the facts. . . . In conclusion, therefore, I do not think Dr. Morton a safe man to quote from." Darwin to Lyell, June 2, 1847, in *The Correspondence of Charles Darwin, 1847–1850*, vol. 4, ed. Frederick Burkhardt and Sydney Smith (Cambridge: Cambridge University Press, 1988), 45–46.

25. All three letters are found in *Louis Agassiz: His Life and Correspondence*, ed. Elizabeth Cary Agassiz, vol. 2 (Boston: Houghton, Mifflin, 1887), 415, 437–38.

26. Christoph Irmscher, *Louis Agassiz: Creator of American Science* (Boston: Houghton Mifflin Harcourt, 2013), 240–41.

27. "Receipt Book for Crania Americana, 1837–1842," Rare Books and Special Collections, Manuscript Division, Princeton University Library; James T. Costa, *Darwin's Backyard: How Small Experiments Led to a Big Theory* (New York: W. W. Norton, 2017), 268–69.

28. Gerald Horne, "Race from Power: U.S. Foreign Policy and the General Crisis of White Supremacy," in *Window on Freedom: Race, Civil Rights, and Foreign Affairs, 1945–1988*, ed. Brenda Gayle Plummer (Chapel Hill: University of North Carolina Press, 2003), 47.

29. Morton, *Brief Remarks*, 21–22. Morton was perhaps referring to the quote from the British poet Alexander Pope, who wrote, "The proper study of mankind is man."

30. Sanford B. Hunt, "Samuel George Morton. 1799-1851," in *Lives of Eminent American Physicians and Surgeons of the Nineteenth Century*, ed. Samuel D. Gross (Philadelphia: Lindsay & Blakiston, 1861), 586, 594.

CHAPTER 2

Karuizawa and Naka Karuizawa

An Origin of Modern Hybrid Japanese Soft Power

Rui Kohiyama

In 2013 the Tōkyō Olympic Games Bid Committee used a Japanese word, *omotenashi*, to persuade the international community to support the Japanese drive to host the Olympic Games in 2020 in Tōkyō.[1] They succeeded in the attempt, although the actual event was postponed and then held in 2021 without spectators because of the COVID-19 pandemic, smashing the intended chance to show off omotenashi. This word signifies a Japanese style of hospitality—thoughtful attentiveness and care given to guests—that is often associated with peculiar Japanese traditions such as *chanoyu* (the tea ceremony), made famous by Tenshin Okakura's long essay, *The Book of Tea* (1906). The concrete elements of omotenashi today depend on the nature of guests and occasions, but politely giving good food, pleasure, and entertainment of some sort seems to be the must. This kind of soft power has recently become increasingly relevant in the case of Japan, where the global popularity of entertainment such as manga and Pokemon has been mobilized internationally in attempts to attract tourists and other types of foreign consumers to boost the country's weakening economy.

In this chapter, I will focus on the history of omotenashi in tourism and specifically in the context of providing pleasure and entertainment for tourists or those who want to rest away from ordinary environments. I aim to analyze its makeup as soft power because this kind of omotenashi has recently been presented as part of unique Japanese culture and attractions that induces foreigners to visit the country.[2]

To achieve the goal, I trace the history of Hoshino Resorts, Inc., which boasts giving "a high level of Omotenashi, Japanese-style hospitality." Since 2001 the company has expanded rapidly and now operates "more than 55 accommodations both in and outside Japan."[3] The ambition of the company's president, Yoshiharu Hoshino, is to export the *Nihon ryokan* (Japanese inn) overseas and establish the category of the Japanese inn in the world of international hotel and resort business. He insists that only by setting out the Japanese tradition powerfully can he acquire international recognition and success in the business.[4] In this chapter, however, I argue that the omotenashi that Hoshino has inherited from his forefathers was not purely Japanese but was a hybrid construction overlapping Western and Japanese practices from its beginning.

The chapter explores histories of the towns of Karuizawa and Kutsukake (Naka Karuizawa), the cradle of Hoshino Resorts, Inc. It first discusses how the traditional Japanese culture of pleasure and entertainment was criticized and reformulated after the mid-1880s in Karuizawa under the improbable influence of an agent of "public diplomacy"—namely, Protestant missionaries. This reformulation revolved especially around the role of entertainment of a sexual nature (geishas, etc.) and thus defined new approaches to the role of morality, gender, and women in Japanese soft power. Next, the chapter discusses how the Japanese in the vicinity adopted the charms of Karuizawa in their own way. In this part, the chapter not only deals with the expansion of Karuizawa but also a new development in Kutsukake, which is located only about four kilometers away from Karuizawa. In the period before World War II, the latter became a Japanese construct of the new modern space for pleasure and entertainment, where the customs introduced by the American and Canadian missionaries were supplemented by elements of the Japanese tradition more strongly than in Karuizawa.

Through examination of Karuizawa and Kutsukake (Naka Karuizawa), this chapter sheds light on two elements—first, the nature of the intervention by American and Canadian missionaries into the Japanese style of entertainment and, second, the Japanese adoption of some of their customs—and how this shaped Japanese soft power. In so doing, it illuminates the hybridity of omotenashi. In other words, the chapter will show how ideas and habits are transferred across national borders to create this particular Japanese form of soft power. Thus, I contribute to understandings of soft power that are firmly integrated in transnational contexts.

ORIGIN OF THE MISSIONARY KARUIZAWA

In hot and humid Asia, Western colonialists at the zenith of Western imperialism in the nineteenth and twentieth centuries usually took refuge in highlands during the hottest months of the year. Called "hill stations," their summer enclaves were established in the first half of nineteenth century in India and then spread to Southeast Asia and East Asia, including Japan. They remain tourist attractions today. Many of them, such as Shimla in India, exert a peculiar charm of the afterglow of the soft power of the imperial reign or hegemony.[5]

Missionaries in Asia also spent summers there. In fact, there were several hill stations that missionaries created and administered according to their satisfaction: Kodaikanal in India, Baguio in the Philippine Islands, Kuling (Lushan) in China, and Karuizawa in Japan.[6] Their culture was different from typical hill stations in their strict observance of Christian principles and habits. A close analysis of Karuizawa in this chapter will clarify the nature of missionaries' moral claim and influence.

The first group of Protestant missionaries arrived in Japan in 1859 as soon as the ports of Yokohama and Nagasaki were opened to Americans according to the Japan-US Treaty of Peace and Amity in 1858. From then until about 1870, most missionaries in Yokohama largely stayed during summer in the foreign settlement built at the port. After 1870 some of them began to spend summers in mountains, such as those near Hakone and Nikkō, or at seashores.[7] In 1874 the government loosened the rules for domestic travels for foreigners. Those living in Yokohama were permitted to stay in Hakone, Atami, Fuji, Nikkō, and Ikaho.[8]

As far as I know, it was in 1876 that Edward Rothesay Miller of the Dutch Reformed Church in America climbed Mount Asama and therefore possibly became the first missionary to pass through the Karuizawa area.[9] In 1881 Ernest Mason Satow and A. G. S. Haws published *A Handbook for Travellers in Central and Northern Japan*, in which they wrote,

> Karuizawa may be . . . only two days' journey from Yedo [Tōkyō], now that the new road over the Usui pass is completed, as the whole distance may be done in a wheeled vehicle. The lofty situation, 3270 ft. above the level of the sea, renders the climate very cool during the summer months and the absence of mosquitoes is another recommendation in its favour as a place of retreat from the unhealthy heat of the plains. There are plenty of decent houses in the village . . . , and the surrounding country affords an innumerable variety of walks and mountain climbing.[10]

In 1886 Alexander Croft Shaw (1846–1902), a Canadian missionary sent by a British society, stayed with a friend in Karuizawa for a month and acquired an abandoned Japanese inn for his summer residence. From then on, missionaries quickly began to occupy Karuizawa.[11]

According to the land register in 1905, 54 percent of the property owners in the core of Karuizawa were missionaries.[12] In 1930 *The Karuizawa Summer Residents' Handbook* noted that among 186 foreigners who owned property in Karuizawa, 147 (about 80 percent) were missionaries.[13] Foreigners' summer houses were concentrated in the core of Karuizawa—that is, the southern slope of Atagoyama, Asamagakure, and Sakura no Sawa (Happy Valley).[14]

There were several reasons for the proliferation of missionaries in Karuizawa. During the Tokugawa period, Karuizawa prospered as a post town on the major road from Yedo (Tōkyō's old name in the Tokugawa period) to Kusatsu where the road merged with Tōkaidō, the main artery between Yedo and Kyōto. The town began to decline after the Meiji Restoration and particularly after 1884 when a new route bypassing Karuizawa was opened. Without hot springs and major shrines or temples, Karuizawa was not a hot spot of tourism for the Japanese, nor was it suitable for farming as the soil was poor. So, the land in Karuizawa was very cheap around 1884, and the inhabitants were willing to sell their useless land for survival. Shaw acquired 2623.5 square meters of land in 1886 and 1888 for just ¥31.80.[15] One can clearly see how cheap the land was when comparing the price to that of the Oku Nikkō area, where foreign diplomats created a summer residents' enclave as Karuizawa emerged as a missionary community. In Oku Nikkō in 1887 William M. H. Kirkwood, an English law adviser to the Japanese government, built a summer house by renting a piece of land for ¥250/year.[16] Land in Karuizawa was cheap enough in the 1880s and the 1890s for missionaries, who were rich compared to the Japanese but not so according to the Western standard, to buy.[17] Further, traveling to Karuizawa was affordable as this area was closer to Tōkyō, and its altitude was moderate compared to Oku Nikkō.[18]

Karuizawa's residents welcomed foreigners because they were accustomed to providing accommodations for strangers, Karuizawa having been a post village on the major road during the Tokugawa period. They soon adapted their traditions to what they perceived to be the expectations of their foreign hosts. In 1891 the villagers decided to refrain from providing geishas, dancing, and music during summer in inns along the main street to meet the missionary standard, although there were many geishas and prostitutes working in the vicinity of Karuizawa for the workers doing railroad construction.[19]

They thus voluntarily began to police the norms for the village. In the beginning, the scope was narrow—just to conform to the missionary standard. However, the concern paid toward the foreign gaze would eventually invent a new way for Japan to present itself to the West.

Some of the villagers were quick to provide hotels and food to suit Western palates.[20] The villagers also welcomed major Tōkyō shops to open summer branches on the main street of Karuizawa, and by the 1900s Karuizawa had become a hot spot for missionaries from the countryside to enjoy shopping.[21] They even invented *karuizawa-bori* (a kind of wood engraving) to decorate furniture for summer houses by inviting from Nikkō engravers who had long served Tōshōgū (the shrine for Ieyasu Tokugawa, the founder of the Tokugawa shogunate). The major pattern of the karuizawa-bori was taken from cherry blossoms, the flower that had often represented Japan.[22] The villagers thus invented a new commodity by appropriating an old tradition that had been long cultivated in Nikkō to satisfy foreign consumers' wish to own a keepsake of their stay in Karuizawa or Japan. If the karuizawa-bori can be interpreted as a small attempt in the line of Eric Hobsbawm and Terence O. Ranger's "invention of tradition," consumerism as well as foreigners' desire for the exotic were involved in this invention.[23]

In short, Karuizawa was affordable for missionaries who were committed to a lifelong residence in Japan and who were in need of a summer retreat for health. As missionaries gathered in Karuizawa and determined the tone of the village according to their religious and middle-class habits and taste, which will be explained below, more missionaries came to stay to enjoy exchanges among their ilk. In the process, Karuizawa began to exert a peculiar atmosphere, a charm originated from missionary communities.

KARUIZAWA AS THE AMERICAN AND CANADIAN MISSIONARY SPACE

Karuizawa shared some of its features with British imperial hill stations like Shimla. The old village had an Anglican church, a mall, and a post office in its center. The place had a restorative function, and the military sent sick or wounded soldiers to its vicinity for recuperation after the Sino-Japanese War and the Russo-Japanese War. It was vibrant, with various outdoor activities and social gatherings. Also, as in the British hill stations, more women than men stayed there. Thus, a part of the taste and practice of imperial Westerners was transferred to the Japanese highlands.[24]

Figure 2.1. Karuizawa's mall and post office sometime before 1945. *Wikimedia Commons*

Of course, the village had more in common with the hill stations that American missionaries built in Asia, such as Kodaikanal in India. In fact, American and Canadian missionaries were dominant in Kaurizawa, as a majority of the Protestant missionaries in Japan were from America and Canada. In 1930, for example, out of 186 summer residents listed in *The Karuizawa Summer Residents' Handbook,* at least 105 (56 percent) can be identified as Americans and Canadians.[25]

Christianity was alive in the village. Alexander Croft Shaw's Anglican Church (1895), the Union Church (informally started in 1897 and formally in 1906), and the Japanese Church (1904, its chapel erected by William Vories in 1912) were in the center of the old village. Sabbath observance was enforced. Missionary conferences and Bible classes were routine during the summer, and missionaries held meetings for the villagers.[26] In the first half of the twentieth century, most of the Japanese children native to Karuizawa went to Sunday school and were mixed with foreign and Japanese children staying in the summer houses.[27] The Christianity practiced in Karuizawa was definitely ecumenical and liberal. Missionaries sent by different denominations worshiped together in the Union Church; the Japanese Church was established also on a union basis, although its upkeep was delegated to Methodists.[28]

As mentioned above, Christian moral rigidity repudiated the Japanese traditional pleasures and entertainments, such as drinking, geisha girls, and prostitution. Of course, such bans hindered the village's attraction for some

Japanese. Novelist Hakuchō Masamune, who visited Karuizawa out of curiosity in 1912, wrote, "There was no hot spring nor could I find a comfortable and convenient inn [which implicitly means an inn that would upon order provide drinking and geishas who might offer sexual services] and so, I thought I should return to Ikaho right away."[29] However, the village provided amusements of its own. Although Karuizawa did not have a luxurious club, the regular feature of imperial hill stations, the Union Church was the center of social activities. Missionaries also introduced innocent, inexpensive, and simple recreations such as walking, hiking, climbing, cycling, music concerts, amateur plays, mutual visiting among friends, and shopping.

Particularly, tennis had become almost the symbol of the village; the public tennis courts adjacent to the Union Church were maintained by the Summer Residents' Association, and they were the place for social exchanges, as described by Kate L. Hansen:

Have I told you about the courts? These four together in a hollow; and just above them on the hill is a sort of covered grandstand which is the special center of Karuizawa for everybody goes there to talk, drink tea and incidentally once in a while, take a look at the games. In the afternoon, everybody puts on her (the men folks wear all sorts of athletic rigs) best bib and tucker, and the stand is a regular reception. I've met all sorts of interesting people.[30]

In other words, under Christian principles, new kinds of amusements—morally acceptable, affordable, and participatory—were introduced in Karuizawa and definitely were sources of attraction.

Differing from the practices in the imperial hill stations in India, missionaries in Karuizawa did not build English cottages or Swiss chalets to create a complete English/European landscape.[31] Rather, many of them adopted the Japanese architectural technology, such as the Japanese cypress bark thatching, and often used a bungalow style with a terrace on the front (which had originated in India), which the British rulers in India tried to avoid building in their hill stations because they wanted to imagine they were back in Britain and forget that they were there as colonialists.[32] The missionaries in Karuizawa did not care, probably because they were in Japan not as colonialists but rather as "friends" mediating between the West and Japan, at least in their imagination, and also because such a choice curbed construction costs. The decision thus created a mixture of the Japanese (and originally Indian) architectural tradition and the Western colonial experience. For the Japanese, it was something familiar in a different shape. Although the bungalow was colonial in style, the missionary bungalow in Karuizawa did not show off Western grandeur and wealth but rather represented a simple and modest life of ingenuity, another source of the attraction and influence of American and Canadian missionaries.

Missionaries in Karuizawa participated vigorously in the civil governance of the village. From early days, they took the initiative in such projects as road construction, collecting donations and opposing taxes.[33] In 1913 they established the Karuizawa Summer Residents' Association, which maintained the public tennis courts, operated a summer clinic, planned various entertainments, etc.[34] The autonomy as a metaphor of freedom and independence was another source of Karuizawa's uniqueness and charm.

Equal participation was another key that defined the character of Karuizawa. In *The Karuizawa Summer Residents' Association Handbook* of 1922 as well as that of 1930, the most striking feature is that all the residents in a particular year are listed under each house number and its owner's name.[35] The map folded in the handbook shows the location of all the numbered houses. In 1922 a person who paid ¥2 would be a member of the association and was eligible to enjoy all the privileges that it offered. The handbook was sold for ¥0.5 to anyone.[36] This means that everyone had easy access to the summer residents' community once they reached Karuizawa. Such openness and assumed equality among summer residents and visitors made a strong contrast to the exclusiveness in the imperial hill stations in India, where no names were given to the lanes "since inhabitants were presumed to possess the same cozy familiarity with their surroundings."[37] A missionary in Japan testified to the atmosphere of Karuizawa:

No one but a missionary, and one who had lived in an isolated interior station at that, could fully appreciate Karuizawa. But any one could enjoy the busy, friendly, Westernized little community, which someone called "A Little America," and another a "Sample of the Kingdom of Heaven." Here tired and worn out workers of all races met and lived in a fraternity far more democratic than a Soviet and more conglomerate than a Republic. To be sure, after the missionaries discovered and developed the place, Japanese nobility and even occasional royalty summered there; but these, too, became democratic and friendly with the hairy barbarians that still outnumbered them in this unique city of their own land.[38]

In short, the Karuizawa community was open and friendly to strangers: anyone who had purchased the handbook could know members' names and addresses. Karuizawa's distinctiveness lay in equality, which connoted American democracy. According to the missionary above, it even got conformity out of the wealthy Japanese who surrounded the missionary core, as will be explained below. Although the democratic community was not without a barrier for entrance, such as fees and a command of English (e.g., the handbook was written in English),[39] its assumed openness and equality attracted many people and contributed to liveliness of the community during summer, which in turn increased its influence.

Women, a definite majority among the summer residents in Karuizawa, as generally was the case in the hill stations in India,[40] were another important element that defined the town's atmosphere. I reviewed arbitrarily fifty-six residents in houses from #610 to #642 listed in *The Karuizawa Summer Residents' Association Handbook* of 1930 and found thirty-three were women (60 percent). Women owned three of the eight houses privately owned by foreigners. This is a reflection of the entire Protestant missionary forces in Japan, where women were more than 60 percent of the personnel.[41]

The feminization endowed Karuizawa with a characteristic of this genre of soft power. As recent scholarship has found out, women's influence was significant in diplomatic negotiations and international relations, such as in European royal courts in the premodern era and in the Wilsonian peace drive in the twentieth century.[42] In the past, women's diplomatic influence was indirect in most cases but powerful (especially in the West) as women defined manners, respectability, and the standard of civility and they controlled the everyday.

As for Karuizawa, women missionaries from all over Japan gathered in the village during summer, and their missionary activities became visible to wider strata of the Japanese. That is, in proselytizing, women missionaries tried to replicate the "Christian home," which was an ideological backbone of the nineteenth-century feminized evangelical Christianity in the United States and probably in Canada as well. It radiated Christian and moral influence, purifying men tainted with secular dirt and religiously inspiring children. The strategy was maintained in Karuizawa, where women missionaries often invited their female students to stay with them.[43] The women and girls emanated the homely atmosphere, not only its religiosity and morality but also its warmth, careful attention, intimacy, and cleanliness, which defined the tone of the village.

Like the ideal Christian home in the US, the summer houses in Karuizawa had no hedges, boundary walls, or fences to mark the border between private and public spaces.[44] In other words, there was no barrier between the home and the community, as if the former's influence was filtering through the latter, thus creating the public sphere.

Further, dominated by women, Karuizawa became a theater of love, romance, and courtship because in Victorian middle-class culture, with which most of the missionaries were familiar, women controlled courtship. They provided occasions for young people to meet and watched over their steps toward marriage. The missionaries in Karuizawa seem to have followed suit, and they attended attentively to young men and women getting to know each other in Karuizawa.[45]

And in fact, another part of Karuiza's peculiar charm was built upon its function as a theater of love, romance, and courtship. "Romantic love" in nineteenth-century American style, with its emphasis on "platonic love" (love without sex before marriage), was something new and foreign in Japan before World War II. Without alcohol and geishas, Karuizawa became an exceptional space for leisure where young Japanese people could meet the opposite sex in the assumed "pure" relationship. The village exerted a peculiar aura in which a romantic relationship without sexual intercourse was approved and fostered. The novelist Tatsuo Hori (1904–53), for example, produced literary constructions of Karuizawa and its vicinity as such a space and contributed to strengthening this aspect of Karuizawa.[46] Later, in the 1950s, upon the background of this meaning of the village, a climatic event was staged in Karuizawa: the current emperor emeritus met the commoner Michiko Shōda (the current empress emerita) on the central tennis courts run by the Karuizawa Summer Residents' Association. According to popular legend, they "fell in love," which symbolized the Japanese adaptation to victorious American democracy.[47]

JAPANESE RESPONSE TO THE MISSIONARY KARUIZAWA

As missionaries established their community in Karuizawa, the Japanese quickly took notice of its charm and began to occupy the land surrounding the missionary core.

For the Japanese, Karuizawa represented an atmosphere of the West that was still far away and adored. At the same time, however, the village seemed friendly and welcoming because missionaries came from the American and Canadian middle classes and their mission was to get closer to the "natives." In this sense, it was different from the aforementioned Oku Nikkō, where some foreign embassies established summer residences and where exclusiveness was maintained, as reflected in its expensive land prices.[48]

The Japanese soon expanded Karuizawa beyond the old core. At first, like in the case of naval captain Yūjirō Hatta (1849–1930), the first Japanese who built a summer house in Karuizawa, they built summer houses there for health reasons. Most of them had experience staying abroad and therefore did not hesitate living among foreigners. Then capitalists quickly began to invest in the early 1890s. Most of the developers built summer houses for wealthy Japanese and the privileged few, such as Yoshihisa Tokugawa (a son of the last shogun) and Moritatsu Hosokawa (a son of the former feudal lord of Kumamoto).[49] Their summer houses represented the power of wealth and status often in the guise of Western-style architecture. For example, some of them bought summer houses from Genjirō Nozawa, who tied up with the Amerika-ya (American House) Construction Co., which imported two-by-four prefabricated houses from Seattle. Nozawa put up about fifty of them on lots that he began to sell in 1915.[50] In a curious twist, the imported American houses represented the power of the wealthy Japanese people, a charm different from the missionary space in the core of the village. As Karuizawa quickly expanded, its magnetism was thus complicated: the missionary frugality and simplicity was surrounded by what seemed to the average Japanese the "Western" luxury enjoyed by the wealthy Japanese. The village's enchantment was built on a mixture of simplicity accessible for the middle-class and luxury beyond their means.

The lifestyle of the wealthy in the "American" houses was different from that of the middle class. The wealthy people created an exclusive golf club and hosted gatherings and dance parties at the Mikasa Hotel, which became Karuizawa's own Rokumeikan (the Tōkyō guest house where foreign visitors were entertained in the 1880s).[51] At the same time, however, they partly complied with the missionary style of living and morality in Karuizawa. For example, Karuizawa was the foremost "town for formal wives," according to the novelist Renzaburō Shibata (1917–78). The hotelier Ichirō Inumaru (1926–2020) explained the situation by quoting a column written by an unknown person in 1932: "Karuizawa as a summer resort has repudiated and rejected the establishment of the red light district to this day and has made efforts to maintain the custom of purity. I am proud of this, comparing Karuizawa with other resorts."[52] Inumaru further confirmed Shibata's observation: "In Karuizawa, everyone buys land through a friend or an acquaintance, builds a house, and gets to know each other as family friends. At grocery stores or in restaurants, you meet people you know very well. For sure, Karuizawa is a town in which you can walk only with your wife [meaning you cannot walk with a mistress]."[53]

In the old Japanese tradition, concubinage was generally accepted when men could afford it, and this permissiveness did not totally disappear until the rise of the "second-wave" feminism in the 1970s. For the wealthy men, "leisure" often meant spending time with concubines or mistresses. Fun from such leisure time was derived largely from its secretiveness and being able to get away from family concerns. In Karuizawa, on the other hand, relations were supposed to be out in the open, and the men at least had to pretend to be good husbands. Karuizawa became a source of the new culture, of a monogamous and family-oriented way to spend leisure time. The wealthy men whose summer houses surrounded the missionary core seem to have respected and even appreciated the new culture, which would become the norm after World War II.

As an anecdote in this line, the wealthy and influential Japanese summer residents in the area surrounding the missionary core as well as the local Japanese opened a "popular summer college" in 1918. Among the leaders of the project were two prominent summer residents, Shinpei Gotō (1857–1929), the home minister, and Inazō Nitobe (1862–1933), the president of Tōkyō Woman's Christian University, soon to become the deputy secretary-general of the League of Nations. The lecture hall for the college, a donation from a developer, was built by the Amerika-ya Construction Co. Although it is said that the idea of the project was taken from the university extension movement in the United Kingdom and the United States, the college was also similar to chautauquas, a popular adult education and social movement in the US initiated by Methodists in 1874. As a kind of summer camp with religious and educational overtones mixed with elements of fun, it was widely popular in rural America till the 1920s. Most of the American missionaries in Japan were familiar with the movement because stories about foreign missions were a regular feature of chautauquas, and therefore various missionary magazines that circulated widely not only among American home-front supporters but also among missionaries reported on chautauquas each summer.[54] Some of the missionaries' Bible and English classes in Karuizawa, by emulation of this movement, showed the local Japanese that learning was a part of summer fun. Presumably, some of the local Japanese promoters of the popular summer college had learned this idea from the practice of missionaries.

HYBRID CONSTRUCTION OF THE
HOSHINO ONSEN RYOKAN

At a glance, the village of Kutsukake (the current Naka Karuizawa), in which the Hoshino Onsen Ryokan (the Hoshino Hot Spring Inn) was opened in 1914, looks like a mere extension of Karuizawa, which is only four kilometers away. However, a close look at its cultural construction reveals its unique way of combining Japanese and Western traditions. An examination of the history of the development of the Hoshino Onsen Ryokan in Kutsukake will serve as a good case study to show the hybrid origin of the contemporary Japanese soft power called omotenashi.

The Hoshinos of the Hoshino Onsen Ryokan came originally from a village called Iwamurada, near Kutsukake. Kasuke Hoshino II (1875–1931), who was born into a prosperous silk-trading family, bought a forest on a mountain in Kutsukake and embarked on the lumber business in 1904. In 1911 he bought the area adjacent to his land, on which was located a hot spring that had been used since the twelfth century. There in 1913 he began to dig for new springs. In the same year, he built a bathhouse. In 1914 the Hoshio Onsen Ryokan launched its operation.[55]

The first definitely Japanese element that the Hoshino Onsen Ryokan incorporated was its hot spring, one of the most important, traditional, and popular forms of relaxation for the Japanese. In the period after the opening of Japan in the 1850s, Western visitors had curiously observed the Japanese habit of mixed bathing in public bath houses, a custom the Japanese government had long tried to change. Even before the opening of the nation to the West, the Tokugawa shogunate worried about promiscuity and tried in vain to ban the practice. The Meiji government reinforced the ban as it was keenly aware of the Western gaze.[56] By the time the British "lady traveler" Isabella Bird (1831–1904) journeyed to Japan in the late 1870s, the public bath house had become a must-see for foreign visitors. In Kuroishi, Aomori Prefecture, the rickshaw man whom Bird employed took her into a public bath house without her asking. She observed, "I noticed that formal politeness prevailed in the bath-house as elsewhere. . . . But the Government is doing its best to prevent promiscuous bathing; and though the reform may travel slowly into those remote regions, it will doubtless arrive sooner or later. The public bath-house is one of the features in Japan."[57]

The Hoshino Onsen Ryokan put *onsen* (hot spring) in its name, making it the facility's main attraction. As explained above, there was no hot spring in Karuizawa proper, and the absence was its serious disadvantage as a tourist resort for the Japanese. But the Hoshino's bath house was not like the one that Isabella Bird saw in the 1870s. It had a partition between spaces for men and women,[58] avoiding the risk of blame for promiscuity. The main building of the Hoshino Onsen Ryokan was in a typical Japanese inn style, with tatami mats that required shoes off, although Kasuke Hoshino II soon built rental summer houses around the main building, some of which seem to have been Western in style, like the one that Kanzō Uchimura (1861–1930), a leading Japanese Christian nationalist, used in the 1920s.[59] Thus, Kasuke II offered a hybrid service by mixing the Japanese traditional pleasure with the Western style of living and morality.

For an outdoor amusement, the Hoshino Onsen Ryokan provided swimming, a sport with which the Japanese had been familiar as an island people. Using the hot spring, the inn built an outdoor swimming pool that could be used even in the relatively cool climate of the highlands.[60]

Every evening in the front garden of the Hoshino Onsen Ryokan, a party of Bon festival dancing was held, in which not only the guests and the workers of the Ryokan participated but also visitors in the vicinity. Bon festival dancing was a traditional Japanese free and easy dancing party held in summer during the Festival of the Dead, which had been often a sex orgy.[61] The Hoshino Onsen Ryokan's Bon festival dancing, however, excluded this particular part of the traditional amusement. Torahiko Terada (1878–1935), a well-known scientist and essayist who visited the Hoshino Onsen Ryokan, wrote in 1933,

> In those days [around 1901], the Bon festival dancing was considered a "barbarous custom and shame if seen by foreigners," and it was banned in public as I remember. The Bon festival dancing has been held secretly, however, in isolated villages far away from a metropolis. . . . But recently, probably as part of an attempt to nurture the spirit of nationalism, with permission from the police, the dancing seems to have revived silently.
>
> In the front garden of the Hoshino Onsen Ryokan . . . , first came little girls and then young people working at the inn's counter and gradually adults, and soon a circle was complete. . . .
>
> There were girls with short hair and Western clothes and young men with trousers, shirts, and Japanese wooden clogs. Mingled with them were visitors in their *yukata* (informal cotton kimonos), covering their heads with Japanese cotton towels, as well as maids of the inn. It was a strange scenery that forced a drastic correction of the old concept of the Bon festival dancing that we had so far held. Further, the music from a gramophone contained sounds of Western instruments. . . . This was an aspect of advancement of the Bon festival dancing and symbolized the current Japanese situation.[62]

On the background of updating the Japanese traditional amusements in the way of eliminating the "promiscuous" elements, there was Christian influence that emanated from the American and Canadian missionaries in nearby Karuizawa. But the Ryokan's *direct* contact with Christianity was not through missionaries but through Kanzō Uchimura, who had attracted many young elitist men with his prophetic social criticism as well as interpretation of the Bible.

In the summer of 1921, Uchimura stayed in one of the rental summer houses of the Hoshino Onsen Ryokan. He gave a special lecture for the Course for Free Education and Arts, which was held at the Hoshino Onsen Ryokan for the first time that year, probably following the example of the popular summer college in Karuizawa, although humbler in scale. Since then, Uchimura spent every summer at one of the rental houses, holding a Bible class on Saturdays and a gathering and worship on Sundays. Among all the peculiarities of Uchimura's interpretation of Christianity,[63] what is important in the context of this chapter is that he disliked North American missionaries and the Western customs they had introduced. He did not belong to any denomination, did not establish a church, and insisted on a form of Christianity that would be viable in the context of Japanese tradition and society. His influence on the Hoshino Onsen Ryokan, therefore, meant an inherent criticism of the Christianity in the old Karuizawa.

Uchimura treated especially kindly the son of Kasuke Hoshino II, who later became Kasuke Hoshino III (1905–82). In 1935 Uchimura wrote for him a list of ten commandments for business success, which included the warning "Don't emulate the American principle that seeks only for success. Keep the Japanese principle of sincerity."[64] He also named the wooden barn that had been used as a lecture hall during summer the Hoshino Hall for Play and Study and wrote this in calligraphy on its doorplate.

Through Kasuke Hoshino III, Uchimura's influence infiltrated into the Hoshino Onsen Ryokan. Although the Christianity was different from the one introduced by the North American missionaries, his influence was Christian nonetheless. In this sense, the Hoshio Onsen Ryokan adopted something of the missionary Karuizawa. Probably for Kasuke III, the difference between Uchimura and the North American missionaries was not so clear or was not as important as for Uchimura. Hoshino described positively the Christian influence on Karuizawa proper: "The mall in Karuizawa was just like a foreign concession. On Sundays, people gathered at the Union Church overcoming the denominational differences. Merchants and craftsmen were influenced by Christians in their lifestyles. On Sundays, there were no sales and work. Further, the local people learned to be punctual, not to tell a lie, enjoy a simple life and tennis, and love nature."[65]

Nevertheless, Kasuke III's approach at the Hoshino Onsen Ryokan was a peculiar mixture of the Japanese tradition and the North American influence through missionaries. For example, he loved nature as he learned from the missionaries, but the love was expressed in his interest in bird watching, which he learned from a Buddhist priest, Godō Nakanishi (1895–1984), the founder of the Wild Birds Society in Japan, who stayed in the Hoshino Onsen Ryokan regularly. Hoshino often sponsored bird walks in Karuizawa and around the Hoshino Onsen Ryokan, which developed into a movement to preserve nature there.[66]

By incorporating elements of Japanese culture in its hybrid approach, he succeeded in obtaining patronage among many well-known Japanese intellectuals, novelists, poets, artists, and others.[67] Most of them belonged to the middle-class in terms of the economy and were not Christians and therefore were probably uncomfortable with the missionary core or with the area for the very wealthy and privileged around the core.

Testifying to the charms of the hybrid culture of the Hoshino Onsen Ryokan, Toyo Kasuga (1881–1962), the founder of the Kasuga school of *kouta* music (a kind of ballad singing accompanied by a stringed instrument called a *shamisen*), stayed at the Hoshino Onsen Ryokan beginning in 1936. Kasuga was the daughter of Englishman and a Japanese woman and had been raised in the culture of Japanese pleasure and entertainment in Asakusa,[68] the center of such culture in Tōkyō. Her Eurasian hybridity must have resonated with the Hoshino Onsen Ryokan and its vicinity.

Thus, the Hoshino Onsen Ryokan advanced a step forward the hybridity that began in Karuizawa and indigenized it in the soil of Kutsukake.

KUTSUKAKE TO NAKA KARUIZAWA

While Kasuke Hoshino III controlled the Hoshino Onsen Ryokan (1931–82), the influence of Kanzō Uchimura remained at the Ryokan. The original Hoshino Hall for Play and Study had been removed and rebuilt and accommodated Christian activities. In 1949 the Asama Kōgen Church was organized at the Ryokan.[69] In 1965 the hall was removed and rebuilt again and was the site of Christian worship "every Sunday as the philosophical basis of the Hoshino Onsen" at least until 1972, when Hoshino wrote a history of his business.[70]

In 1951 the Hoshino Onsen Ryokan was reorganized into the Hoshino Onsen Company Ltd., dropping "Ryokan" and its reference to a Japanese-style inn from the name.[71] In 1957, as mentioned earlier, the legendary romance between the current emperor emeritus, Akihito, and the empress emeritus, Michiko, on Karuizawa's tennis courts boosted the already established fame of the place as a space for love and romance, a situation that North American missionaries had been deeply involved in creating.[72] In 1960 the village of Kutsukake decided to change its name formally to Naka Karuizawa, emphasizing its closeness to Karuizawa.[73] *Naka* means "in between," and thus the naming was incidentally symbolic, implying the village was "half" Karuizawa.

Meanwhile, the eldest son of Kasuke III (later, Kasuke Hoshino IV) studied at Indiana University in the United States in the 1950s.[74] On his return to Japan, he participated in the management of the Hoshino Onsen Company and seems to have begun to utilize more ambitiously the dynamics of hybridity that had taken shape in Karuizawa and Kutsukake, thus turning the attributes of hybridity into the soft power of his business. In 1965 the Hotel New Hoshino was opened on a site nearer to the Naka Karuizawa railway station, and it was on this occasion that the Hoshino Hall for Play and Study was rebuilt on the spot next to the Hotel New Hoshino.[75] At the same time, the hall's name was changed to Karuizawa Kōgen Church.[76] In so doing, the Hoshino Onsen Company was able to sell a Christian wedding ceremony and party as a package. In the latter half of the 1960s, the percentage of "love marriages" in Japan (48.7) exceeded that of traditional arranged marriages (44.9).[77] The company was keen to ride the trend and took advantage of the fame of Karuizawa as a space for romance as well as Hoshino's historical relationship with Christianity, the religion that had long vindicated love marriage in Karuizawa and elsewhere in Japan.[78] In the 1980s when a Christian wedding ceremony became the vogue, Karuizawa Kōgen Church gained wide popularity as one of its meccas.

In 1988 Kasuke IV built the Stone Chapel adjacent to Karuizawa Kōgen Church to commemorate Kanzō Uchimura. As of 2021, the relics that Uchimura left in the Hoshino Onsen Ryokan, such as calligraphies for the Hoshino Hall for Play and Study and the scroll for his commandments for business success, are stored in the chapel's basement, where anyone can go and see them. But obviously the new chapel was built for wedding ceremonies. This is a real irony because Kanzō Uchimura severely criticized the custom of courtship and love marriage introduced by American missionaries.[79] For Kasuke IV, neither Karuizawa Kōgen Church nor the Stone Chapel was meant for a regular Sunday service, although seasonal events such as Christmas illuminations were centered around the church and the chapel. In short, these facilities were not primarily religious but theaters for consumptive events, part of the amusement that the Hoshino Onsen provided for its guests.[80]

In 1991 Yoshiharu Hoshino, the eldest son of Kasuke IV, took over the presidency of the Hoshino Onsen. In 1995 he reorganized the company into

Hoshino Resorts, Inc., which specializes in resort management. At the same time, he demolished the Hotel New Hoshino to build Karuizawa Hotel Bleston Court to continue to sell wedding packages in an updated style as well as "an unforgettable gourmet stay at the refined Karuizawa high-end resort town where you can enjoy the beauty and the delicacies of the changing seasons."[81] In 2005 he tore down the old Hoshino Onsen facilities to build Hoshinoya Karuizawa, again in the flavor of a Japanese inn, and began to sell "nature" around Hoshinoya.[82] The attributes of Kasuke Hoshino III—such as the spirit of nature loving (especially bird watching) of missionary origin—and a Japanese-style inn are all major Hoshinoya sales points. There are even the independent power plants that Kasuke III first installed in 1929, which unexpectedly meet sustainable development guidelines because they use natural energy from the streams in the vicinity.[83] As Yoshiharu Hoshino builds his business on the Hosihno's tradition of hybridity but with more emphatic use of the Japanese elements, he tries to redefine the hybridity as a Japanese soft power, omotenashi.

Yoshiharu Hoshino quickly expanded the business out of Karuizawa and now aims to become a leading resorts developer and hotel management specialist in Japan, as mentioned in the beginning of this chapter. He did not adopt the name of Kasuke, probably to distance from his forefathers. The Hoshino Resorts' idea of "providing high level of Omotenashi, Japanese-style hospitality,"[84] however, has been nurtured in Kutsukake / Naka Karuizawa, where his forefathers tried to adapt to or absorb the missionary influence while selectively keeping the Japanese traditions. Particularly, the missionary standard of morality was important in defining the elements of hospitality, pleasure, and entertainment. Only by conforming to what the missionaries in Karuizawa insisted on in terms of gender and sexuality was a new style of Japanese hospitality born, one respectable enough for Westerners.

The Hoshinos' example should be but one of many that have contributed to what is now an important Japanese soft power in the international arena, omotenashi. However, this examination makes it clear that soft power is not intrinsic to a nation but is created through a long history of adoptions, alterations, and negotiations as well as business aspirations and initiative.

NOTES

This chapter is a reconsideration of my previous articles on Karuizawa regarding soft power. See Rui Kohiyama, "From the Indian Ocean to the Pacific: Missionary Summer Resorts in Asia," in *Indian Ocean*, ed. Kousar J. Azam (New Delhi: Manohar, 2019), 85–103, and Rui Kohiyama, "Senkyōshi Kukan tositeno Karuizawa to Junnai Bunnka

[Karuizawa as a missionary space and the creation of romantic love culture in Japan," *Tōkyō Joshi Daigaku Hikakubunnka Kennkyūjo Kiyo* 81 (January 2020): 1–23.

1. As a result, "omotenashi" became one of the buzzwords of 2013.

2. Searching for "omotenashi and Japanese culture" on the website of the newspaper *Asahi Shimbun* from 1985 to the present, one can get 127 results starting from 1997. Of these, 86 come from the period after 2013.

3. "About Us," Hoshino Resorts, accessed July 3, 2023, https://www.hoshinoresorts.com /en/aboutus/.

4. "Hoshino Rizōto Daihyō, Hoshino Yoshiharu-shi Intabyū" [An interview with Yoshi-haru Hoshino, the president of Hoshino Resorts, Inc.], Premium Japan, accessed July 2, 2023, https://www.premium-j.jp/pastarticles/20180322_1797/.

5. E.g., see "The Ridge, Shimla," Department of Tourism and Civil Aviation, Govern-ment of Himathal Pradesh, accessed July 3, 2023, https://himachaltourism.gov.in /destination/shimla/. As for hill stations in British India, see Dane Kennedy, *The Magic Mountains* (Berkeley: University of California Press, 1996). Shimla, the most famous hill station in India, was in dense forest in the eighteenth century. After the British East India Company took control of the area in the early nineteenth century, British colo-nialists began to spend summers in the area. By 1864, when the decision was made to permanently shift the British Army's headquarters from Calcutta to Shimla, Shimla became the virtual summer capital of British India. See Vipin Pubby, *Shimla, Then and Now: Summer Capital of the Raj*, 2nd ed. (New Delhi: Indus, 1996), chaps. 1 and 2.

6. J. E. Spencer and W. L. Thomas, "The Hill Stations and Summer Resorts of the Orient," *Geographical Review* 38, no. 4 (October, 1948): 643.

7. I have checked missionary letters in the following books: Michio Takaya, ed. and trans., *Hebon Shokan Shū* [Letters of Samuel Hepburn] (Tōkyō: Iwanami Shoten, 1988); Michio Takaya, ed. and trans., *Hebon no Tegami* [Letters of Hepburn] (Yokohama: Yurin-do,1978); Michio Takaya, ed. and trans., *S. R. Brown Shokan Shū* [Letters of S. R. Brown] (Tōkyō: Nihon Kirisutokyōdan Shuppankyoku, 1980); Michio Takaya, ed. and trans., *Furubekki Shokan Shū* [Letters of Verbeck] (Tōkyō: Shinkyō Shuppan-sha, 1978); Ferris Jogakuin, ed. and trans., *Kidā Shokan Shū* [Letters of Mary E. Kidder] (Tōkyō: Kyōbunkan, 1976).

8. Hiroshi Maruyama, "Kindai Tsūrizumu no Reimei" [The dawn of modern tourism], in *19 seiki no Nihon no Jōhō to Shakaihendō* [Information and social change in nineteenth-century Japan], ed. Mitsukuni Yoshida (Kyōto: Kyōto Daigaku Jinbunkagaku Kenkyūjo, 1985), 90–94. I would like to mention here for accuracy that in the Japan-US Treaty of Peace and Amity of 1858, Kanagawa instead of Yokohama was designated as the port to be opened, and the American consulate was actually located there. Soon, however, the Japanese government built a concession in nearby Yokohama, which was closer to the port. Then all the foreigners in Kanagawa were requested to move and live in the concession in Yokohama.

9. Jogakuin, *Kidā Shokan*, 78, 125.

10. Ernest Mason Satow and A. G. S. Haws, *A Handbook for Travellers in Central and North-ern Japan*, 2nd ed. (London: Murray, 1884), 229.

11. Yasuharu Miyahara, *Karuizawa Monogatari* [A Karuizawa story] (Tōkyō: Kōdan-sha, 1991), 61–65.

12. Calculated from the table in Daisuke Satō and Isao Saitō, "Meiji Taishō-ki no Karuizawa niokeru Kōgen Hishochi no Keisei to Bessō Shoyūsha no Hensen" [Hill station

formation and changes in ownership in Karuizawa], *Rekishi Chiri-gaku* 46, no. 3 (June, 2004): 6.

13. Calculated from the table in Toshihiro Hanazato, "Senzenki no Karuizawa no Bessō-chi niokeru Gaikokujin no Shoyū, Taizai to Taijinteki Kankyō no Yōtai" [The status of the ownership and the occupancy by foreigners and the interpersonal environment at the summer retreat areas in prewar Karuizawa], *Nihon Kenchiku Gakkai Keikaku-kei Ronbun-shū* 77, no. 672 (February 2012): 251.

14. From the map in 1911 in Hanazato, 253.

15. Miyahara, *Karuizawa*, 65. In 1890 ten kilograms of rice cost about ¥0.5.

16. Kazumi Fukuda, *Nikkō Masuzuri Shinshi Monogatari* [A story of a trout-fisher gentlemen in Nikkō] (Tōkyō: Yama to Keikoku-sha, 1999), 61.

17. E.g., in 1890 the US Presbyterian Japan Mission paid monthly about ¥200 ($100) to married male missionaries. In 1891 the Japanese male headmaster at Ferris Seminary, a mission girls' school in Yokohama, was paid ¥30 monthly. Letter, T. M. MacNair (December 28, 1891), in Japan Letters, Records of US Presbyterian Missions in Japan, Yokohama Archives of History; *Ferris Jogakuin 150 nenshi* [150 years of Ferris Seminary] (Yokohama: Ferris Jogakuin, 2022), 141n33.

18. The railroad from Tōkyō to Yokokawa was opened in 1885 and a horse-carriage railway from Yokokawa to Karuizawa in 1887, while the railroad from Ueno (Tōkyō) to Utsunomiya was opened in 1885 and from Utsunomiya to Nikkō in 1890. A railway for electric vehicles from Nikkō to Umagaeshi was opened in 1913, and a new road from Umagaeshi to Chūzenji was opened in 1925. Karuizawa is located 934 meters above sea level, while Oku Nikkō (Lake Chūzenji) is at 1269 meters.

19. Miyahara, *Karuizawa*, 95–95.

20. Manpei Satō, who opened Manpei Hotel in 1895, was one such quick Japanese who responded to Westerners' demands.

21. Miyagi Jogakuin Shiryōshitsu, "Hansen-sensei, Rinzē-sensei to Karuizawa Sansō" [Misses Hansen and Lyndsay and the mountain villa in Karuizawa], *Shin, Kibo, Ai*, no. 16 (March 2010): 103.

22. "Dentō Kōgei Karuizawa-bori" [Traditional craft *karuizawa-bori*], Karuizawa Machi Yakuba, accessed July 3, 2023, https://www.town.karuizawa.lg.jp/www/sp/contents/1001000000735/.

23. Eric Hobsbawm and Terence Ranger, eds., *The Invention of Tradition* (Cambridge: Cambridge University Press, 1983).

24. As for general characteristics of imperial hill stations, see Kennedy, *Magic Mountains*. As for Karuizawa, see Osamu Kobayashi, *Hishochi Karuizawa* [Summer resort Karuizawa] (Saku, Nagano: Ichii, 1999), esp. 51–52 for sick and wounded soldiers.

25. Calculated from the table in Hanazato, "Senzenki," 251.

26. In 1889 about one hundred villagers came to one of such meetings according to G. P. Pierson. See Rev. and Mrs. Pierson, *Tenshi wa Futari de Tatsu* [Forty happy years in Japan], 2nd ed. (Kitami: Nihon Kirisutokyōkai Kitami Kyōkai Pierson Bunko, 2011), 53.

27. Miyahara, *Karuizawa*, 194.

28. See also Pierson, *Tenshi*, 54–55, in which the author appreciated exchanges with those who had different theological viewpoints.

29. Hakuchō Masamune, "Karuizawa to Watashi" [Karuizawa and I], *Gunzō* (October 1957), as quoted in Kiyoshi Shimazaki, ed., *Karuizawa Hyaku-nen no Ayumi* [One

hundred years of Karuizawa] (Karuizawa: self-pub., 1985), 41. The translation is mine and hereafter the same for Japanese authors unless noted otherwise. Ikaho is a traditional resort with hot springs and geishas about sixty kilometers from Karuizawa.

30. Kate I. Hansen, postcard, August 7, 1908, in Miyagi Jogakuin Shiryōshitsu, "Hansen-sensei," 102.

31. As for houses on the imperial hill stations in India, see Kennedy, *Magic*, 103–6.

32. Kennedy, 103–6.

33. Miyahara, *Karuizawa*, 205.

34. Miyahara, 203–6.

35. I thank Hiroaki Kinoshita of the Karuizawa National Trust for generously lending me the handbook of 1922. The handbook of 1930 is reprinted in Shōko Komatsu, *Karuizawa to Hisho* [Karuizawa and summering] (Tōkyō: Yumani Shobō, 2009).

36. *The Karuizawa Summer Residents' Association Handbook* (Kobe: Far Eastern Advertising Agency, 1922), cover, 6.

37. Kennedy, *Magic*, 101.

38. Emma Gerberding Lippard, *Second Hand* (Philadelphia: United Lutheran Publication House, 1934), 149.

39. Even early Japanese summer residents in Karuizawa, the exceptional elites in the Japanese society, seem to have felt a certain distance from the foreigners. See Miyahara, *Karuizawa*, 207–8. Further, many Japanese served the summer residents. There was obviously a difference between the serving and the served.

40. As for hill stations in India, see Kennedy, *Magic*, chap. 6.

41. Rui Kohiyama, *Amerika Fujin Senkyōshi: Rainichi no Haikei to Sono Eikyō* [American women missionaries: Their backgrounds and influences] (Tōkyō: University of Tōkyō Press, 1992, 182–83.

42. See Kristin Hoganson, "What's Gender Got to Do with It? Women and Foreign Relations History," *OAH Magazine of History* 19, no. 2 (March 2005): 14–18, and Karin Aggestam and Ann Towns, "The Gender Turn in Diplomacy: A New Research Agenda," *International Feminist Journal of Politics* 21, no. 1 (February 2019): 9–28.

43. E.g., see Miyagi Jogakuin Shiryōshitsu, "Hansen-sensei," and Fumi Sakai, "Karuizawa to Senkyōshitachi" [Karuizawa and missionaries], *Fuen* 70 (January 2013).

44. Natsuko Machida, who worked at a photo shop on Karuizawa's main street testified that there were no fences between houses in Karuizawa until 1930s. See Ichirō Inumaru, *Karuizawa Densetsu* [The Karuizawa legend] (Tōkyō: Kodansha, 2011), 197–98.

45. At least in the imagination of a missionary writer, young male and female missionaries met in Karuizawa and got married. Lippard, *Second Hand*, chap. 26.

46. See, e.g., Tatsuo Hori, *Kaze Tachinu* [The wind has risen] (Tōkyō: Noda Shobō, 1938).

47. See, e.g., "Love That Grew Up in Karuizawa," *Asahi Shinbun*, November 27, 1958.

48. See notes 15 and 16 above. There still remain in Oku Nikkō the former summer houses for the British, Italian, and Belgian ambassadors. Their grandeur makes a good contrast to a humble cottage built by an American missionary in the core of Karuizawa, which was rented and bought by Tatsuo Hori in 1941. The cottage was moved to the grounds of the Literary Museum of Karuizawa in 1985, where you can still see it.

49. Satō and Saitō, "Meiji Taishō-ki," 10–15; Hanazato, "Senzenki," 255; Kobayashi, *Hisho-chi Karuizawa*, 50–58, 86–93, 108–110, 211–13, 235–37, 283; Katsuhiko Shichinohe, "Hōgakusha no Karuizawa" [Karuizawa for a law scholar], *Hōsei Kenkyū* 81, no. 3 (December 2014): 240–47; Shimazaki, *Karuizawa*, 51.

50. Shimazaki, *Karuizawa*, 43–44.

51. As for the Karuizawa Golf Club, see Inumaru, *Karuizawa*, chap. 3. As for the Mikasa Hotel, see "Karuizawa no Rokumeikan" [The guest palace of Karuizawa], NYK Maritime Museum, accessed July 3, 2023, https://museum.nyk.com/kouseki/200205/index.html.

52. Inumaru, *Karuizawa*, 31.

53. Inumaru, 50.

54. As for the popular summer college, see Miyahara, *Karuizawa*, 243–47; *Karuizawa Chōshi Rekishi-hen (Kin-Gendai)* [History of Karuizawa Town (the modern and contemporary period)] (Karuizawa: Karuizawa Chōshi Kankō Iinkai, 1988), 287–98; and Seizō Uchida, "Senzenki niokeru Karuizawa Bessōchi to Yōfū Bessō no Henyō nikansuru Kenkyū" [A study on the changes of the land use and the housing style in Karuizawa before World War II], *Kenkyū Nenpō (Jūsōken)*, no. 27 (2000): 60. As for chatauquas, see Rui Kohiyama, *Teikoku no Fukuin: Rūshī Pībodī to Amerika no Kaigai Dendō* [The gospel of empire: Lucy Peabody and the American foreign mission enterprise] (Tōkyō: University of Tōkyō Press, 2019), 155–56.

55. Kasuke Hoshino, *Yamabōshi* [Kousa dogwood] (Karuizawa: Hoshino Onsen, 1972), 3–9, 15–20.

56. Koushi Shimokawa, *Konyoku to Nihonshi* [Mixed bathing and the history of Japan] (Tōkyō: Chikuma Shobō, 2013), 146–48, 164, 174–76.

57. Isabella L. Bird, *Unbeaten Tracks in Japan*, vol. 1 (New York: G. P. Putnam's Sons, 1881), 398–99.

58. Hoshino, *Yamabōshi*, 207.

59. "Mr. and Mrs. Uchimura in front of the Hoshino Mountain Villa," Uchimura Kanzō Kinen Bunko, accessed July 3, 2023, https://www-lib.icu.ac.jp/Uchimura/DigitalArchive/html/03-22.html.

60. "Mr. and Mrs. Uchimura," photo on the front page and 562.

61. For details, see Koushi Shimokawa, *Bonodori: Rankō no Minzoku-gaku* [Bon festival dancing: Folkfore of the sex orgy] (Tōkyō: Sakuhinsha, 2011).

62. Hoshino, *Yamabōshi*, 223–24.

63. As for peculiar characteristics of Uchimura's version of Christianity, see a brief introduction and references in English at "Uchimura, Kanzō," Boston University, accessed July 2, 2023, https://www.bu.edu/missiology/missionary-biography/t-u-v/uchimura-kanzo-1861-1930/.

64. Hoshino, *Yamabōshi*, 36–42.

65. Hoshino, 96.

66. Hoshino, 71–72, 88–89; "Karuizawa, the Forest for Wild Birds," Ministry of the Environment, accessed July 2, 2023 http://chubu.env.go.jp/shinetsu/[Web]_jp.pdf.

67. Hoshino, *Yamabōshi*, 31–73.

68. Hoshino, 74–82; "The School Founder: Toyo Kasuga," Kasugakai, accessed December 6, 2021, http://kasugakai.jp/toyo.html. Eurasians in Japan often belonged to Japanese mothers' side because the legitimacy was not given by foreigner fathers.

69. *Karuizawa Chōshi*, 686.

70. Hoshino, *Yamabōshi*, 42.

71. Kasuke Hoshino, *Kobushi no Hana* [Magnolia kobus] (self-pub., 1984), 456.

72. See Kohiyama, "Senkyōshi," 17.

73. "Karuizawa Nenpyō" [Time table of Karuizawa], Karuizawa Kankō Kyōkai, accessed June 5, 2022, https://karuizawa-kankokyokai.jp/knowledge/265/; "Karuizawa-chō no Ayumi" [History of the town of Karuizawa], Karuizawa-chō, accessed June 6, 2022, https://www.town.karuizawa.lg.jp/www/contents/1001000000004/index.html.

74. Yoshiharu Hoshino, "History (6): Hoshino Yoshiharu-shi, Hoshino-ke, Taenu Kakushin" [Mr. Yoshiharu Hoshino, the Hoshinos and incessant renovations], *Nikkei Shinbun* [newspaper], September 18, 2020.

75. Hoshino, *Yamabōshi*, 42.

76. "Company History" in "About Us."

77. Ryūichi Kaneko, Tsukasa Sasai, Saori Kamano, Miho Iwasawa, Fusami Mita, and Rie Moriizumi, "Marriage Process and Fertility of Japanese Married Couples: Overview of the Results of the Thirteenth Japanese National Fertility Survey, Married Couples," *Japanese Journal of Population* 6, no. 1 (March 2008): 27.

78. As for the relationship between Christianity, love romance, and marriage in general in Japan, see Rui Kohiyama, "Hokubeishutuji no Joseisenkyōshi niyoru Joshikyōiku to 'Hōmu' no Jitsugen" [Women's education by the North American women missionaries and the realization of "home"], in *Kindai Nihon no Kirisutokyō to Joshikyōiku*, ed. Kirisutokyō Shigakkai (Tōkyō: Kyōbunkan, 2016), 19–48.

79. Kohiyama, 46–47.

80. Kohiyama, "Senkyōshi," 17–18.

81. "A Deluxe Gourmet Stay in a secluded Highland Resort, merely one hour from Tokyo," Hotel Bleston Court, accessed on July 2, 2023, https://www.blestoncourt.com/en/.

82. "Yamaai no Shūraku nite Mori no Koe wo Kiku" [Listening to voices from woods in a village in the mountains], Hoshinoya, accessed July 3, 2023, https://hoshinoya.com/karuizawa/.

83. "Hoshino Resorts' Way of SDGs" and "Company History" in "About Us." As for the history of power generation, also see Hoshino, *Yamabōshi*, 88.

84. "About Us."

CHAPTER 3

Refusing to Be Soft on US Racism

African Americans in the Soviet Union as Soft Power Agents of Black Liberation in the Interwar Era

Meredith L. Roman

In 1932 the African American writer Langston Hughes boarded a train "going South in Russia" to explore firsthand how the Soviet project was transforming the lives of Central Asians. He had arrived in Moscow in June to help make a Soviet film that condemned racism in the United States. Hughes, like some other Black Americans, expressed feelings of internationalist affinity for the populations of the "Soviet South." Although they were not of African descent, Central Asians were fellow persons of color who were liberating themselves from the legacies of czarist Russian oppression. Since Soviet soft power measures sought to convince African Americans that communism provided *the* ideological path to Black liberation, Hughes was shown only the positive aspects of life under Soviet rule. Yet when Hughes wrote about his journey in a 1934 essay for *Crisis* magazine, he focused extensively on the travel itself rather than the destination. Public transportation was one of the most powerful manifestations of American racial apartheid, limiting the freedom of movement of all Blacks—in the US South *and* North, as Hughes emphasized—regardless of age, class, or professional status.[1] The absence of the surveillance and humiliations of Jim Crow segregation on the Moscow-Tashkent Express had a deep emotional impact on him. This Soviet train, Hughes explained, transported him not only physically to Central Asia but also temporally back to a time in his childhood before his mind and body had been traumatized by the institutionalized anti-Black racism that afforded him treatment "like a dog." The journey powerfully affirmed what he had instinctively known as a young boy, that a world—a "South"—without the lie of Black inferiority was possible and constituted the future.[2]

Hughes's powerful commentary about his Soviet experiences underscores the critical role that African Americans who traveled to the USSR in the interwar decades played as soft power agents of Black liberation. In addition to Hughes, several hundred African Americans of diverse political and socioeconomic backgrounds journeyed to the Soviet Union to raise international attention to US racial apartheid while investigating the veracity of Soviet claims of having established a morally superior society where racism was absent. Leaders in Moscow implemented an array of soft power measures that appealed to many African Americans' dreams of a world without the violence and indignities of anti-Black racism. Given the USSR's considerable economic and military inferiority vis-à-vis the capitalist West in the 1920s and 1930s, Soviet authorities lacked the hard power tools to bring about communist revolution in the United States through military force or intensive financial investment. However, if they could persuade African Americans—whom they identified as the most oppressed segment of US society—to support communist revolution, then they could perhaps make this transformation possible.

The Soviet soft power agenda directed at Black Americans assumed greater priority by 1928 with the ascendancy of the militant Third Period (1928–35) of the Communist International (Comintern). Authorities of the Third International posited that an impending crisis in capitalism would bring with it a proliferation of revolutionary opportunities. The Sixth Comintern Congress in Moscow in 1928 officially declared African Americans an oppressed nation with the right to national self-determination and designated them the vanguard among oppressed nations.[3] This decree—which African American communist Harry Haywood was instrumental in crafting—made American Blacks "indispensable allies" to the USSR at a time when the country was embarking on an intensive campaign to build socialism in what Soviet leaders depicted as an extremely antagonistic capitalist world. Despite many African American communists' initial opposition, the 1928 Comintern decree of nationhood was of immense significance. As historian Mark Naison emphasizes, it "endowed the black struggle with unprecedented dignity and importance."[4] Since Western democratic leaders granted national self-determination only to the supposedly "politically mature" peoples of eastern Central Europe after World War II and not their own colonies in Africa, Asia, and the Caribbean, the

Comintern decree was intended to impress African Americans with Moscow's commitment to supporting Black liberation and affirmed their status as valued foreign revolutionaries.[5]

African Americans were, of course, not universally sold on Soviet communism as the antidote to racism. However, many nonetheless rejected the fierce anticommunism that US leaders demanded as a sign of loyalty.[6] As members of a minority group whom US racial capitalism purposefully kept impoverished, disenfranchised, and poorly educated, they lacked the hard power of military or economic strength to force US leaders to implement policies that would make Black equality a reality. Efforts at Black armed self-defense in the early twentieth century in the face of white mob violence and "pogroms" in northern and midwestern cities had been defeated by law enforcement officials, the National Guard, and white vigilante forces that were deputized across the country.[7] The failure of politicians to pass antilynching legislation epitomized their apathy toward Blacks' lack of self-possession and self-determination imperative to genuine freedom.

Without access to hard power, African Americans such as Hughes exercised soft power agency by traveling to the USSR to internationalize the anti-Black violence that the caretakers of American capitalist democracy shamelessly sanctioned. To be sure, before US leaders even established diplomatic recognition with the USSR in November 1933, African Americans practiced their own form of foreign relations by adopting Soviet soft power measures for their own purposes. The representations of Soviet racial equality that they created exemplify the circular nature of soft power politics. While Soviet leaders aspired to sell African Americans on communism, Black sojourners to the USSR such as Hughes sought to persuade US politicians that their continued sanction of Black inequality threatened the nation's security and compromised their prideful claims to be the world's beacon of democracy.[8] They also wanted to encourage fellow Blacks not to surrender the capacity to imagine a world beyond the violent racial apartheid of Jim Crow.

This essay examines the Scottsboro protest campaign as a definitive example of the convergence of African Americans and Soviet leaders' soft power interests. From 1931 through 1932, leaders of the Soviet organization known as the International Organization for Assistance to Revolutionary Fighters (Mezhdunarodnaia Organizatsiia Pomoshchi Bortsam Revoliutsii), known by its Russian acronym MOPR, organized an international campaign to liberate nine male African American teenagers in Scottsboro, Alabama, whom an all-white jury had condemned to death on trumped-up charges of raping two white women. Authorities in Moscow directed the Scottsboro campaign at an African American audience but also used it to instruct the

Soviet populace that their transformation into the morally superior "New Soviet Men" and "New Soviet Women" required them to emphatically reject the biological racism ascendant throughout the globe, to condemn US racial injustices like the Scottsboro legal lynching, and to embrace African Americans as revolutionary allies. Indeed, according to the Soviet ideological interpretation, the so-called Scottsboro Boys were not "boys" but militant workers whose persecution represented the first step in US leaders' preparations to wage an imperialist war against the USSR. African Americans may have not bought the ideological viewpoint, yet they appreciated how it fueled the Soviet commitment to halting the execution of the Scottsboro youth. This commitment also meant that a Soviet-sponsored organization—namely the International Labor Defense (ILD), MOPR's US affiliate—was the first to defend the Scottsboro teenagers. In contrast, the National Association for the Advancement of Colored People (NAACP) initially refused to take on the Scottsboro case because it involved the charge of rape.[9]

While African Americans' and Soviet authorities' soft power interests converged in the Scottsboro campaign, the film project *Black and White* exposed how they simultaneously diverged because of their different priorities. *Black and White* was scheduled to be filmed in the summer of 1932—at the height of the Scottsboro campaign—and was intended to further convince Black Americans of the Soviet commitment to racial equality and justice. It was *the* Soviet soft power measure that served as the direct impetus behind Langston Hughes's travel to the USSR in June 1932 with twenty other African Americans who enthusiastically supported the film project and were supposed to be its cast. *Black and White* was envisioned as a fictional, feature-length film that dramatized the plight of Black workers in Alabama while placing it within the historical context of racial bondage. Yet precisely because of its intended aggressiveness in attacking the US racial regime, officials in Moscow—without consulting the African American cast—canceled the film's production out of fear of potentially jeopardizing US diplomatic recognition. However, the majority of the African American cast members chose not to publicly attack as "soft" the Soviet commitment to antiracism since it meant relinquishing their soft power agency to advance Black liberation. Indeed, Soviet leaders' abandonment of the film reaffirmed the power of US white supremacy and reified Black Americans' resolve that they, unlike leaders of a foreign nation, could not afford to go soft on the struggle to eradicate it. As Hughes's 1934 *Crisis* essay suggests, these cast members, like many other Black American sojourners to the USSR, presented the Soviet Union as a bastion of racial equality not to please leaders in Moscow who would have disapproved of his and others' lack of direct engagement with Marxism-Leninism. Rather, they sought to pressure US leaders into recognizing the imperative of implementing antiracist policies to redeem and defend the security of American democracy. By representing white people, "fair-skinned Russians" as Hughes called them, as more committed to democratic universalism than white supremacy, they also provided evidence that anti-Black racism was unnatural and could be eliminated in their lifetime.

OPPOSING SCOTTSBORO IN THE USSR

Before the nine African American teenagers in Scottsboro became the focus of a protest campaign that touched nearly every corner of the USSR, Soviet cartoons and photographs condemned lynching as a central feature of US capitalist democracy. Given the threat that lynching posed to the physical security of all African Americans, internationalizing these barbaric acts had the potential to win Black Americans' support for communism. One particularly representative lynching cartoon published on the front page of *Rabochaia gazeta* (Workers' newspaper) purported to capture "American 'Democracy,' As It Really Is." The grim reaper is shown disguised as the Statue of Liberty, with ten nooses hanging from her skeletal arms with the bodies of Black American men dangling at the end of five of them. The bottom caption explained that "for Negro-workers in 'free' America there are many free nooses."[10] The publication of lynching photographs in the Soviet press and on postcards conveyed in even starker terms the savagery of these acts of extralegal violence. Such images also no doubt satisfied an interest among Soviet citizens for what scholar Evgeny Steiner calls "sadistic discourse" and replicated the anti-Black violence that their reproduction ostensibly condemned.[11] Yet at the same time the lynching photographs instructed onlookers that this savage conduct was not the behavior of the enlightened "New Soviet Person," who in contrast to their backward white American counterparts recognized their shared humanity and destiny with persons of African descent, whom they embraced as comrades. Indeed, the Soviet press warned that the escalating number of incidents of lynching against their African American allies constituted evidence of the severity of the capitalist threat to the USSR. Moreover, US officials were disturbed by the sale of lynching postcards in the Soviet Union not out of concern for the violence against African Americans that their reproduction replicated but because it fostered a negative image of US democracy within the Soviet populace.[12]

Visual depictions of US lynch law provided a sharp contrast to images in the central press, which showed African Americans being respected as equals in Soviet society. Photographs and sketches of African Americans as laborers working in Soviet factories, visitors touring the country, children attending school, and delegates participating in international conferences symbolically defined the Soviet Union as a place where racism did not exist—that is, which afforded Black Americans, the country's valued revolutionary allies, the opportunity to be students, workers, intellectuals, and leaders without any threat to their physical safety.[13] This message was reinforced by the nationwide press coverage of the August 1930 trial of two white American workers at the Stalingrad Tractor Factory who had attacked Robert Robinson, a Black American laborer. Their sentence of expulsion from the USSR demonstrated that while Soviet citizens and authorities valued US technical expertise, they would not tolerate expressions of anti-Black racism. Thus, if a Black American's safety was compromised as in Robinson's case, then they could be assured that unlike in the United States, the white perpetrators would be swiftly brought to proletarian justice and deported from the country. The implication was that the fate of a Soviet citizen, of whom more was expected, would be far worse.[14]

Representations of Americans racial violence and Soviet racial equality served as the backdrop for the Scottsboro protest campaign—Soviet authorities' most elaborate attempt to impress African Americans with communism's uncompromising opposition to racial injustice. Members of the Soviet intelligentsia were at the forefront of this campaign to save the Black teenagers from the electric chair.[15] Their active involvement in the Scottsboro protest serves as an important reminder of the indispensable role that intellectuals played in soft power initiatives to gain African American support for the Soviet project while also modeling the enlightened antiracist consciousness that citizens were expected to emulate as New Soviet Men and Women. The highly acclaimed Soviet writer Maxim Gorky formed a sixteen-person defense committee known as the Committee for Saving the 9 Negroes that included Black communists George Padmore and Lovett Fort-Whiteman as members. The committee appealed to all male and female workers in the Soviet Union and around the world to "raise a protest against the verdict and execution of 9 Negro workers" and recognize that "saving the lives of the prisoners in Scottsboro rests entirely in the hands of the working masses."[16] They condemned as an old form of "racist 'trickery'" the accusation that the young men, who represented "the doubly oppressed and persecuted Negro proletariat," raped two white women. The real "crime" for which the "bourgeois-fascist American court" made the young Black men "candidates for the electric chair" was their involvement in "rally[ing] black and white workers for the struggle against the unbridled terrorism of the maddened bourgeoisie."[17] Since the "Scottsboro 9" were revolutionary African American workers, their legal lynching signified the continued threat of an imperialist war against the Soviet Union.

Soviet writers and graphic artists also voiced their outrage at the attempted execution of their Scottsboro allies in the form of poems, essays, pamphlets, and cartoons. In "A Song about Alabama," a poem printed in *Literaturnaia gazeta* (Literary newspaper), writer Nikolai Aseev explained that in Alabama if a Black man—above whose head constantly hangs a "long, sturdy noose"—even smiled at a white woman, then he would be "burned alive" by the extralegal means of wood and kerosene or the legal means of electricity. Aseev linked Alabama's systematic terrorism against its "black slaves" to American imperialists' desire to wage war against the Soviet people.[18] Fellow writer Aleksei Tolstoy warned in his *Izvestiia* (News) essay "Liberate Our Black Comrades" that as a result of African Americans' increasing class consciousness, white Americans had resorted to even more desperate measures to inflict violence against them.[19] Maxim Gorky similarly emphasized in a pamphlet titled *Terror against the Negro Workers in America* that the Scottsboro legal lynching and recent atrocities in Camp Hill, Alabama, against Black sharecroppers were the result of the American bourgeoisie's efforts "to scare Negroes"—who had become increasingly militant—back into their "proper," subservient place.[20] Soviet graphic artists drew cartoons that complemented the writings of their literary counterparts. The majority featured an electric chair, noose, and/or the grim reaper (like the aforementioned lynching cartoon) juxtaposed against a defining symbol of American freedom, such as the Statue of Liberty or the American flag. These symbols of death that were synonymous with US racial "democracy" reminded onlookers of the impending fate of the Scottsboro defendants and the eventual fate of the first workers' state if Soviet citizens did not recognize that their destiny was intimately connected to that of their Black American comrades.[21]

Evidence that Soviet workers, students, and collective farmers had mobilized to condemn the legal lynching of their comrades in Alabama appeared consistently in the central press alongside intellectuals' essays, poems, and cartoons. In late May 1931 MOPR's Executive Committee initiated this mobilization process by sending a directive marked "Urgent" to authorities at the national republic, *krai* (region), and *oblast'* (province) levels regarding the need to immediately organize mass meetings at industrial enterprises, schools, and state and collective farms to inform citizens of the status of the revolutionary movement, the plight of American Blacks, and the impending execution of the Scottsboro "proletarians," which they instructed reflected the intensification of the global class struggle.[22] Black American communists George Padmore, Otto Huiswood, and Lloyd Brown produced much of the knowledge about US racism that was presented at these mass meetings, while others, such as Fort-Whiteman, the agronomist Oliver Golden, and Robert Ross, who became an official propagandist, spoke at meetings around the country.[23] In addition, Emma Harris, a sixty-two-year-old African American and a long-time resident of Moscow, spoke at all the rallies in the capital. According to Langston Hughes, although Harris disagreed with many of the Soviet state's policies (having had a successful business under the czarist regime, which the Bolshevik Revolution had ended), she supported its energetic condemnation of US racism.[24] To be sure, African Americans such as Harris realized their presence at these gatherings authenticated the Soviet Union's commitment to Black equality while further embarrassing US leaders.

Soviet newspapers frequently published the protest resolutions that citizens composed at these nationwide meetings after learning of the atrocities of the US racial regime and the impending execution of the Scottsboro prisoners.[25] A disclaimer typically explained that the editorial offices had received so many protest resolutions that it was impossible to print them all. Workers, collective farmers, and students alike often followed their articulation of anger at the impending Scottsboro legal lynching with a pledge to respond to it by fulfilling a certain task or tasks to strengthen socialism. This included forming shock brigades, engaging in socialist competition, organizing voluntary work-days, sowing plots of land, collecting donations, and/or establishing new MOPR cells on behalf of the joint goal of gaining "freedom for the Scottsboro prisoners" and building socialism.[26] The fact that these types of pledges were standard in protest resolutions from around the country is unsurprising. MOPR leaders had instructed lower-level officials that this was the proper way for the "New Soviet People" to demonstrate their antiracist indignation and enlightened awareness that their fate was inseparable from that of their Black allies.

Many African Americans—including those who did not possess Communist Party USA membership cards—attached great value to Soviet leaders' mass mobilization of support for the Scottsboro prisoners and equation of the birth of a new, modern human being with a fierce opposition to anti-Black racism. African American workers Sam Langford, Morris Wikman, and Abraham Lewis, who visited the country in 1931, expressed amazement at the nearly ubiquitous visual presence in the USSR of the Scottsboro defendants, whose likeness they testified adorned public spaces "everywhere—on street corners, in factories, in hotels and clubs."[27] African American Dorothy West, a member of the *Black and White* film cast, was impressed by the knowledge people in Moscow possessed about the Scottsboro prisoners, from whom she learned about developments in the case.[28] Ada Wright, the mother of two of the Scottsboro defendants, who toured Europe in 1932 to raise support for the campaign but who was too ill to address the MOPR congress when she arrived in the USSR, even insisted later that the Russians had been responsible for saving her sons' lives.[29] As Wright's comment suggests, the soft power interests of Soviet authorities and African Americans successfully converged in the Scottsboro campaign. The campaign brought international attention to the violent injustices that American Blacks routinely faced under American capitalist democracy and placed pressure on US authorities to stop the execution of innocent African American male teenagers.[30]

NOT SO *BLACK AND WHITE*

Soviet leaders' decision to abandon the *Black and White* film project in late August 1932—at the height of the Scottsboro campaign—betrayed the USSR's hard power vulnerability on the world stage. It also demonstrated that African Americans' soft power priorities often diverged from those of officials in Moscow. Twenty-one African Americans had agreed to travel to the USSR to make *Black and White* because it promised to be a landmark film in terms of its condemnation of US racism and dignified depiction of African Americans. At the same time, involvement in the project enabled them to investigate Soviet claims to have eliminated racism. The four-month contracts that this group of college students, social and postal workers, and writers and journalists signed in Moscow afforded them salaries unavailable to most Blacks in Depression-era America.[31] The cast's only white member, Alan McKenzie, was the only member of the Communist Party USA. Hughes, as the group's most high-profile figure, was supposed to serve as a consultant on the film's fictional screenplay and write its English-language dialogue.[32]

Yet Hugh L. Cooper, an American engineer and businessman who was instrumental in the construction of the Dnieprostroi Dam—one of the showpieces of socialist industry—was outraged at the arrival in Moscow of *Black and White*'s cast. Cooper met with party leaders Viacheslav Molotov and Lazar Kaganovich in July 1932 and threatened to withdraw his assistance from the dam's construction and support of US diplomatic recognition of the Soviet Union if *Black and White* was made.[33] Newspapers in the United States and throughout Europe reported that Soviet leaders canceled the film's production in August to avoid jeopardizing rapprochement with the United States and to strengthen the USSR's position in the Far East against Japan.[34] Authorities in Moscow had deemed it advantageous to make a film condemning the racial violence that their African American allies suffered as long as the establishment of diplomatic relations with the United States seemed distant. Once diplomatic relations seemed imminent, however, the film became a possible detriment. The mainstream American press celebrated the abandonment of *Black and White* as evidence that Soviet soft power measures directed at American Blacks could be compromised to Great Power politics. Comintern officials denied these reports and insisted that the film had merely been postponed for technical reasons and would be made the following summer.[35]

While political maneuvering sealed its fate, to claim that production of *Black and White* had been canceled is misleading. In the five weeks that the African American cast had been in the USSR, production on the film had not begun. Dissension and incompetence among officials of Mezhrabpom (Mezhdunarodnaia Organizatsiia Rabochei Pomoshchi, or International Workers' Aid) regarding the film's script and the ability of the German director Carl Junghans to make it—rather than the political exigencies of the Soviet state—were the reasons for this inactivity.[36] Yet, notwithstanding the various factors that conspired against its production, *Black and White*'s cancelation constituted the gravest threat to the USSR's antiracist image prior to the 1939 Nazi-Soviet Pact. But of the twenty-one African American cast members, only four publicly accused Soviet leaders of opportunism. In an official statement dated August 22, 1932, Henry Lee Moon, Theodore Poston, Thurston McNairy Lewis, and Laurence Alberga rejected as "unsound, insufficient, and insulting to our intelligence the reasons offered by Meschrabpom Film Corporation for the cancelation of the 'Black and White' film project." Alluding to Cooper's role in the affair, Soviet officials, they charged, conceded to the "racial prejudice of American Capitalism and World Imperialism."[37] In another statement, which Moon and Poston sent from Berlin weeks later, they reiterated that "once again the forces of American race prejudice have triumphed, and this time in a land where it would be least expected—the Union of Soviet Socialist Republics."[38] What is striking about the dissenters' statements is that they used the language of Soviet antiracism to voice their protest. By accusing officials in Moscow of allowing "the forces of American race prejudice" to triumph "in a land where it would be least expected," they invoked the Soviet Union's stated commitment to racial equality and characterized authorities' conduct as racist and anti-Soviet. Hence, even as they sought to separate themselves from the Soviet worldview, they affirmed that it was the one by which leaders ought to be judged.[39]

The majority of the *Black and While* cast members, however, publicly insisted that Soviet leaders had not compromised their commitment to antiracism and had merely postponed the film's production. In a collective public statement, the fifteen cast members also denied erroneous reports—most likely the result of Cooper's misinformation—that they were stranded in Moscow without food, money, or way home. Such slanderous accounts, they emphasized, "are readily utilized by the press" to arouse the distrust of white and Black workers. They added, "We deeply regret these malicious and unfounded attacks upon people whose guests we have been and who are doing everything possible for our comfort and entertainment during our stay in the U.S.S.R."[40] A few cast members issued individual statements affirming as sincere the Soviet commitment to racial equality. For instance, Loren Miller posited, "We have seen with our own eyes how this is the one country where all races and peoples are free, and where they have achieved real equality and self-government. This is a cardinal principle of Soviet life. The Soviet Union is the best friend of the Negro and of all oppressed peoples." Louise Thompson expressed similar sentiments, asserting, "We have been afforded opportunities here that, as Negroes and working people, would never have been open to us in any other country."[41]

Why did four male cast members decide to attack as opportunistic Soviet soft power measures, while fifteen others, conversely, publicly defended as uncompromising Moscow's support of the Black freedom struggle? In addition to these nineteen, the three other Black cast members, Leonard Hill, Katherine Jenkins, and her fiancé, George Sample, remained silent during the controversy, signing their name to neither group's statements. It would be easy to portray the majority of cast members as puppets of Soviet leaders, who were blinded by the equalities afforded them in the USSR and loyally fulfilled Moscow's will. Viewed in this way, the public dissenters acted heroically, unblindly holding Soviet leaders accountable to the antiracist code of conduct that they espoused and condemning their acquiescence to US "race hate."

The reality of the situation was, however, more complex. Personal gain on some level arguably motivated the public discontents. They likely concluded that whatever personal advantage they could garner from the controversy outweighed any intangible soft power agency that came with affirming Soviet intransigence to racism. The path that they chose also promised to eradicate the stigma of disloyalty that accompanied travel to the USSR and involvement in a film project to indict US racism. It furthermore entailed a more immediate tangible financial and professional incentive. The scholar Joy Carew discusses how upon returning to the United States, Poston, Moon, and Lewis "sold their version of the story to the white and black press." The controversy allowed the two journalists, Poston and Moon—the most outspoken critics—to finally fulfill their dreams of appearing in the *New York Times*.[42]

The decision of fifteen cast members to defend the Soviet commitment to antiracism was likewise the result of careful political calculation. They too objected to leaders' decision to cancel the film but strategically chose to do so privately. Anticipating his career as a prominent Los Angeles attorney, Loren Miller acted as the group's spokesperson in written correspondence and meetings with Comintern authorities in which the cast criticized the film's cancelation and Mezhrabpom officials' mistreatment of them. Indicative of their incredulity that the film was merely postponed, Miller used the terms "abandonment" and "cancel" to voice their grievances; he reserved use of the term "postpone" only for public statements. Among the many documents Miller presented to Comintern leaders was a two-and-a-half-page statement detailing the negative political repercussions that would result from *Black and White*'s nonproduction. Implicit in this tactic was the understanding that political reasons motivated the decision to "postpone" the film and that alternate political reasons could alone persuade officials to follow through on its production.[43] Thus the decision to refrain from publicly criticizing Soviet soft power did not mean that most *Black and White* cast members had failed to recognize its limits. They arguably concluded that making their discontent public was futile since it meant surrendering their own soft power agency.

Remaining publicly loyal to the master narrative of Soviet antiracism, as the above discussion indicates, allowed them to voice their complaints to Comintern leaders at length and try to convince them of the urgency of making *Black and White*. It also enabled them to extend their stays in the USSR. To be sure, although Soviet leaders canceled the film, they did not abandon their soft power agenda. To the contrary, they offered the cast members the opportunity to travel and/or seek employment and permanent residence in the USSR. The latter was the option chosen by three male cast members, Wayland Rudd, Homer Smith, and Lloyd Patterson. Indeed, Soviet soft power measures, despite the opportunism that to varying degrees motivated them, translated into a level of equality unavailable to African Americans in the United States—a reality to which Soviet authorities hoped

Black American visitors would continue to attest.[44] Even Laurence Alberga, one of the initial public dissenters, testified to this reality in a private letter to W. A. Domingo, a Harlem intellectual who chaired the Cooperating Committee for the Production of a Soviet Film on Negro Life, which sponsored the cast's journey to Moscow. Alberga outlined his grievances regarding the film's cancelation but also emphasized that they had been "well received" in the Soviet Union and traveled throughout the country as "honored guests."[45] Dorothy West, who remained in Moscow for nearly a year after the film's cancelation, candidly discussed in letters to her mother the impact that this warm reception had on her disposition. In a letter dated November 1932, for example, West commented, "Hope you are as half as happy as I am. Nothing has happened. It's simply that life is very good right through here, and I haven't any worries." Several months later in March 1933, West wrote, "I would never be so carefree again as I have ever been since I've been here."[46]

Indeed, the "carefree" existence that many African Americans enjoyed in the USSR relative to the United States was not lost on Colonel Cooper and the outraged white American businessmen for whom he spoke. When Cooper met with Molotov and Kaganovich in July 1932 "in a spirit of great indignation," he had also threatened the withdrawal of his assistance "'if those niggers are not sent out of Russia by the 10th of August."[47] As his threat indicates, the mere presence of the twenty-one African Americans in Moscow, who were lodged at the prestigious Grand Hotel—which West incidentally described to her mother as "really grand"—had roused considerable discontent among white Americans in the Soviet Union. In debriefings with US consulate officials, one of these white American men remarked with disdain that upon leaving Moscow in September 1932, these African Americans, whom he overestimated as "about forty Negroes from the Harlem district," were still "having a good time playing around Moscow."[48] Given that the white American enemies of Black liberation deemed Soviet soft power dangerous in spite of the "shameless" opportunism that motivated it, it becomes even clearer why most *Black and White* cast members—whom Soviet leaders did not kick out of Moscow as Cooper demanded—refrained from helping them attack it.

Instead, African American sojourners to the USSR continued to challenge the white American opponents of Black equality by writing testimonials—often published in the noncommunist African American press—that praised the superior racial enlightenment of Soviet citizens and leaders. In the 1934 *Crisis* article that opens this essay, Langston Hughes stressed that the crowd that welcomed the Moscow-Tashkent Express once it reached its destination included "brown Asiatics and fair-skinned Russians" but also the African American Bernard Powers of Howard University, who was in Uzbekistan to help build roads. Hughes's emphasis on the shared humanity; interracial solidarity; and collective desire to develop the culture, education, industry, and infrastructure of the Soviet South stood in stark contrast to the "horror," "fear," "terror," "hate," and "violence" that he ascribed to the American South. Hughes's representation of his Soviet journey as a journey into the future was thus intended to transport himself and the *Crisis* reader from the "American nightmare" to the "American dream" of a genuine multiracial democracy where exploitation and anti-Black racism were absent.[49]

In addition to Hughes, Homer Smith was the *Black and White* cast member who consistently used his descriptions of Soviet society in the non-communist African American press to imagine an America that lived up to its promise of equality "without regard to color or race."[50] In the *Chicago Defender* Smith contrasted the Russian people's opposition to anti-Black racism with that of their backward white American counterparts. He claimed that the former treated Blacks like himself as equals not because of their class consciousness but because, unlike the white inhabitants of "Christian" America, they daily practiced the Ten Commandments. For this reason, Smith claimed, "non-Christian," communist Russia was the most "Christian country" in the world. He further reported that Soviet citizens used the materials from the destruction of churches to help those in need and assigned greater significance to the date in the Scottsboro case ("set by a 'Christian' judge, in a 'Christian' state, in a 'Christian' country for the execution of two innocent boys, Patterson and Norris") than the Christmas holiday.[51]

Smith's decision to attribute the enlightened conduct of the Soviet people not to class consciousness but to an innate "Christian" morality that valued human life over material goods underscores how African Americans' representations of Soviet racial equality often deviated from those that Soviet ideologists approved for communist publications. Smith was appealing not to Soviet propagandists but to the hearts and minds of a largely Christian Black readership. And yet even the testimonials that African Americans wrote for communist publications likewise held up Russian people as evidence that whites could treat Black people with dignity and respect. In a representative article from the *Negro Worker*, Margaret Glascoe recounts how her son Lloyd Patterson (who like Smith pursued employment in the USSR after *Black and White*'s cancelation) encouraged her to move to the first workers' state. Although she enthusiastically accepted his invitation, Glascoe confessed that "from force of habit I thought that I would meet with a hostile attitude among the white people here. . . . 'Comrade,' that was the first word I heard. . . . I have quite forgotten that I am black. I feel that

I am a person like everybody else."[52] Unburdened by the weight of being the despised Black other, Glascoe forged such strong bonds of friendship and trust with white people in the Soviet Union that she declared, "'I am Among My Own People in My Own Country.'" As Glascoe's testimonial illustrates, even Soviet-sponsored publications deemed acceptable Blacks' articulation of mistrust of whites because of their experiences with centuries of enslavement and oppression. African Americans in both communist and noncommunist publications therefore used the Soviet Union to prove that racism was not a problem of Black people or alleged Black inferiority as US assimilationist discourse claimed but rather of white people who needed to emulate Soviet citizens and earn Blacks' trust by implementing antiracist policies and respecting them as equals. The degree to which the image of the USSR as a society without racism accurately represented Soviet reality was secondary. What was certain is that this was the American reality for which African Americans aspired.

CONCLUSION

In the late 1920s, as Soviet leaders launched a massive industrialization campaign to acquire the hard power that would make the USSR a dominant player on the world stage, they pursued soft power initiatives to gain allies of communism among nonstate actors such as African Americans. Since they lacked access to hard power tools to advance Black liberation, some Black Americans—many of whom were not members of the Communist Party USA—embraced the soft power agency that they could exercise by adopting Soviet soft power measures to further their own agenda. They sought to pressure US leaders into implementing real antiracist change as a national security imperative while reminding fellow African Americans that it was vital not to relinquish their ability to envision a radically different future beyond the violent indignities of US racial apartheid.

African Americans' effective co-optation of Soviet soft power initiatives is evidenced in the outrage expressed by white American businessmen in the USSR, such as Cooper and his compatriots. They warned US consulate officials in Riga, Latvia, that Black Americans in Moscow had adopted an "extremely offensive" attitude toward white Americans in the Soviet capital. Once they returned to the United States, these Black Americans, they admonished, would demand to be treated with respect and insist on achieving equality with white men.[53] These white American male visitors to the USSR thus identified African Americans' soft power agency as posing a serious threat to America's "democratic" future. They also voiced indignation that their self-conception as good, honest Americans was assaulted by Soviet citizens' frequent inquiries regarding their complicity in discriminating against if not actually lynching African Americans. They deeply resented having their sense of superiority questioned by members of an allegedly inferior, less civilized country that lacked the hard power necessary to impose its will on the world stage.[54]

The informal foreign relations that interwar African American sojourners to the USSR forged with Soviet authorities and intellectuals to advance the Black freedom struggle serve as an important reminder of the circular and malleable nature of state-sponsored soft power initiatives. With war on the continent imminent, the few Black Americans who remained in the Soviet Union in the second half of the 1930s bore witness to the violent xenophobia and Stalinist terror that enveloped the first workers' state. Yelena Khanga, today a Black Russian journalist and former talk show host, claims that her African American grandfather, Oliver Golden, who led a team of Black agricultural specialists to Uzbekistan in 1931 (which included Bernard Powers, whom Hughes met in Tashkent) could have easily been murdered in the Great Terror. However, Golden was not home when the secret police came looking for him in the summer of 1937. By the time he returned from vacation, the local authorities explained that they had already met their arrest quota and left him alone. Khanga's recollection of Golden's fate illuminates the tragedy that the same country that had allowed African Americans like her grandfather to find refuge from the racial terrorism of the US South was also responsible for mass murder and political terror that did not necessarily exclude them.[55] Indeed, the immense atrocities of the Soviet project combined with the signing of the Nazi-Soviet Pact of 1939 undermined Moscow's soft power measures to win Blacks' support of Soviet communism and compromised its efforts to cultivate an enduring antiracist consciousness in the populace of the first workers' state.[56]

NOTES

1. Mia Bay, *Traveling while Black: A Story of Race and Resistance* (Cambridge, MA: Harvard University Press, 2021).
2. Langston Hughes, "Going South in Russia," *Crisis* (June 1934): 162–63.
3. For the Black radical influences on the Comintern decree, see, e.g., *Black Marxism: The Making of the Black Radical Tradition* (Chapel Hill: University of North Carolina Press, 2000), 224–28, and Minkah Makalani, *In the Cause of Freedom: Radical Black Internationalism from Harlem to London, 1917–1939* (Chapel Hill: University of North Carolina Press, 2011).

4. Mark Naison, *Communists in Harlem during the Depression* (New York: Grove Press, 1983), 18. See also Harry Haywood, *A Black Communist in the Freedom Struggle: The Life of Harry Haywood*, ed. Gwendolyn Midlo Hall (Minneapolis: University of Minnesota Press, 2012).

5. See, e.g., Erez Manela, *The Wilsonian Moment: Self-Determination and the International Origins of Anticolonial Nationalism* (New York: Oxford University Press, 2009).

6. John Fousek, *To Lead the Free World: American Nationalism and the Cultural Roots of the Cold War* (Chapel Hill: University of North Carolina Press, 2000).

7. Alfred L. Brophy, *Reconstructing the Dreamland: The Tulsa Riot of 1921; Race, Reparations, and Reconciliation* (New York: Oxford University Press, 2002); Mark Krugler, *1919: The Year of Racial Violence: How African Americans Fought Back* (New York: Cambridge University Press, 2014); Charles Lumpkins, *American Pogrom: The East St. Louis Race Riot and Black Politics* (Athens: Ohio University Press, 2008).

8. The national security component was rooted in US authorities' equation of antiracist initiatives with Bolshevik machination. Mark Ellis, "J. Edgar Hoover and the 'Red Summer' of 1919," *Journal of American Studies* 28, no. 1 (April 1994): 39–59; Theodore Kornweibel Jr., *Seeing Red: Federal Campaigns against Black Militancy, 1919–1925* (Bloomington: Indiana University Press, 1998).

9. Mark Solomon, *The Cry Was Unity: Communists and African Americans, 1917–1936* (Jackson: University Press of Mississippi, 1998), 191–206, 240–49.

10. *Rabochaia gazeta*, August 17, 1931.

11. For photographs, see, e.g., *Trud*, August 28, 1930; *Komsomol'skaia pravda*, August 28 and 30, 1930; *Rabochaia gazeta*, August 14, 1930; *Ogonek*, no. 17 (June 20, 1931): 13; *Workers News*, May 17, 1931. For the term "sadistic discourse," see Evgeny Steiner, *Stories for Little Comrades: Revolutionary Artists and the Making of Early Soviet Children's Books*, trans. Jane Anne Miller (Seattle: University of Washington Press, 1999), 104–5.

12. See RG 84, MLR no. 435, USSR Embassy, 1935, vol. 28, National Archives and Records Administration, College Park, MD, entry 60, 840.1.

13. Examples include *Komsomol'skaia pravda*, August 21 and 23, 1930; *Pravda*, August 13, 27, and 28, 1930; *Trud*, March 8, 1930, and August 10, 13, and 24, 1930; and *Izvestiia*, August 19, 1930.

14. Meredith L. Roman, *Opposing Jim Crow: African Americans and the Soviet Indictment of U.S. Racism, 1928–1937* (Lincoln: University of Nebraska Press, 2012), 25–55.

15. Although evidence in the case was extremely weak, on April 9 an all-white jury found the defendants guilty on all charges. The judge sentenced eight of the defendants to death and sentenced the youngest (who was only thirteen) to life imprisonment. Their execution was initially scheduled for July 10, 1931.

16. "Predvaritel'naia informatsionnaia svodka provedeniia kampanii po spaseniiu deviati negritianskikh iunoshei v skottsboro SASSh," Gosudarstvennyi arkhiv Rossiiskoi Federatsii (GARF; State Archive of the Russian Federation), f. 8265, op. 1, d. 39, ll. 222–25 (esp. l. 222).

17. "Preliminary Informational Summary of the Campaign in Defense of the 9 Negro Youths in Scottsboro, USA, Measures Taken on the Part of the C.C. of the MOPR/IRA Section in the USSR," Rossiiskii gosudarstvennyi arkhiv sotsial'noi i politicheskoi istorii (RGASPI; Russian State Archive of Social and Political History), f. 539, op. 5, d. 127, ll. 105–108 (esp. l. 105). See also "Obrashchenie komiteta sodeistviia MOPR," *Trud*, June 29, 1931.

18. Nikolai Aseev, "Pesenka ob alabame," *Literaturnaia gazeta*, July 30, 1931.

19. A. Tolstoy, "Osvobodite nashikh chernykh tovarishchei!," *Izvestiia*, July 8, 1931. The English-language translation was published as "History Has a Long Memory," *Workers News*, July 16, 1931.

20. "Terror kapitalistov protiv negritianskikh rabochikh v Amerike," RGASPI, f. 539, op. 5, d. 76, ll. 252–53; *Negro Worker* 1 (January 1932): 13–15; *Workers News*, September 1, 1931.

21. See, e.g., *Komsomol'sksia pravda*, January 27, 1932, and March 3, 1932.

22. "Vsem TsK natsrespublik, kraikomam, i obkomam MOPR," GARF, f. 8265, op. 1, d. 41, l. 79.

23. See, e.g., "Linchevanie i presledovanie negritianskikh trudiashchikhsia v SASSh," RGASPI, f. 539, op. 5, d. 126, ll. 43–54; "Osnovnye fakty o protsesse protiv 9 negritianskikh iunoshei v skottsboro," GARF, f. 8265, op. 1, d. 41, ll. 37–56; "ILD (24 April 1932)," RGASPI, f. 515, op. 1, d. 3017, ll. 99–100; and Otto Huiswood, "Ne dadim linchevat' negritianskikh iunoshei," *Mezhdunarodnoe rabochee dvizhenie* 9 (March 1932): 7–9. On Brown, see J. A. Miller, S. D. Pennybacker, and E. Rosenhaft, "Mother Ada Wright and the International Campaign to Free the Scottsboro Boys, 1931–1934," *American Historical Review* 106 (April 2001): 387–430, 401n39.

24. Langston Hughes, *I Wonder as I Wander: An Autobiographical Journey* (New York: Hill & Wang, 1956), 83, 87. On Soviet paternalist treatment of Harris, see Roman, *Opposing Jim Crow*, 117–18.

25. *Komsomol'skaia pravda*, May 27 and 31, 1931; June 9, 1931; March 3 and 27, 1932.

26. "Brigady imeni 8 molodykh negrov," *Komsomol'skaia pravda*, July 4, 1931; "Biuro pechati TsK MOPR o kampanii Skottsboro," RGASPI, f. 515, op. 1, d. 3012, ll. 59–63 (esp. l. 60). Shock brigades and socialist competition were organized to raise productivity rates and demonstrate one's commitment to building socialism.

27. "Negro Workers to Contrast U.S.A. with Soviet Union," *Liberator*, October 17, 1931.

28. "Cast of 'Black and White' Comments on U.S.S.R. and Films," *Moscow Daily News*, July 6, 1932.

29. Pennybacker, "Mother Ada Wright," 401n38.

30. The ILD successfully appealed their convictions and the US Supreme Court, in November 1932, ordered a new trial for the young men because the rights guaranteed them under the Fourteenth Amendment had been violated.

31. Joy Gleason Carew, *Blacks, Reds, and Russians: Sojourners in Search of the Soviet Promise* (New Brunswick, NJ: Rutgers University Press, 2008), 120–23.

32. Hughes, *I Wonder*, 73–77, 95–98.

33. R. W. Davies and Oleg V. Khlevniuk, eds., *The Stalin-Kaganovich Correspondence, 1931–1936* (New Haven, CT: Yale University Press, 2003), 113–15.

34. Norman E. Saul, *Friends or Foes? The United States and Soviet Russia, 1921–1941* (Lawrence: University Press of Kansas, 2006), 216, 254–77.

35. In 1933 D. Manuilsky, head of the Comintern, confirmed circuitously that the film had been canceled to avoid jeopardizing recognition. See "Shorthand record of the conversation of Comrade Manuilsky with students of the Ninth Sector of KUTV," RGASPI, f. 532, op. 1, d. 441, ll. 1–13.

36. "22 Negroes and Meschrabpom," RGASPI, f. 495, op. 72, d. 201, ll. 264–65; "Dear Comrade," RGASPI, f. 495, op. 72, d. 201, l. 198; "Directors Meschrabpom Film, August 25, 1932," RGASPI, f. 495, op. 72, d. 201, l. 208.

37. Alberga was one of sixteen cast members who four days later signed a statement rejecting the minority statement. "WE, the undersigned . . . ," RGASPI, f. 495, op. 72, d. 201,
l. 242.
38. "Say Race Bias Here Halted Film," *New York Times*, October 5, 1932.
39. "Moscow, USSR 8/22/32," RGASPI, f. 495, op. 72, d. 201, l. 205.
40. Comintern officials removed the racialized language from the group's draft and infused
the statement with a class analysis. See "For Immediate Release," RGASPI, f. 495, op.
72, d. 201, ll. 199–200, and "Majority Statement by Members of the Negro Cast for
'Black and White,'" RGASPI, f. 495, op. 72, d. 201, l. 251. The signatories were Louise Thompson, Matt N. Crawford, Mildred Jones, Dorothy West, Constance W. White,
Sylvia Garner, Lloyd Patterson, Langston Hughes, Juanita Lewis, Loren Miller, Alan
McKenzie, Homer Smith, Wayland Rudd, Mollie V. Lewis, and F. Curle Monte.
41. "Negro Actors in USSR Well Provided For," *Liberator*, October 1, 1932.
42. Carew, *Blacks, Reds, and Russians*, 129.
43. "Reasons for Abandonment," RGASPI, f. 495, op. 72, d. 201, ll. 266–67; "Majority
Statement by Members of the Negro Cast for 'Black and White,'" RGASPI, f. 495, op.
72, d. 201, ll. 251–52; "The group would like to . . . ," RGASPI, 495, op. 72, d. 201, l.
269; "Langston Hughes (August 23, 1932)," RGASPI, f. 495, op. 72, d. 201, ll. 213–15.
Comintern leaders, who sought to win the group to communism, expressed distress
that Mezhrabpom did not organize excursions since they feared that their idleness was
corrupting them. See "Odessa, August 9, 1932, Dear Comrade Randolph," RGASPI, f.
495, op.72, d. 201, ll. 202–3.
44. Carew, *Blacks, Reds, and Russians*, 131–32.
45. RGASPI, f. 495, op. 72, d. 201, l. 256.
46. "March 5th Mummy dearest darling," and "Nov 4th Darling mums," Dorothy West Collection (85-M139), carton 1, folder 1, Schlesinger Library, Radcliffe Institute.
47. Records of the Department of the State Relating to Internal Affairs of the Soviet Union,
1930–39, 861.5017—Living Conditions/791.
48. Records of the Department of the State.
49. Hughes, "Going South in Russia," 162–63.
50. Chatwood Hall, "Full Equality of Races and Nations," *Crisis* (September 1936): 268.
Smith often wrote under the pen name "Chatwood Hall."
51. Chatwood Hall, "A Column from Moscow," *Chicago Defender*, December 15, 22, and 29,
1934.
52. "I Am Among My Own People in My Own Country," *Negro Worker* 5 (July/
August 1935): 32–34, was reprinted as "Negro Mother, Now a Shock Worker," in *60
Letters: Foreign Workers Write of Their Life and Work in the USSR*, ed. N. S Rosenblit
and R Schüller (Moscow: Co-operative Publishing Society of Foreign Workers in the
USSR, 1936), 10–14.
53. Records of the Department of State Relating to Internal Affairs, Colonel Hugh L.
Cooper, 861.5017—Living Conditions/519, John M. Pelikan, 861.77—Living Condi-
tions/423, John Stafford Cromelin, 861.5017—Living Conditions/371, Samuel George
Bloomfield, 861.5017—Living Conditions/575, Eugene Szepesi, 861.5017—Living
Conditions/255.
54. Records of the Department of the State Relating to Internal Affairs, 861.5017—Living
Conditions/419 and 861.5017—Living Conditions/623.

55. Yelena Khanga, *Soul to Soul: A Black Russian Jewish Woman's Search for Her Roots* (New York: W. W. Norton, 1992), 90–91. Lovett Fort-Whiteman, who fell out of favor with Soviet authorities and African Americans in Moscow, is the only known African American victim of the Great Terror. See Roman, *Opposing Jim Crow*, 9, and Joshua Yaffa, "A Black Communist's Disappearance in Stalin's Russia," *New Yorker*, October 18, 2021, https://www.newyorker.com/magazine/2021/10/25/a-black-communists-disappearance-in-stalins-russia-lovett-fort-whiteman-gulag.

56. On the escalation of racism in the late 1980s and since the collapse of the USSR, see, e.g., Jeff Sahadeo, *Voices from the Soviet Edge: Southern Migrants in Leningrad and Moscow* (Ithaca, NY: Cornell University Press, 2019), and Nikolai Zakharov, *Race and Racism in Russia* (Basingstoke, UK: Palgrave Macmillan, 2015).

CHAPTER 4

Tensions between Soft Power and Domestic Propaganda

Public Diplomacy toward the Mexican Diaspora in the United States, 1934–40

Sylvia Dummer Scheel

Propaganda was central to Lázaro Cárdenas's government (1934–40) in Mexico. It was under his mandate that the unprecedented Autonomous Department of Press and Publicity (Departamento Autónomo de Prensa y Publicidad, DAPP) was created. The need for propaganda derived from the fact that his administration was the most radical of the postrevolutionary governments: it sought to materialize the promises of the Mexican Revolution of 1910 through a six-year plan that contemplated agrarian reforms, socialist education, and greater state interference. In 1938 Cárdenas led Mexico to the revolutionary climax by decreeing the nationalization of the oil industry. In order to successfully implement his program, Cárdenas needed to overcome various types of resistance, both within the Mexican population and in international public opinion. His domestic propaganda sought to involve Mexicans in his six-year-plan and orient them ideologically by exalting their emotions through a revolutionary nationalism. Its foreign propaganda, for its part, was mainly directed at the United States, where it sought to disprove the image of radicalism and communism disseminated by its enemies there. Powerful interest groups—such as the expropriated oil companies and Roman Catholic groups opposed to Mexican anticlericalism—had organized virulent propaganda campaigns to pressure the US authorities to take action against Mexico. Despite Franklin Delano Roosevelt's Good Neighbor

Policy (GNP), Mexican authorities still feared the threat of historical political and military US interventionism. Thus, in the absence of hard power, soft power was one of the important tools to empower Mexico in its unequal power relationship with its northern neighbor. The Cárdenas government addressed US public opinion in a rational, moderate, and conciliatory tone in order to win at least some of its support.

However, between the domestic and the international propaganda policies, a third public was targeted by the Mexican government, which until now has received little scholarly attention: the Mexican communities living in the United States. These diasporic communities represented an important group in the US, and the Cárdenas government was concerned with strengthening ties with them, trying to bolster their identification with Mexico and its government. This chapter focuses on the public diplomacy directed at these communities. The objective is to understand how these communication efforts developed in the space between domestic propaganda and soft power, generating opportunities but also tensions among them.

Diasporas—which can be defined as "communities of people who left their ancestral homes and settled in foreign countries, but who preserve the memory of and links with the land of their fathers and forefathers"[1]—have not been very prominent in historical studies of soft power.[2] Nicholas Cull notes that it is a side effect of history's fixation with the nation-state that transnational populations like them have not been considered.[3] Therefore, I propose that studying public diplomacy toward diasporas is relevant for two main reasons. First, it allows us to understand governmental communications toward a population that is considered part of the nation but that is not anchored to the national territory or to political sovereignty. Persuading diasporas implies conditions and challenges different from those of domestic propaganda, such as competing with the culture and politics of the host country and the difficulties of promoting government communications in a foreign territory. Second, the study of public diplomacy toward the diasporas allows us to delve into the relationship between domestic propaganda and soft power. As R. S. Zaharna remarks, it seems unanimously accepted that public diplomacy considers the foreign public to be the opposite of the domestic public.[4] In fact, most countries use separate entities to organize their domestic and foreign propaganda, while the United States for decades prohibited the domestic dissemination of its public diplomacy content.[5] However, public diplomacy aimed at diasporas strains this separation, generating a transnational space where soft power and domestic propaganda overlap. Not only is a domestic public addressed in foreign territory, thus resorting to the same actors and channels used in public diplomacy toward the public opinion of that country, but also diasporas, and the propaganda directed toward them, can have different effects on such soft power.

Diasporas are seen by many governments as soft power resources. As a "living transnational network," they can act as natural ambassadors or "intermediary agents" of their home country in the host nation, helping to advance their government's interests there in what is known as "diaspora diplomacy." Of course, emigrants are autonomous groups whose collaboration with the government of origin is not automatic: hence, the importance of turning them into allies through public diplomacy specifically aimed at them.[6] However, here I argue that public diplomacy toward diasporas not only has the potential to strengthen soft power but also to weaken it. Exporting and deploying the message of domestic propaganda on foreign soil makes it difficult to maintain the separation between the two messages, which can be counterproductive if the two discourses oppose each other. Diasporas thus constitute a space where contradictions between internal and external propaganda manifest, an aspect that has been little addressed in soft power studies.

In this chapter, I address the tension between domestic propaganda and transnational public diplomacy in the context of diasporas, studying the Mexican communities in the United States from 1934 to 1940. The chapter is divided into two parts, each of which examines a different side of the same coin. The first focuses on the relationship between domestic propaganda and diasporas and analyzes the contents and mechanisms used by the Cárdenas administration to generate support among Mexican communities in the United States. Although diasporas are often described as a transnational population—given their networks and loyalties both to the host country and to the country of origin—this chapter argues that the Mexican government approached them, through its public diplomacy, more as a domestic audience on foreign soil, merely reinforcing the national identity and sociability of the communities and replicating the same content and search for political allegiance as in domestic propaganda.

The second part addresses the relationship between diasporas and soft power, in which I argue that propaganda toward these communities was not necessarily favorable to the image of Mexico among US citizens. On one hand, the potential role of Mexican emigrants as propagandists was limited given their aforementioned "domestic" rather than "transnational" character. On the other, propaganda toward the diasporas had undesirable effects on Mexico's soft power in the United States: by exporting its domestic propaganda, the Cárdenas government brought a revolutionary and anti-imperialist message to the United States that contradicted the narrative of moderation and friendship offered to US public opinion, thus generating tensions in the United States.

Scholars have argued that using Mexican emigrants as a political platform to influence US foreign policy was not an important goal of postrevolutionary governments since the role emigrants could play in domestic policies was more relevant. Evidence for this view is provided by the Mexican government's dual opposition to emigrants' assimilation into US culture and their interest in achieving US citizenship.[7] The present analysis allows us to agree with this diagnosis within Cárdenas's propaganda framework. Not only did the content of propaganda for the diaspora have a domestic emphasis, but the propagandistic potential of Mexicans in the US was also used for the most part to spread the government's message among the communities themselves. However, I complement this analysis by arguing that this emphasis was not due to a lack of interest in influencing US foreign policy—the Cárdenas government made great efforts in that direction—but because it did not trust the Mexican communities to be the most effective vehicle for doing so, given their low educational/literacy level and poor assimilation (paradoxically encouraged by the government itself). As this chapter demonstrates, in order to exert influence in the spheres where decisions were made in the US, the Mexican government preferred public diplomacy aimed directly at US public opinion and even prioritized it over propaganda for the diaspora when the latter became inconvenient.

Public diplomacy aimed at diasporas—which falls within the field of "state-diaspora studies"—has been theorized in political science and strategic communication,[8] but it has not received much attention from historians.[9] Even in the case of Mexico, whose communities in the United States have been extensively analyzed for the first half of the twentieth century,[10] the issue has not been specifically addressed from this perspective. Rather, studies on contemporary strategic communications toward the Mexican diaspora place their origins, at most, in the 1970s, ignoring their previous history.[11] This chapter seeks to delve deeper into Mexico's early public diplomacy toward its diaspora and to enrich recent studies that have begun to address both domestic and foreign propaganda of the Cárdenas government, adding a transnational perspective.[12]

In this chapter, I follow the definitions of soft power discussed in the introduction of this book, although it is worth adding a qualification. I will use "public diplomacy" to refer to the propaganda *techniques* and *channels* implemented by the Cárdenas government in foreign territory, whether directed at its diaspora or at US public opinion. Then, I will use "soft power" as the possible favorable *effect* of public diplomacy toward US citizens—that is, as the support or positive predispositions that Mexico could find in US public opinion and that in some way could be beneficial (either by attracting tourists or by positively influencing US foreign policy toward Mexico). In other words, soft power is seen as an asset that is achieved through—although not exclusively—public diplomacy. Finally, I will use "foreign propaganda" as a synonym for public diplomacy.

PART I: DOMESTIC PROPAGANDA IN FOREIGN TERRITORY

Promoting Patriotism within the Mexican Diaspora

Although it is difficult to assess its exact size, the Mexican diaspora in the United States was considerable in 1930. The Foreign Affairs Ministry (Secretaría de Relaciones Exteriores, SRE) estimated there were three million emigrants,[13] but more recent studies put the number at 1,729,000.[14] Many Mexicans had emigrated in the first decades of the twentieth century in search of a livelihood. Others emigrated for political reasons or were displaced by the violence of the revolutionary process. Emigrants were concentrated especially in the border states of Texas, Arizona, New Mexico, and California as well as Colorado. Most were poor Mexicans who carried out agricultural work. Others settled in cities farther north, working as laborers in industries or in service industries. In general, these emigrants had low levels of education and high rates of illiteracy, which, together with the historical prejudice against Mexicans in the United States, made integration difficult. There was also a small percentage of emigrants with a high cultural level. These were elite exiles (politicians, intellectuals, journalists, and artists) who managed to become highly visible thanks to their publications or artistic works. Some even founded influential Spanish-language press outlets in the United States.[15]

The Cárdenas government considered the so-called *México de afuera* (Mexico outside of Mexico) as a part of the homeland, reinforcing the idea of a national identity that did not depend on territoriality. An SRE circular described the Mexican communities in the United States as "a true prolongation of Mexico, momentarily detached from the common soil, but whose reincorporation into the country is of serious concern to the national government."[16] In fact, until World War II, postrevolutionary governments were convinced that Mexicans in the United States would eventually return to their native country. Although they knew that Mexico was not economically prepared to receive them all back, they used nationalistic rhetoric to invite them to return. Cárdenas, for example, organized a highly publicized repatriation plan (though it focused on limited groups of emigrants).[17]

Maintaining the emigrants' link with the homeland posed certain challenges for Cárdenas's government. Mexican consuls in the US repeatedly warned that Mexicans who had emigrated long ago had only a vague idea about Mexico. The case was even more serious among the children of emigrants who had been born on US soil, since these so-called Mexican-Americans were more assimilated into US culture than their parents' generation.[18] In the 1920s and 1930s they had begun to organize themselves into groups such as the League of United Latin American Citizens and the Mexican American Movement in order to deepen their integration as US citizens, and many even felt a certain patriotism toward the United States.[19] Therefore, many children of Mexican families opposed the idea of repatriation.[20]

In this scenario, the first major objective of the Cárdenas government's relationship with its diaspora in the United States was to reinforce the Mexican identity of the emigrants and resist their assimilation into North American culture.[21] To this end, the government addressed the México de afuera through techniques that today we would consider typical of public diplomacy, such as talks and events, dissemination through mass media, and generation of networks and cultural diplomacy. This propaganda was left in the hands of the Mexican consuls in the United States, who were the gravitating figures on which the Mexican communities were articulated.[22] They went around their jurisdictions, giving talks to inform about different issues. However, it was not easy to reach the entire Mexican diaspora in the United States with the limited budget available because the communities were scattered and often in suburban areas. Therefore, the key to the relationship with them was to generate a kind of network diplomacy that could take advantage of their existing channels of communication and associativity. The main vehicle of this was the honorary commission, an association that existed in each locality with large Mexican communities. The SRE officially stated that it was the duty of the commissions to keep patriotism alive among Mexicans in the United States and to provide them with knowledge about their country.[23] To ensure the commissions' collaboration, the consuls encouraged patriotic feelings of their leaders.[24] The honorary commissions were indeed very active in this area. Under the supervision of the consulates, they periodically disseminated the government's message to all their members and organized outreach activities in their own meeting places. The Mexican government benefited enormously from their free collaboration and networks, thanks to which it achieved coverage it would not have obtained by other means.

The consulates also established links with Mexican mutual aid organizations, social and sports clubs, women's and mothers' clubs, pro-Mexico clubs, patriotic boards, and associations called "Centros Mexicanos."[25] Many were enthusiastic collaborators who expanded the scope of public diplomacy for Mexico among their compatriots. Some of these organizations offered to serve "as a vehicle between the Mexican metropolis and the numerous Mexican communities" and collaborated in the work of "mexicanizing" emigrants.[26] The consuls, for their part, provided them with propaganda material.[27]

One of the main means used by the Mexican government to reinforce the link with Mexico among emigrants consisted of the celebrations around the patriotic anniversaries of February 5, May 5, and September 16. Mexican-American communities had celebrated these dates autonomously since the nineteenth century, but postrevolutionary consuls sought to influence them,[28] entrusting the organization of the celebrations to the honorary commissions. These were usually joyful gatherings with music and dance, such as the traditional *jarabe tapatío*, performed by orchestras and dancers dressed in traditional costumes. The program also included civic rituals: the national anthem was played, the consul gave a speech and cheered the heroes of independence, Mexican children recited poems. These celebrations were presented as the ideal opportunity for the exacerbation of nationalist sentiment and the generation of narratives and myths associated with the homeland. In addition, they exposed the children of emigrants to aspects of Mexican identity, bringing them closer to the traditions and culture of the country. Such celebrations were extremely crowded, and Mexicans used to walk long distances to reach them.[29]

Mass communication technologies such as cinema and radio were also used to foster emigrants' national identity. DAPP sent documentaries with landscapes and cultural manifestations of Mexico to the honorary commissions and in 1939 created a radio program, *La hora de México* (The Mexican hour), dedicated specifically to Mexicans living in the United States. Combining traditional music with talks about Mexico, its declared objective was to establish a close link with Mexicans abroad, reminding them of the excellence of their homeland and ensuring that their children would grow up in an environment with affection for Mexico.[30] The broadcast was well received by the Mexican communities in the United States, which appreciated that the government organized programs especially for them.[31] Thus, Mexico joined early on the pioneering countries that used radio to maintain the link with their diasporas, such as the Netherlands (1927) and the United Kingdom (1932).[32]

Revolutionary Propaganda

The second main objective of public diplomacy toward México de afuera was, as in domestic propaganda, to ideologically guide Mexican emigrants and generate adhesion to the government's program. Thus, the Cárdenas government did not only seek to link them to Mexico but also to a particular version of the country: the revolutionary Mexico. Consulates reported that among Mexicans in the United States there were numerous "prejudices" about revolutionary Mexico—which again were more serious among the children of Mexicans born in that country—and blamed the US Spanish-language press for ideologically alienating emigrants.[33]

Indeed, in the crusade to link the diaspora with Mexico, the government had to compete with other Mexican leaders who had their own agendas. The country's internal political divisions were replicated in the México de afuera,[34] and the influential groups of exiled Mexicans, many of them media owners, were a powerful adversary there.[35] The most famous was Ignacio E. Lozano, a staunch antirevolutionary who founded two widely circulated newspapers—*La Prensa* and *La Opinión*—which were often the only Spanish-language media to which the Mexican communities had access.[36] Through their pages, Lozano tried to maintain the cohesion of Mexican communities and prevent their assimilation into North American culture.[37] But although he shared this objective with Cárdenas, the Mexican identity he offered to the emigrant communities contradicted the official version. He actively propagandized against revolutionary nationalism and sought to reinforce a prerevolutionary narrative of Mexico within the diaspora.[38] In late 1937, for example, Lozano's newspapers organized a contest among their readers to choose an "anthem of *México de afuera*." The winner was a text that commemorated landmarks and symbols of nineteenth-century conservative Mexico. Cárdenas's government accused them of establishing divisions between Mexico and its diaspora and trying to form groups of "White Mexicans" as did the Russian enemies of their revolution.[39] However, although postrevolutionary governments had banned Lozano's newspapers from circulating within Mexico on several occasions,[40] they did not have the power to censor their adversaries in foreign territory. The only alternative was to reinforce its own propaganda there.

In this scenario, the government sought to awaken revolutionary sentiments within the diaspora and publicize the objectives and progress of its six-year-plan, just as it did in its domestic propaganda. To this end, the associativity of the Mexican communities was once again exploited. News bulletins were sent periodically to all the honorary commissions, with the instruction to disseminate them among the communities.[41] As each group received only one copy, some commissions met weekly with the communities to read the news bulletins to them.[42] Documentaries on government propaganda produced by DAPP were also shown, so that emigrants could "visually appreciate . . . what the government is doing for the benefit of the working classes."[43] In 1936 a Mexican association in Texas wrote to thank the president for the communications received and stated that it was "the first time in the history of our leaders" that they were so extensively informed about national events.[44]

Finally, the emotional exaltation around the ideology of the revolution was enhanced through the dissemination of the presidential messages that Cárdenas offered to the country. The SRE not only distributed in the United States leaflets containing his printed speeches but also instructed the honorary commissions to gather the communities to listen to the messages on the radio.[45] That meant additional challenges for the commissions since the signals of the Mexican radio stations did not have such a long range.[46]

The ideological orientation of Mexicans also focused on children.[47] The Ministry of Education (Secretaría de Educación Pública, SEP) sent out educational material that extended the domestic socialist education program to the diaspora. The community schools received textbooks in which poems, stories, and allegories used revolutionary themes and symbolism, and records with revolutionary hymns.[48]

Within the framework of this ideological propaganda toward the Mexican communities in the United States, the oil expropriation of March 1938 was a key milestone. Although many of these communities were located in oil states such as Texas where the propaganda against Mexico was especially virulent, the expropriation served to stoke nationalist sentiment within the diaspora. Some consuls even considered that the expropriation had served to unify the Mexican communities over their political differences.[49] This mirrored the situation in Mexico, where the measure unleashed a nationalist fervor among all sectors. The oil expropriation, which affected powerful US monopolies such as Standard Oil, was experienced by Mexicans as a triumph against US imperialism and a confirmation of their national sovereignty.

Consuls reinforced public diplomacy among the communities to counteract the oil companies' propaganda against Mexico and to strengthen nationalism.[50] Consulate employees traveled many miles to give speeches to the Mexican communities,[51] used the upcoming patriotic celebrations to inform about the government's position on expropriation,[52] distributed printed propaganda,[53] and exhibited the documentaries that DAPP edited on the subject. Particularly moving was the film *La nacionalización del petróleo*, which, by recording the demonstrations in support of the expropri-ation in Mexico City, brought the nationalist exaltation to Mexicans abroad. The success of these campaigns was reflected by the enthusiastic contribu-tions of the communities to the Mexican fundraising efforts to pay the coun-try's debt after expropriation.[54] By collaborating, the Mexican communities manifested themselves as part of that same nation.

The legal battle for oil extended over the following years, as did the pro-paganda battle between the Mexican government and the oil groups. For the anniversaries of the expropriation, the SRE instructed the consulates to celebrate the milestone together with the communities.[55] March 18 was thus added to the civic calendar of Mexican celebrations in the United States, making it clear that patriotic celebrations did not honor a general version of Mexico but rather revolutionary Mexico specifically.

PART II: MEXICAN COMMUNITIES AND SOFT POWER IN THE UNITED STATES

Mexican Emigrants as Propaganda Agents?

Public diplomacy toward the México de afuera was not only intertwined with Cárdenas's domestic propaganda but also with Mexico's soft power in the United States. First, Mexican emigrants were natural ambassadors in that country: it was an undeniable fact that their important presence in US territory influenced, for better or worse, the ideas that many citizens of that nation had about Mexico and Mexicans. In this regard, Mexican con-suls were concerned about the consequences that the low educational level of Mexicans residing in the United States could have for Mexico's image there. Most of them were illiterate and lived in poor and unhealthy con-ditions.[56] As the Mexican consul in Del Rio, Texas, warned, the degree of ignorance in which they found themselves reinforced the historical preju-dices that US citizens had toward Mexicans. The consul insisted that it was urgent to raise the cultural level of the compatriots in order to "destroy the humiliating concept" that surrounded Mexicans in the United States.[57] SEP, DAPP, and the consulates were effectively engaged in literacy and cultural propaganda campaigns among the communities in the hope that through the knowledge acquired, Mexicans abroad would "dignify the name of the land where they were born."[58] In addition to the aforementioned schools for Mexican children,[59] they created libraries, plays, patriotic history les-sons, and cultural newspapers.[60] The government also sought to make the emigrants themselves understand that they played a role in Mexico's international image, reminding them of the conduct they should observe as "good Mexicans" in that country.[61] This concern was shared by the Mexican elites in the United States. Through *La Prensa*, Lozano taught emigrants how they should behave to counteract the negative stereotypes.[62]

However, if the social composition of the emigrants was not a particular asset for the country's soft power, there was an aspect from which Mexico could benefit: its culture. Although Mexico had a very bad press in the United States for its political processes, its traditional culture had begun to be highly valued in the 1920s and 1930s. Tourism to Mexico, the fame of its muralism, and a fascination with its folklore, music, and popular art generated a true Mexican craze in the United States.[63] The Cárdenas government was aware of this capital and promoted important cultural diplomacy initiatives, including exhibitions, dance, and music.[64] The activities of its diaspora could, therefore, also contribute to this end. The "Mexican festivals" organized by the honorary commissions had this double gain since they were attended by a certain number of US citizens, including the authorities of each locality. Thus, the Mexican emigrants who performed traditional dances or songs during these events became, perhaps unknowingly, vehicles for the cultural propaganda of their homeland. To that end, consulates spent time and money making sure that these festivities were well organized and projected a good image of Mexico. Although they sometimes feared the low educational level of the participants, they also saw in them a valuable resource since they had "the artistic feeling that is innate to our race."[65] This idea echoed an imaginary that was widely installed in the 1920s and 1930s, according to which the artistic expressions of peasant and indigenous groups expressed the national culture with greater purity and genuineness.[66] In turn, the attraction for "primitive" arts fostered in the United States by the cultural relativism of anthropologist Franz Boas created a fertile scenario to value these expressions.[67]

Second, Mexican emigrants were also seen by the government as potential agents of the revolutionary cause, although in this field its contribution to Mexican soft power was also limited, as will be seen at the end of this section. The Cárdenas administration sought to give Mexicans in the United States the tools to undertake propaganda in favor of their government. For example, in the radio program for the diaspora, *La hora de México*, DAPP invited Mexicans in the United States to become "vehement propagators" of Mexico's goodness. The programs educated listeners on social and economic aspects of Mexico and asked them to correct falsehoods they heard in their localities, giving them concrete inputs to do so: the broadcasters selected injurious news stories about Mexico that were circulating at the time in the

United States and provided arguments and data that could serve Mexicans in disproving them.[68] After the oil expropriation, consulates also considered taking advantage of the Mexicans in the United States to make propaganda without incurring in greater expenses.[69] They educated them through lectures, printed materials, and films to be able to explain the government's point of view, which seemed to bear fruit over time. In 1940, on the occasion of the second anniversary of the oil expropriation, members of the Mexican community were invited to justify the policy to the audience. A consul observed that they analyzed the expropriation with a perfect knowledge of its causes and concluded that the emigrants had adequately assimilated the explanations that the consulate had given them.[70] In addition to the individual actions of emigrants, Mexican associations were also a great ally of revolutionary propaganda. They made special efforts to counteract Catholic and oil propaganda against Mexico.[71] Several took advantage of their relationships with other groups across the country to spread their message.

However, the scope of diaspora propaganda was limited. The Cárdenas government could hardly have been confident that the emigrants' defense of Mexico would have a substantial impact on Mexico's soft power in the United States, especially in terms of influencing US foreign policy or diplomatic negotiations on the payment of oil compensation. In those years there were foreign communities in the United States, such as the Irish Americans, who, thanks to their influential leaders and their newspapers, effectively managed to weigh upon spheres of influence.[72] Mexican communities, on the other hand, did not have such a reach. It is true that the educated members of the diaspora had networks and media in the United States, but most of them were opposed to the postrevolutionary governments.[73] The rest of the communities were poorly inserted into US society, spoke poor English, and carried an inferiority complex that pushed them into isolation.[74] Who could they reach with their word? In fact, in its appeals to emigrants, the Mexican government never specified what kind of audiences they should target with their advocacy. But given that propaganda in the communities functioned mainly in oral form on the basis of personal relationships, it is to be assumed that they would reach those with whom they interacted on a daily basis in their localities, mostly Mexicans.

Thus, paradoxically, the Mexican government's effort to discourage the assimilation and nationalization of emigrants in the United States also proved to be a disincentive for them to exert influence there. Meanwhile, those Mexicans who spoke English and were better integrated into US culture, as well as associations of Mexicans that interacted with groups of US citizens, offered better opportunities to spread Mexican advocacy. Labor associations were particularly useful in this regard. Mexican workers who participated in unions alongside US workers, non-Mexican Hispanics, and other nationalities could play an important role in extending support for Cárdenas beyond the Mexican communities, taking advantage of the natural political solidarity of these groups with the cause of the Mexican Revolution.[75] In 1938, for example, the Alaska Cannery Union organized a massive rally of workers to hear Cárdenas's speech on expropriation.[76] Although US workers in unions were perhaps not politically influential as individuals in the United States, as groups they could offer some influence to the Mexican cause.

The Clash with US Public Opinion

Beyond the ambivalent role of propagandists that members of the Mexican diaspora in the United States may have played, the public diplomacy that the Cárdenas government directed specifically toward them also clashed with Mexican soft power there, even jeopardizing part of its narrative. It is important to clarify that the main target of Mexico's public diplomacy in the United States was by no means the México de afuera but, on the contrary, US public opinion. The main resources of foreign propaganda went to them, and consuls were instructed to deliver the ever-scarce publications issued by DAPP to US citizens rather than to the Mexican communities. Public diplomacy directed at the US population sought to promote a foreign policy favorable to Mexico and was aimed primarily at the educated, influential, and progressive US public where the Cárdenas government could find some support for its policies.

In terms of content, these communication campaigns had similarities with those aimed at the diaspora—they sought to refute the propaganda of interest groups and justify the six-year-plan and the oil expropriation—but also presented important differences. The SRE was conscious of the need to adapt its message to US audiences so as not to frighten them with the program of revolutionary Mexico and worked hard to dispel accusations of political radicalism. Mexican propagandists in the United States sought arguments that would dialogue with the values and interests of their audience: they presented the government's program as moderate, insisted on its similarities with Roosevelt's New Deal, and emphasized Mexico's friendship with the United States in reciprocity to the GNP.[77] In this context, the propaganda for the Mexican diaspora generated a number of controversies as far as it reached US audiences. There were some sectors in the United States that resented the patriotic celebrations of the Mexican communities as expressions of foreign nationalism.[78] But more controversial were other aspects of public diplomacy toward the diaspora: their ideological propaganda and anti-American tone. The former generated a truly delicate scenario. The depression that had begun in 1929 had reactivated fears of communist propaganda in the country, and in the following years two committees—the McCormack-Dickstein Committee (1934) and the Dies Committee (1938)—were created in Congress to investigate this type of propaganda.[79] Mexico, in fact, was not spared from being in the crosshairs of these organizations.[80] The anti-Mexican propaganda of Catholic and oil interest groups insisted on accusing the Mexican governments of being communist and wanting to export their revolution throughout the continent. In this scenario, the Cárdenas government was very careful to avoid ideological proselytism in other countries. Through its public diplomacy toward the United States, it denied being communist and insisted there was no intention of exporting the Mexican Revolution. However, this moderation contrasted with the discourse of revolutionary nationalism that was encouraged within Mexico, which was based on radical slogans and symbols of proletarian emancipation. When Mexican institutions carried this domestic propaganda to Mexican communities abroad, the external discourse of moderation was put at risk.

A particular controversy occurred in 1939 with the educational material sent by SEP to schools for Mexican children in the United States. The Coordinating Council of Los Angeles County scrutinized textbooks used in those schools, fearing that they might contain communist tendencies and therefore be contrary to US values. Its reports denounced that in their poems and stories, there were scenes of workers singing *The Internationale*, stories about the exploitation of workers by US owners and calls to rebel against them, statements about workers' rights to own land and machines, and drawings of raised fists, among others. Mexican diplomats expressed concern about this complaint, as the risk of being presented to the Dies Committee was too great. The SRE ordered consuls to remove any books from schools that aroused suspicion, whether "founded or not." Foreign Secretary Eduardo Hay stated that Mexican children living in the United States could indeed read such books but only at home.[81] His directive evidenced two things. The first was the SRE's acceptance of the need to isolate propaganda for the diaspora to its private space. This was not a predesigned public diplomacy guideline but rather a reaction to the circumstances and in fact was not welcomed by either DAPP or SEP.[82] The second was the prioritization of Mexico's reputation as a politically moderate country in the eyes of US public opinion over the ideological orientation of the Mexican communities.

The second controversy arose especially in the face of the oil expropriation propaganda. Oil companies insisted that by expropriating, Mexico was not only attacking them but also the entire United States and its values. They also claimed that there was a strong feeling of anti-Americanism in the country and that Mexico was mocking the GNP.[83] Cardenista counterpropaganda denied these accusations, and the Mexican government tried to prove its goodwill toward the neighboring country, enthusiastically adopting the rhetoric of the GNP. However, it is certain that the discourse that animated Mexicans after the expropriation was markedly anti-American. The oil expropriation was the culminating point of a crusade of defensive nationalism arising from the Mexican Revolution and embodied in the 1917 Constitution, whose raison d'être rested largely on emancipating the country from US intervention and tutelage.[84] Celebrations about the expropriation in Mexico had a strong anti-American rhetoric, as could be seen in the *corridos* that were written for the occasion.[85] Therefore, it was problematic when the propaganda designed as domestic reached Mexicans living in US territory. The first warnings arose shortly after the expropriation. The Mexican consul in Chicago warned in July 1938 about the inconvenience of showing the documentary *La nacionalización del petróleo*, which displayed triumphant public demonstrations celebrating the expropriation in Mexico City. Given that many US groups had censored the measure, the consul warned that the film would only generate a hostile reaction and proposed that it only be shown to the Mexican communities.[86] This recommendation was in line with the directive of circumscribing SEP books to the private domain of the Mexican communities but was more difficult to achieve because these celebrations and the film were public activities that were usually attended by some US citizens. In addition, US authorities were vigilant about foreign propaganda, especially that considered "communist."[87] The proposal to keep the message encapsulated for the diaspora so that it would not reach US ears was not entirely feasible. In 1940 similar controversies surrounding celebrations of the second anniversary of the expropriation showed that this problem was still unresolved.[88]

These cases demonstrated the complexity of extending the effort of ideological orientation of Mexicans to the diaspora. The opposing discourses of domestic and foreign propaganda overlapped on US soil, making their contradictions evident and risking the credibility of Cárdenas's message toward the US public opinion. Thus, the success of the political propaganda for the México de afuera could jeopardize Mexico's soft power in the United States. The SRE, aware of US sensitivities and Mexico's foreign policy objectives, opted to protect Mexico's moderate image in the eyes of US citizens over the nationalist-revolutionary education of the Mexican communities in this country. A clear example of this is when, in 1939, the radio program *La hora de México*—the government's only propaganda initiative specifically aimed at the diaspora in the United States—was sacrificed in order to use this channel for a new radio program, this time aimed at US audiences, titled *La hora del buen vecino* (The good neighbor hour).[89]

CONCLUSION

This chapter has approached diasporas as a hinge that connects domestic propaganda with soft power and allows us to see the possibilities, contradictions, and difficulties that arose in this encounter. To this end, it has studied diasporas in their dual role as recipients of public diplomacy from their government of origin and as potential ambassadors of their country in the host country.

The Cárdenas administration was successful in addressing the México de afuera. Despite the meager communications budget and the widespread location of the diasporic communities, Mexican officials were able to take advantage of their previous networks of sociability to multiply their message among them. In its approach to the Mexican diaspora, however, the government was far from benefiting from its transnational character. Rather, it treated emigrants as an extension of Mexican domestic audience: it only reinforced their Mexican identity and resisted their cultural assimilation in the United States, it delivered to them the same message of revolutionary nationalism of domestic propaganda, and it involved them in national crusades such as the payment of the oil debt. All this had various consequences for Mexico's soft power in the United States.

On one hand, the export of domestic propaganda to US territory generated controversy since its message opposed that delivered by the Cárdenas government to US public opinion. Thus, this case highlights the inconvenience for governments sending contradictory messages in their domestic and foreign propaganda as well as the impossibility of keeping both messages encapsulated, especially when they intersect in intermediate spaces such as the diaspora.

On the other, the Mexican government's resistance to emigrants' assimilation into US culture—reinforced by the low educational level of the emigrants and their poor command of English—was a factor that paradoxically hindered Mexicans' potential as propagandists in the United States. As a result, their reach as propagandists was ambiguous and limited. The emigrants did indeed spread the "typical" Mexican culture in the United States that was so attractive at the time, but in general they did not exert a relevant political influence among US citizens, as did many diasporic communities of other nationalities. Therefore, diasporas are not always useful intermediary agents for a country's soft power since a series of conditions must be in place as well as the political will to take advantage of them.

The Cárdenas government opted for other ways to reinforce its political soft power in the United States. It favored channels of public diplomacy toward Americans that did not pass through the Mexican communities but went directly to influential US citizens. Aside from this audience—which Mexico urgently needed to have on its side as it negotiated various issues with the Roosevelt administration—the diaspora was not the priority of its propaganda abroad. In fact, the SRE went so far as to sacrifice public diplomacy toward the México de afuera when it became inconvenient for its soft power in the United States.

Studying public diplomacy toward the diaspora during the Cárdenas government allowed us to observe the characteristics of these efforts in a context where Mexican communities in the United States were considered by its government to be more a part of Mexico than as a transnational space. This situation changed sharply after World War II, when the assimilation of Mexican Americans was consolidated by the participation of many of them in the US armed forces, and Mexican governments realized that most emigrants would no longer return to Mexico. How these transformations shaped Mexican public diplomacy toward Mexican emigrants in the United States after 1945 remains to be studied.

NOTES

The research on which this chapter is based was funded by the ANID-Fondecyt project number 3200615.

1. Definition by Victor Horboken (2004), quoted in Vanessa Bravo and Maria de Moya, "Mexico's Public Diplomacy Efforts to Engage Its Diaspora across the Border: Case Study of the Programs, Messages and Strategies Employed by the Mexican Embassy in the United States," *Rising Powers Quarterly* 3, no. 3 (2018): 17393, 174.
2. Although this is gradually changing, see note 9.
3. Nicholas J. Cull, "Diasporas and Public Diplomacy: From History to Policy," in *Routledge International Handbook of Diaspora Diplomacy*, ed. Liam Kennedy (New York: Routledge, 2021), 7.
4. R. S. Zaharna, "Relational Spheres and the Primacy of Domestic and Diaspora Publics in Global Public Diplomacy" (paper, Annual Convention of the International Studies Association, Montreal, 2011).
5. Weston R. Sager, "Apple Pie Propaganda: The Smith-Mundt Act before and after the Repeal of the Domestic Dissemination Ban Notes and Comments," *Northwestern University Law Review* 109, no. 2 (2015): 511–46.

6. Kishan S. Rana, "Diaspora Diplomacy and Public Diplomacy," in *Relational, Networked and Collaborative Approaches to Public Diplomacy*, ed. R. S. Zaharna, Amelia Arsenault, and Ali Fisher (New York: Routledge, 2013), 70, 77–79, 177–78; Zaharna, "Relational Spheres"; Bravo and de Moya, "Mexico's Public Diplomacy Efforts," 178; Kennedy, *Routledge International Handbook of Diaspora Diplomacy*, 1.

7. David R Ayón, "La política mexicana y la movilización de los migrantes mexicanos en Estados Unidos," in *Relaciones Estado-diáspora: La perspectiva de América Latina y el Caribe*, ed. Carlos González Gutierrez, vol. 2 (Mexico City: Miguel Ángel Porrúa, 2006), 117; Gilbert G. González, *Mexican Consuls and Labor Organizing: Imperial Politics in the American Southwest*, (Austin: University of Texas Press, 2010).

8. Rana, "Diaspora Diplomacy and Public Diplomacy," 70; Zaharna, "Relational Spheres"; Vanessa Bravo, "The Importance of Diaspora Communities as Key Publics for National Governments around the World," in *International Public Relations and Public Diplomacy: Communication and Engagement*, ed. Guy J. Golan, Sung-Un Yang, and Dennis F. Kinsey, (New York: Peter Lang, 2014), 279–96; Mark Leonard, "Diplomacy by Other Means," *Foreign Policy*, no. 132 (2002): 48–56, https://doi.org/10.2307/3183455.

9. Some exceptions are John Day Tully, "Ethnicity, Security, and Public Diplomacy: Irish-Americans and Ireland's Neutrality in World War II," in *The United States and Public Diplomacy: New Directions in Cultural and International History*, ed. Kenneth A. Osgood and Brian C. Etheridge (Leiden: Brill, 2010); Marie Gillespie and Alban Webb, *Diasporas and Diplomacy: Cosmopolitan Contact Zones at the BBC World Service (1932–2012)* (New York: Routledge, 2013); Charlotte Faucher, *Propaganda, Gender, and Cultural Power: Projections and Perceptions of France in Britain c. 1880–1944* (Oxford: Oxford University Press, 2022); Elisabeth Piller, *Selling Weimar: German Public Diplomacy and the United States, 1918–1933* (Stuttgart: Franz Steiner Verlag / Washington: German Historical Institute, 2020). Cull also provides historical examples in Cull, "Diasporas and Public Diplomacy."

10. See, e.g., José M. Alamillo, "Playing across Borders: Transnational Sports and Identities in Southern California and Mexico, 1930–1945," *Pacific Historical Review* 79, no. 3 (August 1, 2010): 360–92, https://doi.org/10.1525/phr.2010.79.3.360; Fernando Saúl Alanis Enciso, *La comunidad mexicana en Estados Unidos: Aspectos de su historia* (San Luis Potosí, Mex.: El Colegio de San Luis Potosí, 2004); Fernando Saúl Alanís Enciso and Mark Overmyer-Velázquez, *They Should Stay There: The Story of Mexican Migration and Repatriation during the Great Depression* (Chapel Hill: University of North Carolina Press, 2017); Francisco E. Balderrama, *In Defense of La Raza: The Los Angeles Mexican Consulate and the Mexican Community, 1929 to 1936* (Tucson: University of Arizona Press, 1982); González, *Mexican Consuls and Labor Organizing*; Victoria Lerner, "Los exiliados de la Revolución Mexicana en Estados Unidos, 1910–1940," in Alanis Enciso, *La comunidad mexicana en Estados Unidos*, 71–126; George J. Sánchez, *Becoming Mexican American: Ethnicity, Culture, and Identity in Chicano Los Angeles, 1900–1945* (New York: Oxford University Press, 1993).

11. Bravo and de Moya, "Mexico's Public Diplomacy Efforts," 184. For other studies on Mexico's current relationship with its diaspora, see Carlos González Gutierrez, "The Institute of Mexicans Abroad: An Effort to Empower the Diaspora," in *Closing the Distance: How Governments Strengthen Ties with Their Diasporas*, ed. Dovelyn Rannveig Agunias and Migration Policy Institute (Washington, DC: Migration Policy Institute, 2009); Carlos González Gutierrez, "Fostering Identities: Mexico's Relations with Its

Diaspora," *Journal of American History* 86, no. 2 (September 1999): 545, https://doi.org /10.2307/2567045.

12. On domestic propaganda, see Omar Fabián González Salinas, "El discurso patriótico y el aparato propagandístico que sustentaron a la expropiación petrolera durante el cardenismo," *Estudios de historia moderna y contemporánea de México*, no. 52 (December 2016): 88–107, https://doi.org/10.1016/j.ehmcm.2016.06.003. On foreign propaganda, see Sylvia Dummer Scheel, "En defensa de la revolución: Diplomacia pública de México hacia Estados Unidos bajo el gobierno de Lázaro Cárdenas (1934–1940)" (PhD thesis, Berlin, Freie Universität Berlin, 2015); Amelia M. Kiddle, *Mexico's Relations with Latin America during the Cárdenas Era* (Albuquerque: University of New Mexico Press, 2016); Dafne Cruz Porchini, *Arte, propaganda y diplomacia cultural a finales del cardenismo, 1937–1940* (Mexico: Secretaría de Relaciones Exteriores, Dirección General del Acervo Histórico Diplomático, 2016).

13. Alanís Enciso and Overmyer-Velázquez, *They Should Stay There*, 166.

14. Jesús Martínez-Saldaña, "Los Olvidados Become Heroes: The Evolution of Mexico's Policies Towards Citizens Abroad," in *International Migration and Sending Countries: Perceptions, Policies and Transnational Relations*, ed. Eva Østergaard-Nielsen (London: Palgrave Macmillan UK, 2003), 33–56, https://doi.org/10.1057/9780230512429_2.

15. Lerner, "Los exiliados de la Revolución Mexicana," 71–72, 104–5, 109–2; Martínez-Saldaña, "Los Olvidados Become Heroes," 36; Maggie Rivas-Rodriguez, "Ignacio E. Lozano: The Mexican Exile Publisher Who Conquered San Antonio and Los Angeles," *American Journalism* 21 (January 1, 2004): 75–89, https://doi.org/10.1080/08821127 .2004.10677569, 75–83.

16. Secretaría de Relaciones Exteriores de México (Mexican Ministry of Foreign Affairs, hereinafter referred to as SRE), *Circular Nº C-1-8*, 21.1.1938, Archivo General de la Nación, México (hereinafter referred to as AGN), fondo Lázaro Cárdenas del Río (hereinafter referred to as LCR) 575.1/50

17. See Alanís Enciso and Overmyer-Velázquez, *They Should Stay There*.

18. This is often a characteristic problem in dealing with second-generation diasporas. See Mari Toivanen and Bahar Baser, "Diasporas, Development and the Second Generation," in Kennedy, *Routledge International Handbook of Diaspora Diplomacy*.

19. Sánchez, *Becoming Mexican American*; Gustavo Cano and Alexandra Délano, "The Mexican Government and Organised Mexican Immigrants in The United States: A Historical Analysis of Political Transnationalism (1848–2005)," *Journal of Ethnic and Migration Studies* 33, no. 5 (July 1, 2007): 695–725, https://doi.org/10.1080 /13691830701359157; Rivas-Rodriguez, "Ignacio E. Lozano," 83.

20. From Macedonio Platas to Departamento Autónomo de Prensa y Publicidad (hereinafter referred to as DAPP), 29.11.1937, AGN fondo Dirección General de Información (hereinafter referred to as DGI) 301.60/38; From Ernesto Hidalgo, Consular Department SRE, to DAPP, 19.6.1939, AGN-DGI 301.6(73–47)/1.

21. President Álvaro Obregón also worked to prevent the assimilation of Mexicans into US culture in the 1920s. Cano and Délano, "Mexican Government and Organised Mexican Immigrants," 704.

22. Sánchez, *Becoming Mexican American*, 109; Cano and Délano, "Mexican Government and Organised Mexican Immigrants," 703–4.

23. SRE, Annual Report 1933–34, 645–80, Biblioteca de la Secretaría de Relaciones Exteriores.

24. From Carlos Calderón to Mexican consul in San Antonio, 15.3.1940, Archivo Histórico Genaro Estrada, Secretaría de Relaciones Exteriores, México (hereinafter referred to as AHGE) L-E-556.

25. From Ernesto Hidaldo to Secretaría de Educación Pública, México (Mexican Ministry of Education, hereinafter referred to as SEP), 17.9.1937, Archivo Secretaría de Educación Pública (hereinafter referred to as ASEP) Subsecretaria 17/1.

26. From Macedonio Platas to DAPP, 29.11.1937, AGN-DGI 301.60/38; From Sociedad Pro México del sur de Chicago to DAPP, 21.2.1940, AGN-DGI 201(019)/3.

27. From Ernesto Hidalgo to DAPP, 1.6.1938 and 7.6.1938, AGN-DGI 101.1/3MNOPGR; From Mexican consul in Brownville to SRE, 6.11.1939, AGN-DGI 300/616.

28. David Hayes-Bautista, *El Cinco de Mayo: An American Tradition* (Berkeley: University of California Press, 2012), 473; Ayón, "La política mexicana," 116.

29. From M. G. Calderon, Mexican consul in Denver to SRE, 31.3.1934, ASEP, Departamento Bellas Artes c35/6; From Ernesto Hidalgo to Mexican Ministry of Interior, 24.9.1941, AGN-DGI 101.1/3MNOPGR.

30. The program was inspired by *La Hora Nacional* (The national hour), which DAPP aimed at domestic audiences. From Agustín Arroyo Ch., director of DAPP (hereinafter referred to as AACh), to SEP, 3.2.1939, AGN-DGI 301.2/182; "Varios Radiospots," February/March 1939, AGN-DGI 301.2/182.

31. From Ernesto Hidalgo to AACh, 11.3.1939, AGN-DGI 301.2/182.

32. D. R. Browne points out that these countries pioneered the use of radio to communicate with their citizens in their imperial possessions. *International Radio Broadcasting: The Limits of the Limitless Medium* (Westport, CT: Praeger, 1982). Cited in Cull, "Diasporas and Public Diplomacy," 13.

33. From Ernesto Hidalgo to DAPP, 18.11.1938, AGN-DGI 301(73–84)/1; From Ernesto Hidalgo to DAPP, 19.6.1939, AGN-DGI 301.6(73–47)/1.

34. Cano and Délano, "Mexican Government and Organised Mexican Immigrants," 703–4.

35. Lerner, "Los exiliados de la Revolución Mexicana," 110.

36. From Mexican Honorific Association MC Farland to LCR, 5.2.1935, AGN-LCR 704.1/65.

37. Rivas-Rodriguez, "Ignacio E. Lozano," 77, 84; Lerner, "Los exiliados de la Revolución Mexicana," 109–10.

38. E.g., Lozano financed a highly critical biography of Pancho Villa, one of the icons of the revolution. Lerner, "Los exiliados de la Revolución Mexicana," 106.

39. SRE, Annual Report, 1937–38, Biblioteca de la Secretaría de Relaciones Exteriores; SRE, Circular Nº C-1-8 SRE, 21.1.1938, AGN-LCR 575.1/50.

40. Rivas-Rodriguez, "Ignacio E. Lozano," 80.

41. From Comisión Honorífica Mexicana, Carrizo Springs, to LCR, 9.3.1936, AGN-LCR 133.2/38; From SRE to SEP, 23.7.1938, AGN-DGI 301(73–12)/1; From Miguel Calderon, Consular Department SRE, to DAPP, 19.5.1938, AGN-DGI 101.1/3MNOPGR.

42. From Ernesto Hidalgo to DAPP, 4.5.1937, AGN-DGI 101.1/3MNOPGR and 3.6.1937, AGN-DGI 301(73–85)/1; From Sociedad Pro-México Chicago, to DAPP, 21.2.1940, AGN-DGI 201(019)/3.

43. From Ernesto Hidalgo to DAPP, 19.6.1939, AGN-DGI 301.6(73–47)/1.

44. From Comisión Honorífica Mexicana to LCR, 9.3.1936, AGN-LCR 133.2/38.

45. From Mexican vice consul in Alpine to Mexican consul in El Paso, 1.4.1938, AHGE L-E- 559; From *Comisión Honorífica Mexicana* to LCR, 9.3.1936, AGN-LCR 133.2/38.

46. From Luis Duplan, Mexican consul in Houston, to Mexican consul in San Antonio, 14.3.1940, AHGE L-E-556.

47. Public diplomacy aimed at children has also been addressed by Charlotte Faucher, *Propaganda, Gender, and Cultural Power: Projections and Perceptions of France in Britain c. 1880–1944* (Oxford: Oxford University Press, 2022), chap. 6.

48. From Emeterio Esquivel to José Muñoz, SEP, 25.1.1935, and From Rufina Ochoa to SEP, 28.2.1935; ASEP Departamento de Bellas Artes, 52/55. On Mexican schools in the United States during the nineteenth and twentieth centuries, see Philis Barragán Goetz, *Reading, Writing, and Revolution: Escuelitas and the Emergence of a Mexican American Identity in Texas* (Austin: University of Texas Press, 2020).

49. From Rodolfo Salazar, Mexican consul in Chicago, to SRE, 29.3.1938, AHGE L-E-559.

50. From Hector Escalona, Mexican consul in San Francisco, to SRE, 12.4.1939, AHGE L-E-558.

51. From Hector Escalona to SRE, 12.4.1939, AHGE L-E-558; From A. García Toledo to LCR, 20.5.1938, AGN-LCR 432.2/253-8.

52. From Mexican vice consul in Los Angeles, to Mexican honorific associations, 25.4.1938, AHGE L-E-558.

53. From Honorific associations in Pasadena to DAPP, 4.9.1939, AGN-DGI 101.1/3MNOPGR.

54. From Hector Escalona to SRE, 12.4.1939, AHGE L-E-558.

55. From Alejandro Bravo, Mexican consul in Brownsville, to SRE, 1.3.1939, AHGE L-E-559; From Luis Duplán to Mexican consul in San Antonio, 25.3.1940, AHGE L-E-555 and 14.3.1940, AHGE L-E-556; From Omar Josefé, Mexican consul in San Antonio, to SRE, 25.3.1940, AHGE L-E-555; From Carlos Calderón, Mexican consul in Brownsville, to Mexican consul in San Antonio, 15.3.1940, AHGE L-E-556.

56. Alanís Enciso and Overmyer-Velázquez, *They Should Stay There*, 54–57, 60–65.

57. From SRE to SEP, 23.7.1938, AGN-DGI 301(73–12)/1.

58. DAPP, Annual Report 1937, 37, AGN.

59. From Ernesto Hidalgo to DAPP, 4.7.1938, AGN-DGI 301(73–54)/1.

60. From Ernesto Hidalgo to AACh, 13.10.1938; From Manuel Garza, Mexican consul in del Rio to AACh, 18.11.1938, AGN-DGI 301(73–12)/1; From Ernesto Hidalgo to DAPP, 4.7.1938, AGN-DGI 301(73–54)/1; From Alejandro Bravo to SRE, 6.11.1939, AGN-DGI 300/616; SRE, Annual Report 1933–34, 645–80, Biblioteca de la Secretaría de Relaciones Exteriores.

61. From AACh to SEP, 3.2.1939, AGN-DGI 301.2/182.

62. Rivas-Rodriguez, "Ignacio E. Lozano." 84.

63. Helen Delpar, *The Enormous Vogue of Things Mexican* (Tuscaloosa: University of Alabama Press, 1992); Dina Berger, *The Development of Mexico's Tourism Industry: Pyramids by Day, Martinis by Night*, 1st ed. (New York: Palgrave Macmillan, 2006).

64. Cruz Porchini, *Arte, propaganda y diplomacia cultural a finales del cardenismo, 1937–1940*.

65. From M. G. Calderon, Mexican consul in Denver, to SRE, 31.3.1934, ASEP Departamento de Bellas Artes (hereinafter referred to as dBBAA) c35/6.

66. Anthony D. Smith, *Nacionalismo: Teoría, ideología, historia*, trans. Olaf Bernárdez Cabello (Madrid: Alianza, 2004), 44–46. I have explored this idea in the case of Chile in Sylvia Dummer Scheel, "Los desafíos de escenificar el 'alma nacional': Chile en la Exposición Iberoamericana de Sevilla de 1929," *Historia Crítica*, no. 42 (2010): 84–111.

67. Fredrick Braun Pike, *The United States and Latin America: Myths and Stereotypes of Civilization and Nature* (Austin: University of Texas Press, 1992), 262–66.

68. From AACh to SEP, 3.2.1939, and "Varios Radiospots," February/March 1939, AGN-DGI 301.2/182.

69. From A. Cano del Castillo, Mexican consul in Galveston, to SRE, 26.4.1938, AHGE L-E-559.

70. From Omar Josefé to SRE, 25.3.1940, AHGE L-E-555; From Luis Duplan to Mexican consul in San Antonio, 14.3.1940, AHGE L-E-556.

71. From Eugenio Pesqueira, Mexican consul in Chicago, to Luis Rodríguez, private secretary to the president, 6.3.1935, AGN-LCR 545.3/103; From Manuel Ajuria to Luis Rodríguez, n.d., AGN-LCR 545.3/103; From Manuel Ajuria and Rafael Perez to Illinois House of Representatives, 28.2.1935, AGN-LCR 545.3/103; "Comité Pro México," n.d., AGN-LCR 545.3/103; From Asociación Honorífica Mexicana de MC Farland to LCR, 5.2.1935, AGN-LCR 704.1/65; From Mexican consul in Chicago to SRE, 27.3.1939, AHGE L-E-605.

72. Tully, "Ethnicity, Security, and Public Diplomacy."

73. There were exceptions. The owners of the Los Angeles newspapers *El Eco de Mexico* and *El Paladín* published propaganda in favor of the Cárdenas government. From Agustin Leñero to AACh, 28.9.1939, AGN-DGI 300/588; From Ignacio Mejías to Alfonso Teja Zabre, 14.1.1940, AGN-DGI 128 300/622.

74. From SER to SEP, 23.7.1938, AGN-DGI 301(73–12)/1.

75. US labor organizations were in fact an important source of US support for expropriation. See Dummer Scheel, "En defensa de la revolución," 493–94. On the participation of Mexicans in North American unions, see Sánchez, *Becoming Mexican American*, 227–52.

76. From Hector Escalona to SRE, 18.4.1938, AHGE L-E- 558.

77. See Ramón Beteta, *En defensa de la revolución* (Mexico City: DAPP, 1937).

78. From Ira Rice, editor-in-chief of *Chronicle*, Raymondville, to Raúl G. Domínguez, Mexican consul in Brownsville, 1938, AGN-LCR 573.12/16.

79. Harold D. 1902–1978 Lasswell and Dorothy Blumenstock, *World Revolutionary Propaganda: A Chicago Study*, 2018; Brett Garry, *The Nervous Liberals: Propaganda Anxieties from World War I to the Cold War* (New York: Columbia University Press, 1999), 175–98. These two committees were predecessors to the House Committee on Un-American Activities.

80. From Efraín Domínguez, Mexican consul in Laredo, to Mexican consul in San Antonio, 14.3.1940, AHGE L-E-556.

81. From Eduardo Hay to SEP; 15.6.1939, from SEP to Eduardo Hay, 21.6.1939; SRE, "Memorandum," 1.8.1939, ASEP Subsecretaría 27/21.

82. I analyzed this issue in Sylvia Dummer Scheel, "¿De quién es la diplomacia pública? El rol del Departamento Autónomo de Prensa y Publicidad (DAPP) en la propaganda exterior cardenista," *Estudios de Historia Moderna Contemporanea de Mexico*, no. 55 (June 1, 2018): 279–312, https://doi.org/10.22201/iih.24485004e.2018.55.63301.

83. From Moisés Saenz to AACh, 6.4.1938, FAACh, "abril-mayo-1938."

84. Martínez-Saldaña, "Los Olvidados Become Heroes," 37.

85. The corrido is a Mexican musical style that expresses popular historical, political or sentimental narratives. During the Mexican Revolution it played an important role as an informative and subversive medium.

86. From Eduardo Hay to AACh, 4.7.1938, AGN DGI c173, 301.60/89; From Rodolfo Salazar to SRE, 20.7.1938, AGN-DGI 301.60/89.
87. Garry, *The Nervous Liberals*, 175–98.
88. From Efraín Domínguez to Mexican consul in San Antonio, 14.3.1940, and from Carlos Calderón to Mexican consul in San Antonio, 15.3.1940, AHGE L-E-556; From Omar Josefé to SRE, 25.3.1940, AHGE L-E-555.
89. From [illegible] to AACh, 23.4.1939, FAACh 18-L; From Quintín Rueda to AACh, 1.6.1939, FAACh 20-R.

CHAPTER 5

A Universal Mission

The Propaganda and Folklore of Robert Boutet from Morocco to Occupied Germany, 1931–49

Drew Flanagan

From the late nineteenth century to the early 1960s, France ruled a colonial empire that included possessions scattered across North and sub-Saharan Africa, Southeast Asia, the Caribbean, the South Pacific, and beyond. That empire gave rise to a justifying ideology, known to scholars as the "universal civilizing mission," that assumed the superiority and universality of French values and France's ability—and responsibility—to spread those values abroad.[1] Civilizing mission ideology became especially important during the Third Republic (1870–1940) but continued to structure the French colonial project well into the period of decolonization.

Colonial policymakers and practitioners understood that it was not enough to dominate a conquered people with force—it was also necessary that the colonized population viewed France's colonial project as legitimate. Therefore, ideas about soft power were fundamental to French civilizing ideology. Agents of the French colonial project sought to promote France's *rayonnement*, the supposedly universal attraction and influence of French culture, through education, propaganda, and other co-optive means.[2] Literally, rayonnement referred to French cultural, intellectual, and political influence, generally presented as pacifying, civilizing, and rational. As a metaphor, it evoked images of the light of French civilization radiating out from a center (metropolitan France) and illuminating faraway places.[3]

With the collapse of the National Socialist regime in May 1945, the French became one of four occupying powers in a defeated Germany. The goals and practices of the French occupation were shaped by the belief that German militarism and National Socialist ideology had arisen from Germany's deficit of "civilization." In the French zone of occupation, located along the Upper and Middle Rhine in southwestern Germany, French military and civilian officials sought to orient the occupied population toward the values and norms of Frenchness and "occidental" Christian civilization. Their mission was, to borrow an expression from Konrad Jarausch, to "re-civilize Germans."[4] The French recivilizing mission in southwestern Germany was strongly influenced by French colonial experience and ideology, and many of the military and civilian personnel who carried it out had extensive colonial experience. They brought ideas about the exercise of French power to the French zone of occupation with them, ideas that reflected their understanding of France as a civilizing power.

To better understand how colonial soft power practices crossed over from Morocco to postwar Germany, this chapter analyzes the career of folklorist, ethnologist, orientalist, and propagandist Robert Boutet. Boutet began his career as an agent of France's rayonnement in the protectorate of Morocco. From the early 1930s to the end of World War II, he undertook scholarly research, wrote propaganda for the colonial authorities, and edited the staunchly procolonial newspaper *La vigie marocaine*. He also studied Berber culture and religious practices, using his scholarly knowledge to compose literary works in the style of Berber folklore. These works had a dual purpose: to offer his French readers a window into "the Moroccan mind" and to influence French-speaking Moroccans in the direction of what he viewed as the virtues of French civilization. In 1945 Boutet joined the French occupation in southwestern Germany as an editor of the official magazine of the army of occupation. There he applied research and propaganda methods he had originally developed for use on Moroccans to the military government's mission—remaking the post-Nazi Germans into peaceful, civilized European partners for France.

Both in Morocco and Germany, Boutet occupied an ambiguous position as a state-adjacent actor. He consciously inserted himself into two French soft power projects—first the civilizing mission in Morocco, then the recivilizing mission of democratic reeducation and re-Christianization in Germany. In both locations, his work focused on reaching and influencing a young audience and reflected an apparently sincere commitment to winning hearts and minds for France. While he occasionally cooperated directly with the French Army as an embedded journalist and propagandist and even worked directly for it in Germany as an editor of the official magazine for the occupation troops, he also undertook apparently spontaneous independent scholarly and propaganda work that supported France's soft power ambitions in each place. That output was sanctioned and promoted by the colonial state, the army, and the military government in Germany, indicating that at least some military and administrative leaders saw Boutet as an asset.[5]

Boutet's work in both contexts should be understood as a form of public diplomacy. Jan Melissen has described public diplomacy as "one of soft power's key instruments," distinguished from traditional diplomacy by the fact that it is addressed to "the general public in foreign societies and more specific non-official groups, organizations, and individuals."[6] Joseph S. Nye divides public diplomacy into two broad categories: "broadcasting" a state's point of view and policy goals directly to a foreign population through media and more equal "exchanges" between peoples.[7] Effective public diplomacy implies a delicate act of translation based on detailed knowledge of the target culture. Done crudely, it threatens to degenerate into heavy-handed, arrogant propaganda that "not only fails to convince, but can undercut soft power."[8]

This chapter makes several contributions to the study of soft power and public diplomacy. First, it demonstrates concrete links between early Cold War–era soft power practices and French colonial civilizing practices. Second, while the protectorate of Morocco is usually treated as peripheral to the Europe-centered history of Cold War soft power, this chapter shows that it was in fact a center for the development of French ideas about cultural influence and public diplomacy. Third, it considers an understudied practice of public diplomacy—the use of folklore. In imitating the style of Arab and Berber "wonder tales" and of German fairy tales, Boutet sought to appeal to the aesthetic tastes and cultural norms of his readers in order to subtly promote his notion of French and Western Christian values and the French civilizing mission. Folktales seem to have been an ideal delivery method for what Nye has called "soft, co-optive power."[9] Informed by close study of the indigenous culture and with moralistic rather than overtly political messages, they were calculated to reach a young audience that was likely to mistrust more overt forms of propaganda.

Boutet's efforts in these two settings reveal important commonalities between the French civilizing project in colonial Morocco and its recivilizing mission in post-Nazi Germany. In both locations, Boutet put his ethnographic and folkloric knowledge to work, first to understand the indigenous culture, then to attempt to shape that culture with his writings. In Morocco the public diplomacy efforts of the colonial state and state-adjacent actors could ease the operation of French power by discouraging resistance and helping to encourage a positive identification with France among the indigenous population. In Germany French public diplomacy aimed to discourage resistance to Allied policy aims and, eventually, to build Germans' sense of identification with French and Western civilization. In both locations, Boutet's soft power efforts were made possible by overwhelming French hard power—a colonial protectorate in Morocco and a military occupation in Germany—a fact that is consistent with Ludovic Tournès's insight that public consent to the operation of power does not only result from the "intrinsic magic of attractiveness" but is also "the result of a relation of force" and that therefore "power is never soft, always hard."[10]

Comparing Boutet's projects in Morocco and occupied Germany also reveals important differences between them. On one hand, Boutet seems to have viewed the basic flaw of Moroccan and German culture as analogous: a tendency toward irrationalism and neopaganism. On the other, his folkloric writings reveal his different views of German and Moroccan civilizations. In *Le voleur de lumière* (1942), Boutet treated paganism and irrationalism as fundamental to the cultural and religious traditions of the Berbers. By contrast, *Der Seezwerg* (1946) treats German neopaganism and irrationalism as an aberration. His German characters appear as needing only to reactivate the better aspects of their own cultural tradition—to be recivilized, rather than civilized from scratch. In other words, Germans were—or could become—Europeans.

BOUTET IN MOROCCO

By the early 1930s Boutet was already a prominent figure in the *colon*, or French colonist, community in French Morocco. He wrote prolifically on numerous topics relevant to France's civilizing efforts in the protectorate, including scholarly works in archaeology and ethnography, works of procolonial propaganda, and works of journalism. Boutet's varied roles as a scholar, journalist, and promoter of the French colonial project overlapped and complemented one another, such that it would be artificial to separate Boutet the propagandist from Boutet the scholar. Similarly, Boutet's role as a propagandist for the French "pacification" of Morocco was intertwined with his role as an agent of French public diplomacy, promoting the values and outlook of the French civilizing project to the Moroccan population through his folkloric writings.

Throughout the 1930s and 1940s, Boutet's work regularly received glowing reviews in colonial newspapers and journals such as *Le petit marocain,*

Les annales coloniales, and *La chronique coloniale,* and his work as an archaeologist and scholar of Berber folklore and religious practices was remarked upon in the *Journal de la société des africanistes.*[11] At the age of thirty-two, Boutet won the Prix Littéraire du Maroc for his book *Outka, légende berbère.*[12] By 1934 he had taken up residence in Rabat as editor of the colon newspaper *La vigie marocaine.* Founded in 1908 at the behest of Gen. Albert d'Amade "for the defense of French interests and the extension of French influence in Morocco" and purchased by colon press magnate Pierre Mas in 1920, *La vigie marocaine* had the reputation of ultraimperialism.[13]

As both a journalist and a scholar, Boutet gained a reputation as a skilled interpreter of Moroccan culture and religion for French audiences. His works frequently blend literary and scholarly styles. *Les gens de la poussière* (1931) describes the lives of ordinary and poor Moroccans from infancy to old age, combining sociological observations with common orientalist tropes and stereotypes.[14] Already in this work, we can see evidence of Boutet's concern with the themes of superstition, magical practices, and the continuation of "pagan" practices within monotheistic cultures, a topic that would remain one of his principal preoccupations for the next two decades. Of Moroccan women, he wrote, "They have, actually, beneath the mysterious appearance that the *haik* [a type of veil] gives them, the same mentality as the peasants from home. Their passions do not have other causes, nor do their pains; the marabout like the chapel hears the same prayers; the sorcerer and the soothsayer are consulted for the same purpose; same hopes, same joys, same griefs"[15] Critical responses to Boutet's work emphasized both his literary talents and his conscientious scholarship. In his foreword to Boutet's 1942 literary work *Le voleur de lumière,* journalist Christian Funck-Brentano states that "among those who consecrate their time or their leisure to the knowledge of Morocco, M. Robert Boutet is one of those who is engaged with the most tempting, the most arduous path, that which seeks to lead us into the Moroccan mind."[16] Boutet's interest in Moroccan religious practices, especially when they diverged from an ideal form of "revealed religion," is best understood in the context of French civilizing mission ideology. His writings on Moroccan culture reflect both a measure of respect for that culture and a desire to identify and address its supposed shortcomings—those features most in need of French "civilizing" influence.

At the same time, Boutet also lent his literary and scholarly talents to the project of publicizing and legitimizing the French colonial project in the protectorate. Thus, he was more than a commentator on colonial affairs—he was a conscious agent of the *mission civilisatrice.* In the spring of 1934 Boutet traveled deep into the interior of Morocco and Mauritania alongside French,

Moroccan, and Algerian troops of the Armée d'Afrique to participate in the symbolic completion of the pacification of Morocco, begun under Gen. Hubert Lyautey in 1912. As a "special envoy" of *La vigie marocaine*, his aim was to produce a book extolling the success of French efforts at "pacifying" the Western Sahara. The result was 1935's *Caravanes d'acier*. Along with a journey across the Sahara by car and armored vehicle (the titular steel caravans) to link up with troops and aircraft from Mauritania and French West Africa at el-Guardane (Sebt Gardane), Boutet made use of his knowledge of ethnography, history, and Moroccan folklore to provide context and picturesque details.[17] In a review for *Le petit marocain*, Jean Sermaye described the expedition of the "steel caravans" as having made "concrete, in the eyes of the nomads, the radiant French peace [*la paix française rayonnante*]."[18] He described Boutet as an expert on the Berber people of the Anti-Atlas Mountains as well as a "delicate storyteller" uniquely capable of reviving the "forgotten names" (both Moroccan and French) who had made successful pacification possible.

Caravanes d'acier was both a literary work informed by scholarly research and a sophisticated piece of procolonial propaganda. It was not Boutet's last. In 1940 he coauthored an account of the pilgrimages to Mecca organized by the French Army with the Tunisian Islamic cleric Nourredine Ben Mahmoud. Luc Chantre has described this work as an example of the use of the pilgrimages for procolonial propaganda, demonstrating France's role as a *puissance musulmane* (Muslim power) committed to the spiritual welfare of its Muslim subjects.[19] Boutet's commitment to advancing France's colonial mission in North Africa can be seen in other ways as well. In December 1938 the far-right Paris newspaper *Action française* reported that Boutet had entered a contest to select a new marching song for the Armée d'Afrique. His original lyrics won second place and a F3,000 prize.[20]

FOLKLORE AS PUBLIC DIPLOMACY:
LE VOLEUR DE LUMIÈRE

Edward Said famously identified Orientalism as "power-knowledge" in the Foucauldian sense—a way of knowing that served the needs of European colonial empires by constructing the Orient as in need of European influence and intervention in order to become civilized.[21] Boutet's apparently sincere commitment to the colonial project was inseparable from his scholarly preoccupations. In taking French people, colons or otherwise, on journeys into "the Moroccan mind" through his writings, he lent the authority of his knowledge and his pen to justify and affirm the French colonial project. As we will see, Boutet also used his research to inform folkloric writings for Moroccan consumption. Those writings, which can be understood as a kind of colonial public diplomacy, carried with them the assumptions and values of the French civilizing mission.

Boutet's 1942 storybook *Le voleur de lumière* is an illustrative example of his public diplomacy methods. A morality tale set in Morocco, it makes use of Boutet's knowledge of Moroccan culture and religion and co-opts the form of a "wonder tale" in the North African tradition to deliver a message in line with the priorities of the French civilizing mission. It also reflects many of the preoccupations of Boutet's writings for French audiences and should be considered to have two intended audiences—Moroccan youth and French colonists seeking to better understand the "Moroccan mind."

Le voleur de lumière tells the story of Abdelmalek, a young Moroccan man whose beloved is murdered by her jealous ex-husband. Seeking revenge on her killer, Abdelmalek travels south to visit a sorcerer and, through him, to seek "the complicity of demons, without the aid of which, on earth, a being remains in submission to the strict laws of nature."[22] Adbelmalek soon decides to become a sorcerer himself. In order to gain unnatural powers, he travels deep into the Berber lands in the Atlas Mountains to visit the "tomb of a demon." He goes into a cave to live there for fourteen days, during which time he ritually purifies himself and says a mix of "orthodox prayers and numberless invocations called 'dabroussia' and [reads] treatises on sorcery."[23] Having convinced the "demon" to enter his service, Abdelmalek is transformed physically and spiritually—he has "nothing left of his defunct love but his hate, memories of a tomb."[24]

Abdelmalek, now a sorcerer, has a daughter named Kinza who is described as looking just like his lost love. He raises her imprisoned within his house, fearing that harm will come to her. In spite of this, she manages to meet a young boy named Ghanem. Ghanem tells her about God. "Everything you see, everything you touch, everything you eat," he says to her, "it is to God that you owe it."[25] But Kinza tells Ghanem that it is to the demons that she and her father owe their livelihood. Ghanem tells her not to blaspheme, claiming, "Your father abuses you, your father lies to you. He has, in addition, passed into the service of the Liar who is the enemy of those who love God. Believe me, Kinza, the sovereign master is the only one whose power knows no limits. He created the sky and the earth, the light of the sun, the animals and men."[26] In addition to informing Kinza about the one true God, he helps her sneak out of her house to explore the city with him.

Ghanem and Kinza fall in love, and Kinza tells her father about their relationship. Her father informs her that love is "a lie."[27] He calls upon the powers of hell to turn Ghanem into a death's-head moth.[28] Ghanem (in moth form) flies out the window and goes to ask the animals for help. Eventually, Ghanem is transformed back into a human being and returns to Abdelmalek's house. When the sorcerer asks his daughter how it happened, she replies, "By the grace of God!" Abdelmalek begs her not to say that, saying, "There are words that one cannot say in front of me!"[29] In response to Kinza and Ghanem's prayers, God strips Abdelmalek of his infernal powers. The story ends with Abdelmalek admitting his faults and praying desperately for God's forgiveness.

While it may seem like an innocuous and picturesque story about a fascinating and exotic culture, *Le voleur de lumière* (literally "the light thief") reflects Boutet's core preoccupations as an agent of France's civilizing mission in Morocco. Above all, it reflects his concern about the survival of pre-Islamic pagan practices in the Berber lands of the interior of Morocco. As in his other writings, these practices are presented as reflective of the backwardness of rural Moroccans and the ever-present temptation toward barbarism. Interestingly, that temptation is equated with the lure of Satanic forces—it is Satan and his demons who tempt Abdelmalek to become a sorcerer and to imprison his daughter, denying her the "light" of true monotheist religion as well as, implicitly, the light of civilization. Ghanem can be read as representing the civilizing project itself. He is young, implying a generational split—the Moroccan youth were widely considered to be more open to the values of French and Western civilization than their elders. He teaches Kinza religious and moral lessons as well as shows her the realities of urban modernity by taking her on a tour of the city.

Understood as an effort at public diplomacy aimed at Moroccan youth, *Le voleur de lumière* is a revealing example of Boutet's understanding of the civilizational failings of Morocco and the aims of the French civilizing project there. Of course, the available sources give us a better idea of the attitudes of French colonizers than of the responses of Moroccan youth. The reviews we have are all from the pens of French journalists and writers, many of whom had their own commitments to the civilizing mission and were inclined to see Boutet's picture of Moroccan civilization as accurate. Judging from the number of extant copies on the used book market today, *Le voleur de lumière* was clearly printed in large quantities, and the success of his folkloric project made him a celebrity in the protectorate. In 1945 he would carry his civilizing preoccupations and his public diplomacy methods with him to the French zone of occupied Germany.

THE PROBLEM WITH GERMANNESS

In the spring of 1945 the French First Army advanced into southwestern Germany. That army, two thirds of which was drawn from France's North African possessions (Morocco, Tunisia, and Algeria), was responsible for conquering lands that became the basis for a French zone of occupation. Alongside their British, American, and Soviet allies, they sought to diagnose the reasons for Germany's turn to fascism, aggressive war, and genocide and to address the roots of those problems through the four Ds: de-Nazification, demilitarization, decartelization, and democratic reeducation of the German population.

Within the French zone, Germany's political dysfunction was broadly understood as the result of a deficit of "civilization," with National Socialist authoritarianism and militarism simply the most recent manifestations of a deep-seated German mentality.[30] Germany's supposed tendencies toward authoritarianism, obedience to authority, and militarism were often ascribed to the influence of "Prussianism," the ideology imposed by the "Iron Kingdom" of Prussia in the process of creating a unified German Reich in the mid-nineteenth century.[31]

While Germany's civilizational problems were sometimes treated as ancient in origin, French military and civilian officials saw National Socialism as having reduced the Germans to a lower level of civilization through its brutalizing education and propaganda. They viewed the regime's narrow nationalism as having made the Germans intellectually isolated and backward and its supposedly anti-Christian and neopagan elements as having undermined the country morally and spiritually. According to Christophe Baginski, the French military government in Baden-Baden saw the publication of Alfred Rosenberg's *The Myth of the 20th Century* in 1930 as having led to "disenchantment and neo-paganism" as well as the "de-Christianization of the youth" and the "suppression of religious education."[32] Re-Christianization was therefore a major aim of French policy in occupied Germany, not only because it was thought to be the basis for Germany's moral renewal but also because it was seen as a basis for Franco-German rapprochement on the basis of the two countries' shared "occidental" Christian values.[33]

The French military government's Cultural Affairs Division worked for the "cultural expansion" of France and sought to spread the rayonnement of French civilization.[34] Through the soft power of French culture, the French occupation authorities sought to orient the Germans psychologically toward France and the West and to solicit German support for France's broader policy goals in Germany and Europe. Colonial experience was crucial to those efforts. Jerôme Vaillant has written that "in contrast to the Anglo-Saxon model, the French practiced a policy of intervention into German indigenous affairs that was much more direct: they followed more or less consciously their model of colonial administration."[35]

Within the French zone, Germans' supposed cultural shortcomings were sometimes discussed by analogy with those of France's colonial subjects. Geographer and political commentator André Siegfried, speaking at the opening of a training session for the French military administration in Germany, argued, "One must never forget that the Germans bow before force. . . . A certain liberalism will be interpreted by them as weakness. They must be treated as one treats Orientals."[36]

BOUTET IN OCCUPIED GERMANY

By October of 1945 Robert Boutet had relocated to occupied southwestern Germany and become one of the editors of the official magazine of the French army of occupation, the *Revue d'information des troupes françaises en Allemagne*. In that role, he would once again undertake a hybrid scholarly and literary project that sought to demonstrate the legitimacy of the occupation to the French occupiers and solicit German support for French interests through anthropologically informed folklore aimed at the German youth. This new public diplomacy project had much in common with Boutet's previous soft power work in Morocco but also had novel features that reflect the differences between the French missions in Morocco and in postwar Germany.

Initially Boutet's work for the *Revue* consisted mainly of journalistic and literary pieces focusing on the religious and cultural practices of North African soldiers serving in the French zone. These were informed by Boutet's preexisting interests in Moroccan culture and history, and many reflected his interest in the themes of superstition, sorcery, and neopaganism. One such story appears in the February 1946 edition of the *Revue*. Titled *Que doit-on croire?* (What should one believe?), it recounts a conversation between two French Christian officers and a Moroccan Muslim officer regarding the existence or nonexistence of magic. The Moroccan describes how, long ago, he had come to be acquainted with a sorcerer. In response to his account of the sorcerer's uncanny, apparently magical powers, the French officers at first insist that they were all hallucinations brought on by the Moroccan's suggestible mental state. When he produces further evidence of sorcerer's powers, they appear to be convinced. The Moroccan concludes that "only

God knows" what really happened. Finally, a French soldier who had sat silently throughout the conversation speaks up in support of the Moroccan's interpretation. He notes that St. Augustine said the same—that God can do whatever he likes and that "demons, angelic creatures, it's true, though corrupted by their faults, can do nothing . . . without the permission of Him whose judgments are sometimes obscure, never unjust."[37]

However, Boutet would soon develop a new project—one that sought to apply the mix of ethnographic and folkloric methods he had developed as an agent of French colonization in Morocco to his investigation of the civilizational roots of German National Socialism. His jumping-off point was the study of German carnival traditions, many of which he considered to be pagan in origin. In February 1948 he wrote an article for the *Revue* focusing on neopaganism at the German carnival. It begins by describing the many vain attempts made by church authorities to stamp out the cults of the Norse gods in southwestern Germany beginning in the seventh century AD and concludes by comparing the iconography of the cults of Wotan and Freya, a common feature of the region's carnival celebrations, to what he claims are similar traditions among Moroccan Berbers.[38]

That article was just one part of a larger project—a comparative study of German neopaganism and Berber pagan traditions. In the spring of 1949 that book-length work was published by the official press of the French troops of occupation under the title *Sorcellerie, magie, et paganisme dans l'Allemagne de sud-ouest dans le moyen-âge au XVII siècle*. It was also promoted by an advertising campaign in the *Revue*, including a glowing review by the journalist Jacques Nobécourt. According to Nobécourt, Boutet's central concern was to understand the genesis of National Socialist neopaganism and irrationalism in the context of the long history of the German mentality and by comparison with the mentality of Moroccan Muslims. Nobécourt summarizes the book as revealing the results of the "conjunction of a revealed religion" (Christianity) with "more worldly practices" and the long-term impact of that combination. Nobécourt identified those questions as "proper for penetrating the psychology of the German people."[39] According to Nobécourt, Boutet's comparative approach to explaining "the Germanic rites by their differences with similar Islamic rites" was especially clarifying. He continued:

From his synthesis, a primordial conclusion separates itself; such a survival of paganism is the sign that marks the soul of a whole people, such that one sees voluntary resurrections at fixed periods. To understand the full importance of these resurrections, it suffices to imagine what a peal of laughter would greet the man who tried to revive Celtic customs in France to make of them a faith and a morality. Well! Germans in our time have found themselves wanting to become devotees of Wotan, and with the greatest conviction. M. Robert Boutet's book gives a singular weight to the condemnation that all sane men hold for them.[40]

In short, rural Germany's problem was the same as rural Morocco's: a backward, superstitious culture prone to religious and political atavism.

Boutet's decision to blame superstition and neopaganism for the problems of German society is part of a larger trend in his work—the championing of "revealed" monotheistic religion against superstition and paganism. At the root, his advocacy for a certain type of "modern" rationalist Christianity as a source of values is based on a certain idea of civilization. Civilized people, for Boutet and Nobécourt alike, are at once rationalists who reject superstition and practitioners of something like Christian morality. In Morocco, Boutet's view of civilization had led him to become a vocal supporter of the French colonial project. In Germany, it would make him an agent of French soft power vis-à-vis the Germans—a promoter of reeducation and re-Christianization of the Germans under French tutelage.

To see how Boutet adapted his methods of public diplomacy from the Moroccan context to the German one, let us consider his 1947 German-language storybook *Der Seezwerg* (The dwarf from the lake). Published with the approval of the French military government in Germany and intended for the consumption of German children, *Der Seezwerg* is written in the style of a traditional German fairy tale. Like *Le voleur de lumière* before it, *Der Seezwerg* makes use of a folkloric idiom to convey a message intended to influence Germans away from neopaganism and National Socialism and toward Christianity and Western Civilization. Also like *Le voleur de lumière*, it promotes French policy aims and interests not through explicit political advocacy but through subtle efforts at making what Boutet understood to be French and Western civilizational values attractive to his audience.

Der Seezwerg tells of a German tenant farmer named Hermann, his wife, Gertrud, and their children, Franz and Gretl, who live on the banks of the Wildsee in the Black Forest. All four members of the family are described as hardworking and dedicated to helping one another. Hermann, whom Boutet describes as being as thrifty as he is hardworking, had hoped to pay off the lease on his farm and become a property owner. However, his hopes were dashed by the unexpected outbreak of a war between rival lords.[41] When their town is attacked by enemy troops, Hermann's family returns to find their belongings looted and their home burned.

Hermann remains optimistic, telling his wife and children that the old house was dilapidated anyway and that they could rebuild within a month. Soon after, a storm breaks out and a frost descends. When Hermann's lord asks him if he has the money for the lease, Hermann explains that the soldiers and the storm destroyed his goods. However, the lord says that does not free him of his debt.[42] In his grief, Hermann comes to the bank of the lake. He calls out for someone to help him and is answered by a dwarf. The dwarf tells Hermann to seek a rich man named Wolf who will help him to get a new house. Hermann visits Wolf at his home and, to his surprise, Wolf offers him food and soon has a new house built for Hermann's family.[43]

When Christmastime comes, the children want to give back to the dwarf for all he's done for their family. The family gathers to exchange gifts, inviting the dwarf to join them. Much of the remaining pages of the story recount Christmas traditions interspersed with the lyrics to carols sung in honor of the birth of Christ. The family's gifts for the dwarf—a suit made by the mother, a "pearl of the orient" purchased by the father, the son's walking stick, and the daughter's embroidery are all described as miraculous and beautiful.[44] Yet the dwarf turns them all down. Hinting that he is an angelic being, he tells the family that God's law forbids him from accepting payment in exchange for his protection. Finally, he reminds the family to "do good for the sake of the good."[45]

The structural and functional similarities between *Le voleur de lumière* and *Der Seezwerg* reveal a unifying logic behind Boutet's work in both Germany and Morocco. Both texts make use of culturally specific folkloric forms to transmit a moral message with political implications. *Der Seezwerg* and *Le voleur de lumière* share an emphasis on submission to God and resistance to superstition as the basis of a good life. In *Le voleur de lumière*, the true Islamic faith (along with youth, progress, and freedom) championed by Ghanem vanquishes paganism and sorcery. *Der Seezwerg* calls upon the German tradition of the fairy tale, in which dwarves, fairies, and elves—creatures with pre-Christian roots—frequently have magical powers. The titular dwarf is eventually revealed to be in service of the Christian God rather than getting his power from other sources that Boutet would likely have considered satanic.

Le voleur de lumière presents backwardness and superstition as endemic to Moroccan society. Abdelmalek's devil worship appears a part of an ancient Moroccan tradition, associating it with the older generation and the remote mountains of the country's southern Berber region. By contrast, *Der Seezwerg* draws upon the supposed virtues of the southwestern German peasantry, presenting its protagonists as thrifty, hardworking, and morally upright. Hermann's family's suffering due to war in *Der Seezwerg* is apparently intended to parallel the experience of the southwestern German peasantry during and after the Allied invasion of 1945. Interestingly, Boutet treats the peasants as helpless victims of a war between equally distant and anonymous rival lords. Their virtue is never called into question, and it is never implied that they were in any way complicit with the lords'— or Hitler's—violence. Boutet presents hard work, faith, and adherence to true Christianity free of superstition as the solution for their problems and, implicitly, for Germany's.

CONCLUSION

In the aftermath of World War II, the French zone of occupation attracted many French people whose lives and careers had been made in France's empire. Transplanted to southwestern Germany, agents of French power (both soft and hard) brought their methods and their preoccupations with them. The case of Robert Boutet reveals two ways in which ideas about how to study and influence foreign cultures migrated from the colonial context to the context of occupied Germany and helped to shape French propaganda there. On one hand, Boutet's academic work on German religion and superstition sought to lead the readers of the *Revue d'information des troupes françaises en Allemagne* into the "German mind" as he had led others into the Moroccan one. As it happened, the picture he painted of the German mind was one that was in need of the very things the French occupiers claimed to be bringing to Germany—moral and spiritual reeducation, re-Christianization, and reintegration into occidental civilization.

At the same time, Boutet wrote folklore intended to function as a form of public diplomacy as defined by Joseph S. Nye. Both *Le voleur de lumière* and *Der Seezwerg* put Boutet's skillfully co-opted elements of Moroccan and German culture, respectively, seeking to encourage spontaneous identification between his readers and French policies and interests. Rather than attempting to explicitly impose French values upon either group, he framed their task as adhering to the more civilized aspects of their own cultural and religious traditions.

Both Morocco and southwestern Germany were under French military and political control during Boutet's time there, and his work cannot be understood outside of the context of that "hard power" domination. Yet public diplomacy work like Boutet's had the function of encouraging identification with France's goals, thus avoiding the need to impose France's will exclusively by force.[46] His emphasis on shared values, as when he acknowledged Christianity and Islam's shared theological and moral understandings in *Que doit-on croire?* (1946), reflected the logic of "association" between peoples that continued to inform French policy until Morocco became independent in 1956.[47] It was also compatible with the growing emphasis by French authorities in Germany on rapprochement and the ideal of European integration, an emphasis that grew in importance with the emergence of an independent Federal Republic of Germany in 1949.

Boutet's use of folklore allowed him to combine his scholarly interests, political commitments, and literary skills into one package that was calculated to appeal to audiences that might have resisted less subtle forms of propaganda. The aesthetic appeal of his folkloric output, its ability to reach a young audience, and its lack of overt political messages made it a clever medium for the exercise of public diplomacy intended to encourage spontaneous identification with French goals—to get the Moroccans, then the Germans, to want what France wanted. There is further work to be done on folklore and soft power, especially with regard to its impact and reception. My sources give little account of either indigenous Moroccan or German responses to Boutet's works. The fact that numerous copies continue to be available on the antique book market suggests that his stories were widely read but gives little indication of where and why they were read and whether they had the intended effect on their audiences. Further research into the reception of Boutet's stories by the German- and Arabic-language media could clarify the impact and limitations of his project and shed valuable light on the effectiveness of folklore as public diplomacy.

Boutet's comparative work on Moroccan and German superstition and neopaganism raises interesting interpretive questions. On one hand, he appears to have believed that certain features of a culture could pose long-term risks of atavism and violence. On the other, in both Morocco and occupied Germany, Boutet wrote for multiple audiences and multiple—sometimes contradictory—purposes. When writing about Moroccan culture for French consumption, his work was shaped by French desires for picturesque stories about exotic places. His writings on German culture also present Germany as at once strange, threatening, and fascinating. They cannot help but reflect the long history of Franco-German rivalry and the desire of the victors to humiliate the vanquished—even if that entailed comparing them to supposedly "barbaric" North African peoples.

However, Boutet does not seem to have written his extensive body of work out of a purely cynical desire to justify French power. As a state-adjacent agent of French soft power, Boutet's belief in the beneficial nature of French civilizing influence appears to have been sincere. His work went far beyond his job description as an employee of the French Army in Germany, comprising scholarly research and literary writing undertaken independently. His work reflects what Laure Humbert has called, "the active, often bottom-up nature of the reaffirmation of French national identity and reassertion of its international influence in the aftermath of Vichy and the Nazi occupation."[48] Like the work of United Nations Relief and Rehabilitation Administration officials that Humbert has studied, Boutet's cultural diplomacy efforts reflected his belief in the superiority of French civilization and his willingness to promote it abroad. It also reveals his apparently genuine interest in, and respect for, aspects of both Moroccan and German cultures. It could not have been otherwise as his method of folklore as public diplomacy required him to familiarize himself with the indigenous culture—at least to the point of being able to manipulate it. Considering the ambiguities of state-adjacent actors' roles in public diplomacy and their motivations for taking part would be a fruitful avenue for future research.

Boutet's public diplomacy efforts reveal how the pacification and colonization of the protectorate of Morocco provided models that guided agents of French soft power one the front lines of the Cold War in occupied Germany. This connection shows the centrality of a locale that is often treated as peripheral to the history of classic-period Cold War soft power. It contributes to breaking down the often artificial separation between European history and "colonial history," reminding us how profoundly European ideas about culture, power, and peacemaking have relied upon the image of the non-European other.

NOTES

1. As discussed in Alice L. Conklin, *A Mission to Civilize: The Republican Idea of Empire in France and West Africa, 1895–1930* (Stanford, CA: Stanford University Press, 1997); Dino Costantini, *Mission civilisatrice: Le rôle de l'histoire coloniale dans la construction de l'identité politique française* (Paris: La Découverte, 2008).

2. Discussed in Janet Horne, "'To Spread the French Language Is to Extend the *Patrie*': The Colonial Mission of the Alliance Française," *French Historical Studies* 40, no. 1 (February 1, 2017): 98, https://doi.org/10.1215/00161071-3686068.

3. Jules Ferry, one of the key framers of the *mission civilisatrice*, once suggestively stated that "to radiate without acting, that is, without getting involved in the affairs of the world" through colonization, was mere "political metaphysics," thus aligning French hard power with its soft power as fundamentally interdependent. Jules Ferry, "Les fondements de la politique coloniale (28 juillet 1885)," Assemblée Nationale, http://www2.assemblee-nationale.fr/decouvrir-l-assemblee/histoire/grands-moments-d-eloquence/jules-ferry-1885-les-fondements-de-la-politique-coloniale-28-juillet-1885.

4. Konrad Hugo Jarausch, *After Hitler: Recivilizing Germans, 1945–1995* (Oxford: Oxford University Press, 2006).

5. Boutet's ambiguous position reflects Spencer Segalla's insight that ethnology was "a product of empire, but the relationship between the two was ambiguous" as ethnographic research could either challenge or support colonial ideologies. Spencer D. Segalla, *The Moroccan Soul: French Education, Colonial Ethnology, and Muslim Resistance, 1912–1956*, France Overseas (Lincoln: University of Nebraska Press, 2009), 16.

6. Jan Melissen, *The New Public Diplomacy: Soft Power in International Relations*, Studies in Diplomacy and International Relations (Basingstoke, UK: Palgrave Macmillan, 2005), 5.

7. Joseph S. Nye, "Public Diplomacy and Soft Power," *Annals of the American Academy of Political and Social Science* 616 (2008): 103.

8. Nye, 108.

9. Joseph S. Nye, "Soft Power," *Foreign Policy*, no. 80 (Autumn 1990): 167.

10. Ludovic Tournès, *Américanisation: Une histoire mondiale (XVIIIe–XXIe siècle)* (Paris: Fayard, 2020), 209.

11. A 1934 article details his archaeological work in the south of Morocco and identifies him as a journalist, ethnographer, and editor of *La vigie marocaine*. L. Joleaud and R. Lafitte, "Découvertes archéologiques de M. Robert Boutet dans le sud marocain," *Journal de la Société des Africanistes* 4, no. 2 (1934): 320.

12. "Prix littéraire du Maroc," *L'écho d'Alger*, December 25, 1932.

13. During World War II, *La vigie marocaine* and the rest of Mas's press empire became deeply implicated with Pétainism, for which the paper was sanctioned by the provisional government and Mas was placed under house arrest. In spite of the legal action taken against him, Mas maintained control of *La vigie marocaine* and *L'écho du Maroc* indirectly. Louis Gravier, "Mort de Pierre Mas, magnat de la presse française sous la protectorat," *Le Monde*, December 10, 1970.

14. E.g., Boutet writes the following about courtesans: "O Courtesan! You are a woman, that is to say a subtle mixture of animality and spirituality." Robert Boutet, *Les gens de la poussière* (Casablanca: Imprimeries Réunies, 1931), 44.

15. Boutet, 40.

16. Robert Boutet, *Le voleur de lumière* (Casablanca: Editions Marco-Presse, 1942).

17. Robert Boutet, *Les caravanes d'acier* (Casablanca: Les Éditions du Moghreb, 1935).

18. Jean Sermaye, "Review of Boutet," *Le petit marocain*, June 15, 1935.

19. Luc Chantre, *Pèlerinages d'empire: Une histoire européen du pèlerinage à la Mecque* (Paris: Éditions de la Sorbonne, 2018). Robert Boutet and Noureddine Ben Mahmoud, *Pèlerinage de guerre de l'Afrique du nord aux lieux saints de l'Islam* (Casablanca: Imprimeries Réunies de la Vigie Marocaine et du Petit Marocain, 1940).

20. "Nouvelles des lettres, des sciences, et des arts," *Action française*, December 11, 1938.

21. Edward W Said, *Orientalism* (London: Penguin Books, 2019).

22. Boutet, *Le voleur de lumière*, 14.

23. Boutet, 23.

24. Boutet, 46.

25. Boutet, 82.

26. Boutet, 86.

27. Boutet, 109.

28. Boutet, 137.

29. Boutet, 177.

30. Discussed in Emmanuelle Picard, "Des usages de l'Allemagne: Politique culturelle française en Allemagne et rapprochement franco-allemand 1945–1963" (doctoral diss., Institut d'Études Politiques, Paris, 1999), and Hélène Miard-Delacroix, *Question nationale allemande et nationalisme: Perceptions françaises d'une problématique allemande au début des années cinquante* (Villeneuve-d'Ascq, Fr.: Presses Universitaires du Septentrion, 2004).

31. According to Cyril Buffet, "the French established an abusive amalgam between militarism, Prussia and German unity: the first structured the second which presided over the third which realized itself at the expense of France. Through that lens, it is in sum logical to destroy the Siegessäule, which represented militarism and Prussianism, and to reduce greatly the centralist role of Berlin, which incarnated German unity." Cyril Buffet, *Mourir pour Berlin: La France et l'Allemagne, 1945–1949* (Paris: A. Colin, 1991), 35.

32. Christophe Baginski and Jérôme Vaillant, *La politique religieuse de la France en Allemagne occupée: 1945–1949* (Villeneuve-d'Ascq, Fr.: Presses Universitaires du Septentrion, 1997), 29.

33. Monique Mombert, *Jeunesse et livre en zone française d'occupation: 1945–1949* (Strasbourg: Presses Universitaires de Strasbourg, 1995), 80.

34. As discussed in Corine Defrance, *La politique culturelle de la France sur la rive gauche du Rhin, 1945–1955* (Strasbourg: Presses Universitaires de Strasbourg, 1994), and Karina Günther, "Rayonnement culturel: Kulturpolitische Bedingungen und Aktivitäten in der französischen Besatzungszone 1945–1948" (Frankfurt am Main, Ger.: Lang, 2011).

35. Baginski and Vaillant, *La politique religieuse,* 8.

36. Miard-Delacroix, *Question nationale allemande et nationalisme,* 407.

37. Robert Boutet, "Que doit-on croire?," *Revue d'information des troupes françaises en Allemagne* 5 (February 1946): 33–34.

38. Robert Boutet, "La culte de Wodan et Freya dans le carnaval allemande," *Revue d'information des troupes françaises en Allemagne,* February 1948.

39. Jacques Nobecourt, untitled review, *Revue d'information des troupes françaises en Allemagne,* April 20, 1949, 23.

40. Nobecourt, 23.

41. Robert Boutet, *Der Seezwerg: Ein Maerchen* (Waldkirch, Ger.: Waldkircher Verlagsgesellschaft, 1947), 1.

42. The term *Schuld,* or debt, also means guilt—as in the German term for "collective guilt," *Kollektivschuld.* Boutet, 2–3.

43. Boutet, 9.

44. Boutet, 19.

45. Boutet, 21.

46. In the Moroccan context, Spencer Segalla has noted the hegemonic (in Antonio Gramsci's sense) intentions of colonial education, which had the goal of "convincing the locals that it was in their best interest to comply with the French colonial agenda" and soliciting their "spontaneous" consent. Segalla, *Moroccan Soul,* 8.

47. Segalla, 9.

48. Laure Humbert, *Reinventing French Aid: The Politics of Humanitarian Relief in French-Occupied Germany, 1945–1952* (Cambridge: University Press, 2021), 13.

CHAPTER 6

The Soft Power of Brigitte Bardot
Creation of a Global French Feminine Ideal

Kelly R. Colvin

On March 5, 2017, at the height of a recent campaign for the French presidency, the far-right candidate from the National Front Party, Marine Le Pen, sat down for an interview with the American television news magazine *60 Minutes*. Asked about immigration and the changing face of France, Le Pen caustically answered, "France isn't burkinis on the beach. France is Brigitte Bardot. That's France."[1]

Locating national identity in the person of a female film star seems a somewhat curious definition of the nation of France specifically and really of any nation. And yet it fits in well with current rhetoric about French nationalism and identity. In recent years, many scholars have delved deeply into debates surrounding gender and the practice of veiling.[2] Joan Scott in particular has argued that discussions about veiling in France are, in fact, about anxiety over France's role in a globalizing world, with gender as the masking language. But Scott also isolates how debates about veiling reveal a particularity of women's corporal obligation to liberal democracy, something that is not required of men. She argues that rhetoric around veiling demonstrates that male visual access to women's bodies is, in fact, a requirement of female liberal democratic citizenship.[3] Put more plainly, in order to be a proper female citizen of the Western world, a woman must display her body to the male gaze. The veil disrupts that requirement, blocking men's visual access to the female form. In this piece, I am most interested in the second part of Le Pen's statement—that France is Brigitte Bardot—and how Scott's visual interpretation of female citizenship can be applied to that seemingly strange equation.

This chapter will unpack exactly how Bardot's "preferred" standard of French femininity came about, how it expanded through the French and American press, and finally its broad implications for women and citizenship. As such, it helps explain how French actors in government, tourism, and beyond wielded Bardot's femininity as a marker of soft power, a theory originated by international relations theorist Joseph S. Nye, who defined soft power as "the ability to get what you want through attraction rather than coercion or payments. It arises from the attractiveness of a country's culture, political ideals, and policies."[4] France here represents a particularly intense case, given its existing reputation for cultural superiority and historical significance as well as its investment in soft power. Indeed Nye pays special attention to France and the French in his analysis of soft power, largely because, as of his writing, "France spends close to $1 billion a year to spread French civilization around the world. . . . France's soft power has been clearly maintained or even increased in the past fifty years [1954–2004], although Paris may no longer be the prime intellectual, cultural, and philosophical capital of the world."[5] The French investment in attracting the world has clearly paid dividends.

This chapter adds a gendered component to the idea that nations profit from their "attractiveness." In recent years, scholars of foreign relations have increasingly used gender as a category of analysis to explain how nations interact with one another and how perceptions of masculinity or femininity impact a nation's standing in the world.[6] Indeed many, such as Emily Rosenberg and Kristin Hoganson, have called for greater inclusion of gender to expand the field of the history of foreign relations. This chapter then builds upon their call, demonstrating how assumptions about French women could be co-opted by officials in the government to access the fruits of soft power, in effect actively deploying femininity as a commodity. As such, the chapter argues that in postwar France the cultural joined firmly with the political in the physical form of Brigitte Bardot, a young, famous actress who ultimately performed an important service for France. Through her films, and specifically her physicality, she helped render France desirable—and hence hopefully relevant—on the world stage.

To some extent, in deploying Bardot's image as an ambassador of French femininity, French officials were capitalizing on a longstanding association between Frenchness and sensuality. However, prior to World War II, the French also had a reputation for military greatness, economic strength, and imperial prowess. After the war, each of these arenas lay in something of a shambles. As the historian Mary Louise Roberts has demonstrated, however, the link between Frenchness and erotic femininity remained quite strong, especially in the minds of Americans. Indeed, she argues, American GIs were literally "seduced" into fighting, as recruiters capitalized on Americans' ideas of permissive French women.[7]

Why is American buy-in so important in this particular moment? Postwar French economic recovery depended in large part on Americans and their spending prowess. Indeed, much of the reason for French authorities' revived willingness to showcase its women to the world could be located in two arenas: the struggling French economy and the all-consuming quest for global prestige. First, the nation was desperate for money at the end of the war, and many people in the government particularly coveted American dollars.[8] Much of the country's infrastructure had been destroyed in the war, leading to the striking statistic that industrial production in 1945 was just 38 percent of what it had been in 1938.[9] Tourism boosters in the government and beyond trumpeted their cause, strains that did not fall on deaf ears.[10] As early as 1946 tourism had become France's second-leading industry,[11] and its champions clamored for American spending.[12] By 1949 American tourist spending in France was equivalent to four-fifths of French exports to the United States, meaning that American tourism was just as important to France's economy as its exports. Indeed, according to the historian Christopher Endy, economic statistics show that from 1945 to 1949, American tourists were injecting almost another 10 percent of the entire Marshall Plan's value through their spending, making them a crucial component of the country's economic health.[13] French officials were therefore desperate to at least maintain, if not grow, the flow of dollars into the economy. The equation of France with eroticism helped boost tourist numbers, particularly as the Cold War intensified and Americans sought to escape the political tensions at home.[14]

Other historians, including (but not limited to) Endy, Richard Kuisel, and Whitney Walton, have persuasively addressed cultural Franco-American relations during the Cold War and the era of decolonization, and still more historians, such as Vanessa Schwartz and Ginette Vincendeau, have discussed the import of French film and Bardot in particular, but no one has focused on the specific combination of celebrity, tourism, and gender as a source of French soft power.[15] If tourism was the second-largest industry in France by 1946 and women and their sexuality were already the firm center of that industry, then it merits a serious look.[16] While Bardot, as we will see, may have had somewhat mixed emotions about her life and image being capitalized upon by the government, this chapter articulates the idealization of a specific version of femininity that actors within government purported Bardot to embody, one that has had profound staying power over time.

BRIGITTE BARDOT AS THE NATION OF FRANCE

In 1969 Brigitte Bardot became the face of Marianne, the long-standing female symbol of the French nation, indeed the visual embodiment of the republic. Statues, images, and busts of Marianne had, by tradition, long been displayed in mayor's offices and government buildings across the nation and the world, exposing her image not only to local citizens but also to international dignitaries and visitors. The conflation of Bardot and this widespread French symbol is pregnant with meaning, especially given that Marianne had been an unattributed, anonymous personage prior to Bardot's appointment. The French state actively chose to make Marianne specific to one actual woman, Brigitte Bardot, for the very first time. This act bears questions about the specifics of Bardot, known commonly as BB in France, and why her brand of femininity was so attractive, so important, that the state itself held it up as an international aspiration.[17]

The choice of Bardot as Marianne was largely the result of a campaign led by Jean-Jacques Servan-Schreiber, the famous intellectual and erstwhile leader of the Radical Socialist Party.[18] Servan-Schreiber, for his part, appears to have been somewhat enthralled (obsessed?) by BB, asking people to call *him* by *his* initials as well and even using her likeness as a backdrop for his press conferences, which generally dealt with matters of politics, economics, and literature, not film, women, and celebrity. JJSS was wholly committed to Bardot's sexual international power, once commenting that she was "as valuable to French exports as 'Roquefort cheese or Bordeaux wine,'"[19] rhetorically equating Bardot's image to actual inanimate objects that the world associated with France and enjoyed consuming as well as to objects that come from French soil, hinting that she, as well, was one such object.

In his quest to remodel Marianne and proffer a new vision of France to the world, Servan-Schreiber apparently deployed what he thought was his best weapon: Bardot's considerable physical assets. In a press conference, when asked why Bardot was the right model, he famously gestured to the proposed statue and quipped that "the reasons for the choice of her bust as symbol of France are evident."[20] Coverage of the news conference agreed. One article cited Bardot's qualifications as the "nation's best known sex symbol," while another described the statue as "republican hagiography—or bust."[21] One newspaper coined Bardot "a perfect 38,000," in reference to the number of towns and cities where she would be displayed, all while touting the number—and her—as a "round figure" and "well-rounded."[22] Even further, one article attributed the decision to "two very good reasons," a nauseating description for any modern reader of why a particular woman ought to embody her nation.[23]

That the incarnation of France was located in one particular woman is problematic enough. There are many possible iterations of French femininity, and to point out one as *the* ideal delineates the boundaries of French feminine identity in extraordinarily narrow terms. And yet the equation of Bardot's qualifications for the status of national symbol—again, this is the very first time that Marianne was embodied by a real woman—with her voluptuousness and sexuality necessarily points to the fact that women's sexuality constituted their most fundamental attribute in national—and international—representation. France's national symbol, the way it presented itself both within the borders of mainland France and globally was now defined by a woman's seductive fecundity, not her brain or her achievements. Maurice Agulhon, the foremost scholar of Marianne imagery, called the modeling of Marianne on Bardot "radically new" for the republic in that people would be accepting a "fully recognizable" image of one woman to represent the whole country.[24] The choice of that woman, then, carried extra symbolic weight.

Interestingly, it appears that Bardot herself never posed or modeled for the Marianne image, nor did she sanction it publicly. Instead, a well-known pin-up artist, Aslan, created the initial statue from several pictures of her. In one article, Aslan attributed the inspiration for Bardot as Marianne to a dinner he had in the company of a small-town mayor from Normandy. Aslan speculatively asked the mayor what he would do if he had a statue of Bardot in place of the Marianne bust he currently displayed. "'I'd grab it,' exulted the mayor."[25] The bust's national adoption seems to have been something of a grassroots, haphazard enterprise. A mayor from the Loire region placed the statue in his own town hall, and it grew from there. Agulhon explains that Bardot's Marianne captivated the populace quickly, having "become the new Marianne in an almost enigmatic way."[26] Soon JJSS found and requested a personal copy of the statue, as did André Malraux, the former minister of culture, who displayed it above the hearth in his country house.[27] Ultimately, the state itself adopted the image officially. Here, the state and other stakeholders deployed and possessed Bardot's images at will, while simultaneously not imbuing the woman herself with either agency of self-determination or the potential power inherent within those kinds of gestures.

THE QUESTION OF THE AMERICANS AND THE ALMIGHTY DOLLAR

Why were the French so eager to promote Brigitte Bardot? In a word: tourism. In her heyday, Bardot's femininity massively appealed to Americans, who equated her with a specifically Gallic sensuality, which they sometimes measured against a more buttoned-up Anglo-American mentality. "The hottest thing since fire" and "the screen's most fiery temptress" was how reporter Anthony Noel described Brigitte Bardot in 1958, soon after she debuted across American screens in *And God Created Woman*.[28] In the late 1950s and 1960s, Brigitte Bardot was arguably the most famous woman in the world, a rare designation for a French film actress. Indeed, one newspaper deemed her "the most instantly recognizable female face" in the world.[29] Bardot's captivation of the French and the world began early, when she modeled for the cover of *Elle* magazine at the age of fifteen and was then discovered by the director Roger Vadim, who ubiquitously credited himself with molding and creating Bardot. Her early defining role, a "spectacular breakthrough," according to the film scholar Ginette Vincendeau, came in the 1956 film *And God Created Woman*, which shocked viewers with its candid sexuality.[30] The poster for the film depicted Bardot in the foreground, her head thrown back, eyes closed, mouth open, and topless, with the ends of her hair covering the tips of her breasts. In the background of the poster, three clearly perturbed men looked either at Bardot or at the viewer, as if challenging ownership of the star. The poster reflects both the plot of the film, in which Bardot portrayed a sexually free woman who tempted three jealous men, and the way in which Bardot's sexuality belonged to male interests, not to herself, without her even necessarily recognizing it. As one ad for the film put it, emphasizing her tantalizing image, "'And God Created Woman' . . . But the Devil Invented BRIGITTE BARDOT."[31]

Interestingly, the film was not a great success in France initially but rather first entranced the American film-going public.[32] It came at a fortuitous moment, when the US market was by far the most important one for French exports and when the French desperately wanted to attract US attention and dollars. This US-centric enchantment with Bardot, then, informed the French that they had a special commodity on their hands in her, one that they could mold and shape to serve economic and cultural interests. As the film scholar Diana Holmes put it, Bardot's "international success ricocheted back to France: Bardot became a major export, not only an asset to the national economy but also a representation abroad of that sexy, male-oriented femininity on which French culture has long prided itself."[33] As a whole, as Sarah Fishman notes, mass culture in France had become more diffuse in the 1960s, although, Fishman concedes, despite the diffusion, "every woman's magazine regularly featured Brigitte Bardot."[34]

American reviews of *And God Created Woman* focused almost entirely on Bardot's sexuality. The well-known film critic William Zinsser penned a review of the film that typified the genre. He described Bardot as "the newest love queen of France . . . that amatory land. Her films send men panting to the boxoffice [*sic*] in huge numbers, and it is safe to assume that her photograph hangs on walls from Picardy to Provence." Zinsser devoted almost every word in his review to Bardot and her body, a fact he readily stipulated. "What elusive quality does the girl have?" he pondered. Responding to his own query, he wrote, "Call it sex, for lack of a better word." Zinsser used words like "undulate" and "ripe," and he referred to her body as "a study in rounded surfaces for anyone who likes to study rounded surfaces." Bardot's clothing in the film also inspired fits of sensual wordsmithing from Zinsser, who accused Bardot of "breaking all skirt-raising records," "unbuttoning her blouse to admit the Mediterranean winds," and "wearing a series of garments notable only for their brevity, including a bikini that looks like a Band-Aid." Most seductive of all, Zinsser noted, "she looks like she enjoys every minute." Reinforcing Bardot's French identity along with her femininity, Zinsser reminded the reader that the film was a "Gallic fable" with a director who "wants to make sure you understand this girl's effect on a man—especially if you are a man."[35] In Zinsser's review, he touches on Bardot's sensuality and her Frenchness, establishing a relationship between the two that would set the tone for other American critics and viewers.

Zinsser's review established the themes—clothing, bodies, and overall French sensuality—for the other Americans who stretched the limits of their sensual thesauruses to explain Bardot's film. Bardot's clothing—or lack thereof—captivated reviewers. One writer in the *New York Times* expounded, "She is looked at in slacks and sweaters, in shorts and Bikini bathing suits. She wears a bedsheet on two or three occasions, and, once, she shows nude behind a thin screen."[36] The construction of this sentence is interesting, in that it grammatically renders Bardot an object, a focus of the viewer's gaze, through the writer's use of passive voice ("she is looked at"). Another reviewer, who wrote for the *Boston Globe*, directly equated

Bardot's sartorial scantiness with her sensuality: "She has no inhibitions and she wears almost no clothes." For another, Bardot's bikini was a major focus: "Her bathing suit, if such as it can be called, wouldn't cover a 2 year old."[37] Yet another reporter added a titillating detail about Bardot's dress: "The only time she wears undergarments is when there is a stiff wind blowing."[38]

If Bardot was the main attraction of the movie, it was because of her body, which became in turn the main attraction for reviewers. "The leading glamour girl of France today is a lithe blonde," announced a profile about Bardot that appeared on the front page of the *New York Herald Tribune*.[39] Similarly, the *New York Times* called her a "round and voluptuous little French miss" who "is put on spectacular display and is rather brazenly ogled from every allowable point of view."[40] That writer later floridly described her as "a perambulating peril for all males. She tempts them with her unrestrained gyrations. She joys in having them chase after her."[41] And Marjory Adams, writing for the *Boston Globe*, described Bardot as "a girl with the kind of figure men dream about."[42]

These reviews made it quite clear that Bardot—with her specifically French brand of bodily, sartorial sensuality—was the bright, shining reason to see the film. One profiler even equated Bardot's sexiness with a French national monument: Bardot "looked sexy, which is like saying the Louvre is a museum."[43] By this trick of writing, Bardot's sexiness was not simply a given—it was a French national treasure. According to the reviewers, there was just something about Bardot that drew people to see her. As one writer put it, "even with all the censor board trims, sexy Parisian star Brigitte Bardot's shemoting in 'And God Created Woman' is still plenty, plenty (and biz is big, big)."[44] Melvin Maddocks titled his review "Brigitte Bardot at the Gary," with no mention of the film's title whatsoever.[45] Marjory Adams in the *Globe* described Bardot as having "an undoubted and dazzling fascination."[46] Still another review in the *Los Angeles Times* oozed that Bardot was "the most fabulous wench of the decade" and was "smoking up the screen."[47] In the *Baltimore Sun*, reviewer R. H. Gardner pondered the appeal of the film, which had broken local box office records, and he came away with the conclusion that Bardot's openness about sex, which he described as a French quality, was absolutely the key ingredient. Further, he argued, the sex on screen was of a sort that appealed greatly to viewers of the film, suggesting that the "French-produced" Bardot and her film "knew exactly how to appeal" to men in the audiences.[48] Film reviewers clearly established that Bardot and France shared a certain sex appeal.

The film itself was secondary for reviewers, most of whom barely mentioned the plot. One reporter, as though under a spell, wrote that "the most remarkable thing about BB is that after one has seen the film, one comes out trying to remember if she can act."[49] Bosley Crowther praised the visuals of Saint-Tropez in the film, going on to paint Bardot as simply part of that scenery: "the outstanding feature of the scenery is undoubtedly Mlle. Bardot." Crowther continued, ending his review with the complete objectification and muting of Bardot as a person: "She is a thing of mobile contours—a phenomenon you have to see to believe."[50] Perhaps even more stultifying for Bardot, far removed as she was from the era of silent movies, one film reviewer argued that dialogue was unnecessary for Bardot in films. "At best," he wrote, "words are for her merely adjuncts like background music and one can listen or not, for like the Grand Canyon she is essentially a natural feature. The fact that she is also animated [i.e., alive and human] one must regard as something of a stroke of genius."[51]

The objectification of Brigitte Bardot is overwhelming in the reviews of her American film debut, but early on it became clear that the French state also sought to profit from her reputation for sensuality, rendering France itself attractive and sensual precisely because of her presence. The French Senate, debating the appropriation of funds for the French film industry, bemoaned the "crisis in French cinema," particularly focusing on how the money previously allotted seemed to have been misallocated. Senators especially rued that French film stars seemed to think they deserved elevated salaries. The special investigator they appointed, Édouard Bonnefous, echoed the senators' disenchantment, with one major exception: "With Brigitte Bardot," Bonnefous explained, "I would pay her anything."[52] Similarly, in a government publication, a budget-minded writer argued that stars usually were not worth their large salaries, but he stipulated that Bardot was an exception, precisely because of her attraction for Americans. Pay her handsomely, the writer argued, because "everyone knows that Brigitte Bardot has an elevated value in the American market."[53] And the minister of finance and economic affairs (and former prime minister), Antoine Pinay, informed Bardot that following her American success in *And God Created Woman*, she was more valuable to the France economy than that erstwhile symbol of French success, the Renault automobile.[54] Reactions to Bardot's onscreen roles, then, catapulted her into international fame, which in turn caused French officials to look to her when commodifying French femininity.

THE MODEL ENDURES

As Bardot aged, her "attractiveness," both in the sense of cultural perceptions of her physicality and Nye's articulation of soft power, waned. However, the

Bardot experiment, that of literally banking on femininity to render a nation more enticing, did not. France found other forms for people to emulate. If the 1950s and 1960s saw the meteoric rise of Brigitte Bardot, whose curves were celebrated everywhere from film to media to the official representation of Marianne, the 1970s in France belonged to the lithe British-French actress Jane Birkin.[55]

In fact, Brigitte Bardot and Jane Birkin once both occupied the screen in the same film and, according to film historians, not to Bardot's benefit. *Don Juan 73* was a 1973 Roger Vadim–directed project in which Bardot portrayed a female Don Juan and Birkin a young innocent. In the film, as the historian Leila Wimmer describes it, Birkin is "braless and wears unisex jeans, projecting an unthreatening image of femininity, as opposed to Bardot's experienced, confident and desiring persona. Bardot's pronounced bust and hips, overtly sexual mouth and eyes and accentuated make-up signify an explicit sexuality quite at odds with Birkin's slenderness and lack of curves that had become a new body type and a reconfiguration of the feminine ideal."[56] According to the film historian Ginette Vincendeau, an expert on Bardot, this is the film in which Bardot loses her gamine status, her unquestioned sex appeal, and becomes less relevant to moviegoers, especially in the face of Birkin's fresher, breezier, even less attainable—but also less threatening—style.[57] In contrast with Bardot's apparently overproofed curves and overt sexuality, then, Birkin was a sensual child, an image that appealed both to the ascendant youth cultures of the late 1960s and to the idea that a woman should have a sleek, almost childlike body, rendering her both sexy and nonthreatening to the status quo.

Birkin's body, like that of Bardot, captured the imaginations—and pens—of contemporary observers. Describing her first French film, *Slogan*, the film historian Leila Wimmer calls Birkin "the incarnation of a new kind of beauty: young, slim, with long straight hair and long legs," a new sort of model for moviegoers to admire.[58] And they did. Writing about the film *Cannabis*, with Serge Gainsbourg, the film critic for *Le Monde* described Birkin's body as a "long, fragile caressing vine." Her physical form, the prominent film writer Jean de Baroncelli noted, was a centerpiece of the film for the director, who filmed "around her body with a mixture of restraint and shamelessness, in a clever arabesque."[59] In other reviews Baroncelli called her alternatively a "delicious stripper,"[60] "supercharged," "whimsical, sparkling, tangy like an English candy,"[61] and "open to life, comfortable in her skin, available, ingenuously perverse"[62] In yet another review, Jacques Ciclier referred to her as a "body-object."[63]

Jane Birkin's physical appeal—and ensuing commentary—traversed the Atlantic much like Bardot's had a decade earlier. The *New York Times* film critic called her a "shapely, exuberant morsel" and Gainsbourg's "plaything" in *Slogan*.[64] In *Catherine & Co.*, she played what was called a "well-endowed English girl in Paris."[65] And in reviewing "Love at the Top," Charles Michener referred to Birkin as one of the "most dazzling starlets on the continent."[66] As such, Birkin became a model for the era, an aspirational physical emblem for women in France and beyond. Here, cinema, fashion, and the pressure on the individual woman combined to create an unattainable vision of the body, one that women had to strive for constantly.

As the example of Birkin shows, this official profiteering off Bardot is not isolated but rather presents a concerted pattern in how stakeholders in the postwar era successfully identified France's attractions for external observers—in this case alluring female bodies—and weaponized them in order to bring prestige and power to the state of France. It is a striking example of how a state can cunningly use soft power, as well as the power of gender, to promote itself. The fact that Americans tapped into assertions of Bardot's (and later all French women's, as my broader project argues) feminine sensuality so profoundly stands as proof of the state's success. And yet for Bardot herself, she seemingly was absent from the processes that commodified her sensuality, her femininity, and her national identity. She was what I would call "an object of the state."

CONCLUSION

Even in Brigitte Bardot's well-documented fall from grace, the result of her extreme and hate-filled racist, xenophobic, and misogynist political views, her body remained the center of critical language.[67] When he pulled her statue from his town hall in 1996, François-Henri de Virieu, the mayor of a small town near Paris, stated, "Brigitte Bardot was chosen as the model of Marianne because she had generous curves. . . . Today, she has ideas that we don't find generous."[68] "Support Is Sagging," was the headline for the same Associated Press story in another newspaper, while a third newspaper laughed, "Bardot's bust is sagging."[69] Bardot's body, the qualification for her presence as Marianne, was again deployed linguistically in her downfall.

In many ways Bardot is but one figure in a larger project in which the French government placed alluring women in extremely public and visible positions, hoping to capitalize on their attractiveness to foreign visitors.[70]

Government-run Air France carefully selected thin, elegant air hostesses, major events such as the Grenoble Olympics were staffed by fashionable beautiful women, and other French film stars—less known than Bardot but still famous—graced the pages of the world's magazines. Bardot, however, is clearly a singular figure in this story, given her literal position as symbol of France. Attesting to the success of Bardot-as-Marianne, the feminine symbol of France has been embodied by a real, beautiful woman ever since.[71]

While the question of cultural impact is always difficult to answer convincingly, in this case there is a clear sense that the French government needed to attract more tourists to France and that one of the main ways to do so was through marketing and commodifying the image of one of France's most beautiful, sexy women. Tourism to France skyrocketed throughout the 1950s and 1960s, and France today—pandemic-related lags aside—remains the most visited nation on earth.

French femininity has also had a disproportionate impact on conceptions of femininity in the West. Assumptions about the superiority of French femininity have remained stubbornly persistent. A perusal of the feminine and self-help presses reveals French women's apparent authority on any number of subjects: they "don't get fat,"[72] they have "Parisian chic,"[73] they know better beauty secrets,[74] they have better marriages and sex,[75] they are ageless,[76] they raise their children better,[77] and they just generally live better than *you*.[78] Its adaptability across different platforms is also noteworthy. Social media teems with "French girl" style and beauty accounts, and even a basic Internet search reveals how style and beauty websites seek out and curate French influencers and then advertise them to an apparently rapacious audience.[79]

Clearly this celebration of French femininity is not a cottage industry but rather a well-developed powerhouse based on the combination of femininity and soft power, a national identity/beauty–industrial complex that sells the world on an aspirational image of French female superiority. The perfection of the French woman is astoundingly diverse in these idealized manifestations, and the pressure on both sides of that equation—on the French women to uphold that standard and on other women around the world, who are taught to aspire to it and yet are always found wanting—seems immense. In understanding how soft power operates, it is crucial to untangle the threads it can weave in the service of a larger institutional project. For Bardot, *And God Created Woman* is a misleading title. Rather, Bardot's image was a careful construct, meant to benefit large institutions and not the woman herself.

If judging success on the basis of duration and financial gains, the model of French femininity is undoubtedly triumphant. If, however, judging on the basis of the millions of small cuts and large wounds women feel for not reaching that aesthetic pinnacle, for not looking and feeling alluring and thin and elegant at all moments, then the model is problematic, if not outright dangerous.

NOTES

1. Anderson Cooper, "France's Marine Le Pen Says She's Not Waging a Religious War," CBS News, March 5, 2017, https://www.cbsnews.com/news/frances-marine-le-pen -says-shes-not-waging-a-religious-war/.

2. See, e.g., the work of Mayanthi Fernando, Naomi Davidson, and Joan Scott.

3. Joan Wallach Scott, *The Politics of the Veil* (Princeton, NJ: Princeton University Press, 2007), 160–70.

4. Joseph S. Nye Jr., *Soft Power: The Means to Success in World Politics* (New York: PublicAffairs, 2004), x.

5. Nye, 76. There are some historians of France who have employed Nye's theory within the context of mainland France. Perhaps most notably, François Chaubet has delved into France's linguistic outreaches, starting with the Alliance Française in the nineteenth century and extending into France's campaign to ensure that French remains a dominant language in developing regions. My project's innovation comes in combining gender with soft power and showing how France commodified its women in order to remain relevant—and economically powerful—during a time when neither its relevancy nor its economy stood on especially solid ground.

6. See Kristin Lee Hoganson, "What's Gender Got to Do with It? Women and Foreign Relations History," *OAH Magazine of History* 19, no. 2 (2005): 14–8. See also Emily S. Rosenberg's "A Round Table Explaining the History of American Foreign Relations: Gender," *Journal of American History* 77 (June 1990): 116–24. In the piece, Rosenberg offered pioneering advice on how to incorporate gender into that particular field.

7. Mary Louise Roberts, *What Soldiers Do: Sex and the American GI in World War II France* (Chicago: University of Chicago Press, 2013), 63. See especially part 1, "Romance." Harvey Levenstein has also chronicled the long-standing link between American tourism and alleged French sexual permissiveness in *Seductive Journey: American Tourists in France from Jefferson to the Jazz Age* (Chicago: University of Chicago Press, 1998), and *We'll Always Have Paris: American Tourists in France since 1930* (Chicago: University of Chicago Press, 2004).

8. Communists, as Christopher Endy shows, and some others on the French left were ambivalent about American dollars and corresponding US influence. See Christopher Endy, *Cold War Holidays: American Tourism in France* (Chapel Hill: University of North Carolina Press, 2004), 57.

9. Robert Gildea, *France since 1945* (Oxford: Oxford University Press, 1998), 10.

10. Cynthia Enloe points out the gendered implications of dismissing tourism from serious studies of international relations: "That conventional political commentators do not discuss tourism as seriously as oil or weaponry may tell us more about those commentators' own ideological constructions of 'seriousness' than it does about the politics of tourism." Cynthia Enloe, *Bananas, Beaches, and Bases: Making Feminist Sense of International Politics* (Berkeley: University of California Press, 2014), 69.

11. Endy, *Cold War Holidays*, 57.

12. The love was not one-sided. American interests also called for increased aid and leisure spending in the context of the Cold War and preventing communism from gaining a hold in France. Endy, 204.

13. Endy, 54.

14. Endy, 101–4.

15. Endy mentions the French antirudeness campaign, Walton discusses the resumption of study abroad after World War II, and Kuisel focuses on France's protectionist measures in the face of American cultural invasion.

16. See Kelly Colvin, *Charm Offensive: Commodifying Femininity in Postwar France* (Toronto: University of Toronto Press, 2023), for a discussion of how state programs, such as the Air France air hostess program, came to dominate much of the postwar discourse about how to increase tourism numbers. In so doing, officials in the French government deployed gender as a means of luring tourists to France. Brigitte Bardot was but one very potent weapon in their arsenal.

17. While other historians have analyzed Bardot, French film content of the time, and Hollywood's attraction to Paris, here I analyze how she came to serve as the standard for all French women in the American mind, not through the plots of her films or those of other contemporary French actresses but from reviews and reactions to Bardot and the sexualized, gendered form they took. See, e.g., the scholarship of Ginette Vincendeau, Vanessa Schwartz, and Felicity Chaplin, whose excellent works deal with these three subjects in varying proportions. The use of "BB" is in and of itself a somewhat controversial moniker, as in the French language, BB sounds like *bébé*, which translates to baby. In this way, BB is further infantilized.

18. JJSS was tapping into/creating a popular sentiment for this shift. A marketing firm polled the populace at 55 percent in favor of modeling Marianne on a living woman in 1970. See Nesta Roberts, "Letter from Paris," *Guardian*, April 3, 1971.

19. Richard Vinen, "Bikinis and Breastplates," *History Today* 56 no. 4 (April 2006): 50–52, quote from 51.

20. "Names in the News," *Atlanta Constitution*, March 11, 1971.

21. "Why Brigitte? For 2 Very Good Reasons," *Los Angeles Times*, March 11, 1971; Nesta Roberts, "Republican Hagiography . . . Or Bust," *Guardian*, February 19, 1972.

22. "Considers Bardot a Perfect 38,000," *Chicago Tribune*, March 11, 1971.

23. "Why Brigitte?," 2.

24. Maurice Agulhon, "Marianne: Réflexions sur un histoire," *Annales Historiques de la Révolution Française*, no. 289 (1992): 313–22, 320.

25. "French Symbol to Show Bardot Influence," *Baltimore Sun*, April 25, 1971.

26. "Marianne de l'an 2000," *Le nouvel observateur*, October 14, 1999.

27. "French Symbol to Show Bardot Influence," *Baltimore Sun*, April 25, 1971.

28. Anthony Noel, "Sexy Roles Out for Brigitte, Says Producer," *Atlanta Journal-Constitution*, September 21, 1958.

29. Patricia Pullan, "Still Fun in Future for Bardot after 40," *Baltimore Sun*, September 24, 1974.

30. Ginette Vincendeau, *Companion to French Cinema* (London: Cassell, 1996), 26.

31. Advertisement for Congress and Portage Movie Theaters, *Chicago Tribune*, April 19, 1958.

32. Nat Hentoff, "Bob Dylan, the Wanderer," *New Yorker*, October 24, 1964.

33. Diana Holmes, "'A Girl of Today': Brigitte Bardot," in *Stardom in Postwar France*, ed. John Gaffney and Diana Holmes (New York: Berghahn Books, 2011), 51. While I think that French culture was in the process of creating a specific brand of femininity rather than it being eternal, Holmes's point about Bardot's marketability is well taken. Vanessa Schwartz also points out the fact that the French government and film industry tilled the soil of film quite productively on the international scene and especially in the United States, thereby paving the way for Bardot's arrival and domination. See Vanessa R. Schwartz, "Who Killed Brigitte Bardot? Perspectives on the New Wave at Fifty," *Cinema Journal* 49, no. 4 (2010): 145–52, 149.

34. Sarah Fishman, *From Vichy to the Sexual Revolution: Gender and Family Life in Postwar France* (New York: Oxford University Press, 2017), 117.

35. William K. Zinsser, "On: 'And God Created Woman,'" *New York Herald Tribune*, October 22, 1957.

36. Bosley Crowther, "French Import Brigitte Bardot Stars in 'And God Created Woman,'" *New York Times*, October 22, 1957.

37. Marjory Adams, "'And God Created Woman': Brigitte Bardot, Sinful Siren," *Boston Globe*, October 31, 1957.

38. Joe Hyams, "Brigitte Bardot: Magic Mirror," *New York Herald Tribune*, July 12, 1956.

39. Hyams.

40. Crowther, "French Import Brigitte Bardot."

41. Crowther.

42. Adams, "'And God Created Woman.'"

43. Dick Schaap, "She Looked Sexy, Which Is Like Saying the Louvre Is a Museum: Not Like in Pottstown," *Boston Globe*, December 17, 1965.

44. Herb Lyon, "Tower Ticker," *Chicago Tribune*, December 27, 1957.

45. Melvin Maddocks, "Brigitte Bardot at the Gary," *Christian Science Monitor*, October 30, 1957.

46. Adams, "'And God Created Woman.'"

47. GMW, "Brigitte Bardot Real Dazzler in New Film," *Los Angeles Times*, December 27, 1957.

48. R. H. Gardner, "Sex Sold the Movie by Bardot," *Baltimore Sun*, April 13, 1958.

49. GMW, "Brigitte Bardot Real Dazzler."

50. Crowther, "French Import Brigitte Bardot."

51. Paul V. Beckley, "The Formidable Brigitte Bardot," *New York Herald Tribune*, May 18, 1958.

52. Sénat de France, Notes from Séance du February 5, 1963, M. Edouard Bonnefous, rapporteur spécial de la commission des finances, du contrôle budgétaire et des comptes économiques de la nation (cinéma), 441, http://www.senat.fr/comptes-rendus -seances/5eme/pdf/1963/02/s19630205_1_0437_0456.pdf.

53. "La production des films," *Informations sociales: Bulletin mensuel à l'usage des services sociaux*, Union Nationale des Caisses d'Allocations Familiales, June 1960, 27. Interestingly, at her peak Bardot was earning about $350,000 a film, a far cry from her male counterparts, such as Alain Delon and Jean-Paul Belmondo, who commanded $500,000. See Paul Sarlat, "The Industry: Actors' Salaries; Let's Make a Deal," *Film Comment* 11, no. 4 (1975): 30–31, statistics from 31.

54. Jean-Pierre Rioux, *The Fourth Republic* (Cambridge: Cambridge University Press, 1987), 441.

55. Dominique Veillon argues that Birkin shares the decade with Catherine Deneuve, but that Deneuve was so unapproachable that she was "never copied but always admired." See Veillon, "Corps, beauté, mode, et modes de vie: De 'plaire' au 'plaisir' à travers les magazines féminins (1958–1975)," in Geneviève Dreyfus-Armand et al., *Les années 68: Le temps de contestation* (Paris: Broché, 2008), 176.

56. Leila Wimmer, "Jane Birkin: From English Rose to French Icon," in *Je t'Aime . . . Moi Non Plus: Franco-British Cinematic Relations*, ed. Lucy Mazdon and Catherine Wheatley (New York: Berghahn Books, 2010), 228–29.

57. Ginette Vincendeau, "Family Plots: The Fathers and Daughters of French Cinema," *Sight and Sound*, March 1992, 14–17.

58. Wimmer, "Jane Birkin," 226.

59. Jean de Baroncelli, "Cannabis," *Le Monde*, September 8, 1970.

60. J. B., "Comment réussir dans la vie quand on est C . . . et Pleurnichard," *Le Monde*, June 22, 1974.

61. J. B., "La course à l'échalote," *Le Monde*, October 15, 1975.

62. J. B., "Le diable au coeur," *Le Monde*, June 11, 1976.

63. Jacques Ciclier, "Du côté de chez Santelli," *Le Monde*, December 24, 1971.

64. Howard Thompson, "'Slogan,' from France, at Cine Malibu," *New York Times*, March 17, 1970.

65. Ann Barry, "Arts and Leisure Guide," *New York Times*, March 7, 1976.

66. Charles Michener, "French Twists," *Newsweek*, January 27, 1975, 67.

67. In 2021 Bardot received her sixth fine from the French government for "inciting racial hatred," this time for referring to residents of the French island of Réunion as "savages" in an open letter to multiple French news outlets. Her previous offenses addressed comments she made about Islam and Muslims. See Talpin, Jérôme, "Injures raciales: Une amende de 25 000 euros requise contre Brigitte Bardot," *Le Monde*, October 8, 2021.

68. "Friday Newsmakers," *Detroit News*, December 6, 1996.

69. "Bardot Busts Removed," *Edmonton Observer*, December 6, 1996; "And Brigitte Created Quite a Controversy," *Spokesman Review*, December 10, 1996; "Friday Newsmakers."

70. This was a departure from more conservative visions of femininity of the past, as seen in Whitney Walton's work on the *jeune femme* of the interwar period, for example. See Whitney A. Walton, *Internationalism, National Identities, and Study Abroad: France and the United States, 1890–1970* (Palo Alto, CA: Stanford University Press, 2010), 88–89.

71. Women used have included the actress Catherine Deneuve and the models Inès de la Fressange and Laetitia Casta.

72. Mireille Guiliano, *French Women Don't Get Fat* (New York: Vintage, 2007). Guiliano also has a similarly titled cookbook and a book of "secrets" of French women as well as the amazingly titled *Frenchwomen Don't Get Facelifts*, a guide to aging like a French woman.

73. Inès de la Fressange, *Parisian Chic: A Style Guide* (Paris: Flammarion, 2011). See also Anne Berest, *How to Be Parisian Wherever You Are* (New York: Doubleday, 2014); Tish Jett, *Forever Chic: Frenchwomen's Secrets for Timeless Beauty, Style, and Substance* (New York: Rizzoli Ex Libris, 2013); Jennifer L. Scott, *Lessons from Madame Chic: 20 Stylish Secrets I Learned while Living in Paris* (New York: Simon & Schuster, 2012); and Isabelle Thomas, *Paris Street Style: A Guide to Effortless Chic* (New York: Abrams Image, 2013).

74. Mathilde Thomas, *The French Beauty Solution* (New York: Avery, 2015); Chrissie Callahan, *The Paris Bath and Beauty Book: Embrace Your Natural Beauty with Timeless Secrets and Recipes from the French* (Kennebunkport, ME: Cider Hill Press, 2016).

75. Jamie Cat Callan, *French Women Don't Sleep Alone: Pleasurable Secrets to Finding Love* (New York: Citadel, 2009); Debra Ollivier, *What French Women Know: About Love, Sex, and Other Matters of the Heart and Mind* (New York: Berkley Books, 2010); Danielle Postel-Vinay, *Home Sweet Maison: The French Art of Making a Home* (New York: Dey Street Books, 2018).

76. Clémence Von Mueffling, *Ageless Beauty the French Way: Secrets from Three Generations of French Beauty Editors* (New York: St. Martin's, 2018).

77. Pamela Druckerman, *Bringing Up Bébé: One American Mother Discovers the Wisdom of French Parenting* (New York: Penguin, 2014); Karen Le Billon, *French Kids Eat Everything: How Our Family Moved to France, Cured Picky Eating, Banned Snacking, and Discovered 10 Simple Rules for Raising Happy, Healthy Eaters* (New York: William Morrow, 2014); Pamela Druckerman, *French Children Don't Throw Food* (London: Black Swan, 2001).

78. Jamie Cat Callan, *Parisian Charm School: French Secrets for Cultivating Love, Joy, and That Certain Je Ne Sais Quoi* (New York: TarcherPerigee, 2018); Catherine Malandrino, *Une Femme Française: The Seductive Style of French Women* (New York: St. Martin's, 2017); Helena Frith-Powell, *All You Need to Be Impossibly French: A Witty Investigation into the Lives, Lusts, and Little Secrets of French Women* (New York: Plume, 2006); Debra Ollivier, *Entre Nous: A Woman's Guide to Finding Her Inner French Girl* (New York: St. Martin's Griffin, 2004).

79. Pulled from one basic Internet search for "French girl Instagram": "9 French Girls to Follow on Instagram for Endless Style Inspiration," https://www.huffpost.com/entry/french-girls-instagram_l_5cae25d0e4b03ab9f24f8314; "In Honor of Bastille Day, Here Is Our Guide to Instagram's Chicest French Girls," https://www.lofficielusa.com/fashion/french-girls-instagram-fashion-follow; "25 Effortlessly Chic French Style Influencers to Follow on Instagram," https://frenchstyle.co/french-style-influencers/.

CHAPTER 7

Soft Power or Propaganda?
China's "People-to-People" Diplomacy during the Cold War

Cyril Cordoba

Since the integration of the expression "soft power" (*ruǎn shílì*) into the Chinese Communist Party's (CCP) lexicon in 2007, Beijing's increasing presence on the international stage has been a growing source of polemics. With the 2008 and the 2022 Olympic Games, the 2010 Shanghai World Expo, the (co)production of Chinese blockbusters, the promotion of the Chinese Dream, and the multiplication of Confucius Institutes around the world,[1] the People's Republic of China (RPC) has been trying to change its authoritarian image into one of a stable, pacific, and harmonious country. To this end, inside the CCP a United Front Work Department is in charge of developing "friendly" relationships abroad and "people-to-people" exchanges with influential individuals in order to have them "align" with the official discourse.[2] Those strategies are anything but new, and not only have the CCP's efforts to strengthen its attractiveness and prestige with cultural activities always been disqualified by Western powers as mere propaganda, but Beijing's "foreign friends" (*wàiguó péngyou*) have also long been considered as simple puppets of the regime.

In order to break its isolation after its foundation on October 1, 1949, the PRC indeed deployed many efforts to gain recognition on the international scene. Formally founded in 1954, the Chinese People's Association for the Friendship with Foreign Countries (CPAFFC)[3] oversaw China's people's diplomacy (*rénmín wàijiāo*) or people-to-people relationships (*mínjiān wàijiāo*) during the Cold War.[4] In her pioneering and unequivocal book, Anne-Marie Brady demonstrates how the CPAFFC's mission consisted of "making the foreign serve China."[5] However, her analysis does not address the modus operandi of the CPAFFC's international partners, who were crucial intermediaries for improving the PRC's image beyond the Bamboo Curtain, understood here as the geopolitical and sociocultural barrier separating China not only from noncommunist Asian states but more generally from the Western bloc. These key assets, called the friendship associations,[6] were not formally created or controlled by Beijing, and they acted at the margins of official diplomacy after having "spr[u]ng up spontaneously" in civil society.[7] Yet these organizations only interacted with state-controlled agencies in China, and they heavily depended on the Maoist propaganda apparatus. How, then, should their action be apprehended, and how should Beijing's relations with its foreign supporters be designated? More generally, what do these hybrid intermediary agents tell us about Chinese soft power *avant la lettre* and its changing nature?

In order to answer these questions, this chapter proposes to shed light on the ambiguous position of these cultural mediators and political agents entirely dedicated to the promotion of China in the West. As the following pages will demonstrate, friendship associations throughout the world were caught in an unequal relationship with the PRC, which led them to unquestioningly repeat the doxa fixed by Beijing. Despite their claims of being nonpolitical, these groups cautiously respected the watchwords of the regime to preserve their status of privileged partners of the CPAFFC and to keep access to material and symbolic resources, key to their success.

STATE OF THE ART AND RESEARCH OUTLINE

Today it is commonplace to introduce a research paper dealing with the concept of soft power by insisting on the confused, vague, and ubiquitous nature of this notion because of its lack of theoretical framing by Joseph S. Nye and the vast number of researchers who used it after him. This is particularly true when it comes to its reappropriation in the PRC,[8] whose recent soft power efforts, fitting "the party state's approach to propaganda,"[9] have generated countless studies since the 2000s.[10] China has a long tradition of "culture winning over an enemy" and of considering "culture and politics as entwined, with culture manifesting political ideology and helping mobilize the public in support of [its] policies."[11] Nevertheless, recent academic literature about the PRC's use of soft power unquestioningly brushed aside the pre-1978 period (before the death of Mao Zedong and Deng Xiaoping's "reform and opening up"), which has generally been considered irrelevant to the topic. Even if Nye's formulation (and its introduction in China) only dates back to the early 1990s, this chapter postulates that Beijing's use of friendship associations during the Cold War offers interesting perspectives on how the country exported its "political ideology and ruling methods" by using cultural attraction and that it can help clear the blurred theoretical line between soft power and propaganda.[12]

Nye himself, who explained that "when governments are perceived as manipulative and information is seen as propaganda, credibility is destroyed," recognized that "soft power does not depend upon being true" and that "if propaganda attracts, it can produce soft power."[13] That is why, instead of opposing the two terms, we will consider soft power "a process by which one country can non-coercively spread knowledge of its culture and ideas to other countries due to their attractive characteristics."[14] This chapter will remind that soft power, far from being "a synonym for cultural attractiveness,"[15] relies just as importantly on ideological values and foreign policy.[16] As to the notion of propaganda, generally used to delegitimize the discourse of the other, which is nowadays euphemized thanks to less polemical expressions such as "publicity," "public diplomacy," and "public relations,"[17] it will be primarily considered in the following pages as a form of communication seeking, typically under the guise of information or entertainment, to convince, which is to say to modify or create an opinion or a behavior.[18] In this respect, China's external propaganda (*duìwài xuānchuán*) will not be simply depicted as coercion,[19] but rather it will be described as generating "positive attraction and persuasion."[20]

To do so, this chapter will analyze the central role played by Western friendship associations with China in Beijing's soft power strategies from 1949 to 1989. It will draw on archival material collected in Switzerland, the United States, France, and Belgium, consisting mainly of internal documents of pro-Chinese organizations as well as ego-documents—self-reflective material such as personal diaries and travel accounts—collected during interviews with (former) friends of China. It goes without saying that pro-Chinese groups around the world differed according to the relative power of the local communist movement, the prominence of racial issues, the development of sinology, and the presence of a Chinese diaspora in each country. Therefore, our aim will be to address the most prominent common feature of Western friendship associations: their dependency on the PRC's authorities. Focused on the intermediaries between the source and the target of Chinese propaganda, the chapter will demonstrate that Beijing's so-called people-to-people diplomacy corresponded neither to a symmetrical and disinterested system of exchanges nor to a gross manipulation. It will present how friendship associations were created in the 1950s, radicalized in the 1960s, and professionalized in the late 1970s and early 1980s. Thereby, it will argue that China's people's diplomacy was in fact the expression of a transnational clientelist system that required loyalty to the CCP.

FORTY YEARS OF "FRIENDSHIP"

In the early 1950s, the PRC was isolated on the international stage. Taiwan was widely recognized as the legitimate government of China by Western countries and by the United Nations, and the United States imposed an embargo on Beijing following its intervention in the Korean War. Consequently, the Maoist regime created networks bypassing traditional canals of diplomacy to break through the Bamboo Curtain.[21] China sought to "win friends and allies" and advance its agenda by reshaping foreign audiences' perception of the country and by contradicting the "anti-Chinese lies" of the mass media[22]—that is to say, information unfavorable to Beijing.[23] The Maoist government thus developed, in parallel to its official exchanges with partner states and brother parties, alternative networks based on relationships with foreign sympathizers from civil society. The CPAFFC was in charge of developing such relations with foreign institutions and personalities likely to help improve China's image in the public sphere.

In Britain (1950), Japan (1950), Sweden (1952), Chile (1952), France (1952), New Zealand (1952), West Germany (1957), and Mexico (1957), local friendship associations with China were founded by sinologists, businesspeople, and left-wing activists. In their early days, the work of these associations was mainly to disseminate information about the PRC and to organize events to help develop economic or cultural exchanges with Beijing. Although most of them did not hide their sympathy for the regime, many others were only interested in informing their members about Chinese civilization, doing business in East Asia, or simply offering their members opportunities to travel to the PRC. In any case, the strategy of these organizations was met with unquestionable success.

Officially apolitical, these associations promoted the development of their own country's relations with the PRC, but on this rather consensual foundation, their concrete role was in fact to pressure their own government into recognizing the PRC as the sole and legitimate China and cease all relations with Taiwan. It thus seemed very clear from the start that those groups had a political agenda. Yet they sought to gather people beyond left-wing circles, which had already been won over to socialist ideas, to reach populations a priori hostile or indifferent to communism and build a sort of united front rallying "as many allies as possible in order to achieve a common cause."[24] To do so, they organized many different cultural activities.

At first, they mainly distributed propaganda material produced by the Beijing Foreign Languages Press: political brochures, newspapers, and magazines (e.g., *Peking Review*, *China im Aufbau*, *Littérature chinoise*, and *El popola ĉinio*) but also illustrated books for children and general documentation about China (language, geography, art, medicine, etc.). They also regularly organized shows of Chinese artistic troupes touring the world (ballets, acrobatics, operas, etc.), sold Chinese products (handicraft, papercutting, spring rolls), screened Chinese movies, and set up photograph and painting exhibitions with material they received from Beijing or that they brought back themselves. Concretely, friendship associations thus heavily relied on the support of Beijing to obtain the resources necessary to their activity. And this situation further increased after the Sino-Soviet Split of the early 1960s and the emergence of Maoist parties around the globe.[25]

For the friendship movement, the 1960s undeniably marked a phase of radicalization since the majority of the pro-Chinese associations in the world came under the almost exclusive leadership of Marxist-Leninist militants. In most countries they succeeded in attracting several thousand members. According to the Leninist terminology, they became "mass organizations" of "vanguard parties," but as the head of the Svensk-Kinesiska Vänskapsförbundet (Swedish-Chinese Friendship Association) explained, "many people did not understand . . . the distinction between a Party and a Friendship organization."[26] The proximity of these two types of entities was the same in most of the countries where the pro-China movement had developed to a sufficient extent. In the United States, the Revolutionary Communist Party took the lead in many sections of the US-China Peoples Friendship Association. In Belgium, it was the AMADA (All the Power to the Workers) group that for a time exercised a decisive influence within the Belgium-China Association,[27] while in France, the Parti Communiste Marxiste-Léniniste de France had itself hatched out of a local committee of the Asssociation des Amitiés Franco-Chinoises in Marseille.[28]

It became clear for the supporters of Beijing that the objective of friendship associations was not to promote China's ancient culture and civilization but rather to support contemporary political campaigns such as the Great Cultural Proletarian Revolution (1966–76).[29] In the late 1960s a certain "Maomania" spread throughout the world, and artifacts such as the so-called

Little Red Book and Mao suits—political instruments of Mao's growing personality cult—even became trendy among certain youth.[30] These historical circumstances assured a growing popularity to friendship associations with China. Nevertheless, the CPAFFC always gave its guidance to the associations. For example, in Switzerland, where public opinion and the authorities were particularly supportive of Taiwan and Tibet,[31] the CPAFFC suggested local friendship associations retaliate against the "the anti-Chinese activities of the Chiang Kai-shek gang and of the Dalai Lama in Switzerland [through] cultural troupes such as acrobatics, ballet, painting exhibitions, etc."[32]

The CPAFFC, which had relations with seventy organizations in fifty countries, reminded the local associations how to organize themselves and make sure they were on the right track. One should neither "give power to those who are interested in only one aspect of China" (e.g., sinologists or lovers of Chinese culture) or to those "who attack China virulently and defame it" (e.g., anyone who has expressed reservations about Beijing's foreign policy) nor, above all, exclude "revolutionary comrades" who were in line with the regime's ideology.[33] The internal documents of friendship associations were full of formulas such as "the Chinese suggest . . ." and "our Chinese friends consider that . . . ," to remind them that exemplary loyalty was required. In addition, CPAFFC gave the associations several points of reference, such as the facts that in Japan their counterparts were too openly left-wing and that in the United States some leaders were too critical of the CCP.[34] On the contrary, the Scandinavian models, and in particular Swedish ones, were presented as examples to follow because of their balance between political convictions and openness to the general public. The pro-Chinese activists thus had to remain open to noncommunists while staying completely loyal to Chinese foreign policy, which at that time underwent unexpected reversals.

From 1971 onward, when the PRC sought to build new international alliances, the friendship associations took on a strategic role, becoming, for example, the centerpieces of the "ping-pong diplomacy" that marked the Sino-US rapprochement.[35] After the PRC's accession to the United Nations and its recognition by most Western states, China progressively reopened to international tourism and allowed for thousands of foreigners to visit the country each year. Thanks to their close ties with the authorities, friendship associations enjoyed a preferential treatment on the allocation of Chinese visas, and their guided tours thus attracted many travelers. Preparatory meetings and constant supervision assured that after their return, the vast majority of the tourists would praise the great achievements of the regime. Riding the wave of the PRC's popularity in the West, Beijing's friends played on the blurred lines between the appeal of Chinese culture and civilization on one hand and enthusiasm for the Cultural Revolution experience on the other. By advertising traditional arts, culture, and folklore as well as contemporary political campaigns, the activists relied on the USSR's experience with regard to propaganda in order to gather as many people as possible to plead the cause of the PRC. This mixture of genres was ultimately the core of their strategy as Maoist parties were strongly encouraged by the CPAFFC to maintain control over friendship associations while remaining behind the scenes.

The material and symbolic resources that Beijing dangled through these alternative networks became real power issues, and in some countries governments tried to create their own friendship organizations in an attempt to weaken Beijing's hand. However, with the death of Mao Zedong in 1976, this international machinery quickly jammed, until the whole system broke down in the 1980s. In just a few weeks, the international partners of the CPAFFC were asked to disavow everything they told about China during the past ten years and promote the PRC's new path toward "socialism with Chinese characteristics" (e.g., opening to foreign investments). As the political changes at the head of the PRC led to the disappearance of all the egalitarian ideals defended until then by the CCP, Maoism lost its ideological appeal and quickly ran out of steam worldwide. After the Sino-Vietnamese War, it became increasingly difficult for the leaders of the friendship associations to praise Beijing's foreign policy,[36] and the Maoist parties no longer dictated their ideological line.

In the 1980s pro-Chinese organizations were forced to adopt a new orientation, much less revolutionary but just as political. In order to find their place among the various "China watchers" and travel agencies of various kinds that sprang up after 1978, some, like the US-China Peoples Friendship Association, chose to lobby and to become one filament in "a vast web of interconnections between government structures, agencies, enterprises, institutions and private citizens."[37] Many of them managed to take the decisive turn in the 1980s by getting closer to the most influential circles and joining the camp of the triumphant liberal ideology, which allowed their leaders to rub shoulders with cultural, economic, and political elites.[38] Consequently, the friends of China's political spectrum broadened, in parallel with growing prospects for economic exchange with the PRC. China's people's diplomacy thus took on a new dimension, abandoning the logic that had been in place for decades. From then on it was no longer a question of developing alternative channels on the fringes of official exchanges and expanding its influence over different strata of the population but rather of participating in the intensification of bilateral relations with foreign countries and integrating the highly profitable field of economic partnerships. Thus, the friendship associations no longer tried to bypass diplomatic channels and instead tried to fit in as comfortably as possible.

After countless exhibitions on the regime's great achievements and endless screenings of revolutionary operas in the 1960s and 1970s, the associations organized talks on topics such as calligraphy, martial arts, acupuncture, archaeology, and Buddhism as well as Chinese language and cooking courses. Nevertheless, the main task of the friends of the PRC remained the same: to win Beijing sympathizers by spreading information favorable to the regime. What passed for a depoliticization was in reality a professionalization (with full-time positions within the associations, the creation of travel agencies, collaborations with public and private partners, etc.) since the pro-Chinese continued to defend the vision of the PRC, which seemed to be moving ever closer to a capitalist economy, a modern state, and, as some had hoped in vain, a liberal democracy.[39] The associations did not, therefore, become mere documentation centers on China but continued to serve as a counterweight to the mass media, which focused, for instance, on the environmental problems in the PRC and on the various campaigns against "spiritual pollution" launched by the CCP. As a result, friendship associations in the 1980s mainly organized conferences focusing on the positive aspects of Chinese modernization, such as the miracles of the special economic zones and the peaceful nature of Beijing's foreign policy. In other words, they continued to serve the political agenda of the PRC.

In fact, determined to benefit from the modernization of the country, the friendship associations did not disavow their loyalty to the Chinese government, on which they remained dependent in many ways. It was essential for them to stay in favor with Chinese diplomats in order to receive sufficient visas, since travel to China still was their main source of income. But even if the CPAFFC still expected unwavering loyalty from its foreign friends, after the repression of the Tiananmen Square demonstration in 1989 most of the associations funded in the 1950s and 1960s disappeared. After many abrupt and radical reversals over the past two decades, the massacres perpetrated by the Chinese army marked a point of no return for many friends of China. However, some organizations that were very comfortable in their new role as lobbyists or business partners managed to get through this fateful period and thrive to this day by collaborating with Confucius Institutes, one of Beijing's new instruments to "promote the mutual understanding and the friendship" between the Chinese people and the rest of the world.[40]

FRIENDS OR CLIENTS?

The rhetoric of "friendship between the people," omnipresent in political and diplomatic language,[41] was extensively used by communist powers during the Cold War.[42] Yet like the pro-Soviet groups before them, the friendship associations with China were long regarded by Western governments as agents of subversion.[43] However, in countries such as Belgium and Japan,[44] the business community quickly realized the value of unofficial channels for developing commercial contacts with Beijing, and in countries such as Sweden and the United Kingdom,[45] sinologists were willing to work with Maoists in order to maintain cultural exchanges with the PRC. Throughout the world, the techniques employed by Beijing's friends were very similar: promotion of highly supervised trips, projection of grandiloquent films, organization of public conferences, and distribution of stereotypical magazines. Pro-Chinese organizations all over the world complied entirely with the injunctions of Chinese diplomacy and followed the same strategy: not to address Marxist-Leninists as a priority but rather to seduce those who had no inclination to Chinese socialism.

Beijing's people's diplomacy was a privileged instrument to extend its influence abroad. The CPAFFC's patronage of the pro-Chinese movement made the designation "friend of the PRC" a title of nobility that gave the groups that claimed it real power and access to material and symbolic resources.[46] Friendship associations around the world, therefore, acted in such a way as to maintain their advantages with Beijing. Even in the absence of a "Chinese Comintern" to coordinate their action internationally, they respected the dogmas of the propaganda with disconcerting zeal, as if they were risking formal exclusion from the CCP.[47] It is, therefore, at the price of a restricted freedom of expression that they were able to impose themselves as privileged partners of the regime.

In this sense, most friendship associations did not contribute to meaningful cultural transfers between their own country and the PRC since they were more concerned with reproducing the codes of Chinese propaganda than with reinterpreting a thousand-year-old civilization in forms adapted to their own environment. The blurred line between cultural action and political promotion, which was at the heart of Chinese soft power practices, thus turned the pro-Chinese associations into agents of gray propaganda. The objective of the messages they relayed was in no way hidden from the general public (as with black propaganda). However, not all the ins and outs of their work on behalf of the PRC were necessarily openly assumed (as with white propaganda). For all these reasons, the notion of friendship with

China involved very elaborate discourses, which contrasted with its apparent spontaneity.

As alternative practices beyond official diplomatic circuits based on deeply political principles, which required "clients" to be highly loyal in order to maintain their advantages with their "boss," Beijing's people's diplomacy highly resembled a clientelist system. The asymmetrical relationship of friendship associations with Chinese institutions was based on the allocation of material and symbolic resources (such as propaganda material and Chinese visas but also mentions in the *Peking Review* and invitations to sumptuous banquets),[48] which depended on the goodwill of the CPAFFC. Through the exchange of gifts and countergifts,[49] each side benefited from its privileged links beyond the Bamboo Curtain. In this sense, the voluntary work of the friendship associations was not done for free, even if the gratifications that resulted from it were generally unconscious, secondary, or repressed.[50] In other words, as the political scientist Jean-Louis Briquet reminded, "rather than the pragmatic exchange itself, what specifies the clientelist relationship is the perception of this exchange as a disinterested moral duty, both on the part of the boss (who acts out of devotion or friendship) and on the part of the client (who acts out of loyalty or fidelity)."[51] Of course, one should not forget the affects, the genuine interest, and the political motivations of the protagonists, who united for a common cause and a shared passion. The clientelist nature of the notion of friendship did not alter the sincerity and the altruism of those who claimed it or the legitimacy of their anti-imperialist beliefs.

It is nevertheless necessary to clarify the limits of this characterization of Beijing's people-to-people diplomacy as a clientelist system. These lie mainly in the difficulty in accessing sources. As long as Chinese archives (and in particular those of the Ministry of Foreign Affairs) remain closed to research, it will be hard to analyze the rhetoric of friendship employed by the PRC in greater depth. Concepts such as *rénqíng*, *bào*, and *guānxì*—which could be summarily translated as "exchanges of favors, indebtedness," "reciprocity," and "inter-personal connections, social ties"—should also be further integrated in a reflection about Western interactions with China to better understand which hierarchies, instrumental ties, and degrees of intimacy were at stake and maybe misinterpreted by Westerners.[52] Key questions remain to be answered in terms of how reciprocal or asymmetrical this patronage relationship was: What exactly were the commitments, and perhaps even obligations, of the CPAFFC to its foreign friends? What could they demand from Beijing to continue to advocate on its behalf when the context called for a renegotiation of the terms of their agreement? Since today friendship associations with China "are increasingly attempting to court political influence,"[53] it seems particularly relevant to determine what really is at stake, considering Beijing's insistence on promoting "win-win exchanges" with its international partners.[54]

Finally, it is worth mentioning that since the 2010s another concept blurring the lines between soft power and propaganda has attracted attention when it comes to Beijing's promotion of its political model abroad: sharp power.[55] This notion, generally attributed to authoritarian regimes, underlies the gray zone between what Nye designates as coercion ("getting others to want what you want") and cooptation ("getting others to do what you want").[56] Sharp power consists of using the enemy's inner rifts to destabilize and rallying public opinion to your cause through intimidation, subversion, and manipulation via "entities acting on behalf of the communist party-state [that] disguise their initiative as commercial ventures or as grassroots civil society initiatives."[57] Abandoning the modest and cautious attitude dictated by Deng Xiaoping after the Tiananmen Square massacre (maintain a low profile, and do not claim leadership), the PRC has now shifted to a more assertive and proactive diplomacy toward Western countries, often deemed combative and aggressive. Named after a patriotic action movie, this so-called wolf warrior diplomacy involves offensively defending China's national interests, notably by countering the "anti-Chinese lies" in Western mass and social media with "controversial Chinese narratives" on topics such as the COVID-19 pandemic.[58] This shift was described by French political scientists as "a Machiavellian moment" in which China would consider it "safer to be feared than to be loved."[59] Despite Xi Jinping's call to create a "trustsworthy, loveable and respectable" image for the country, it is indeed not certain that Xuexi Qiangguo, the mobile app that, like a digital Little Red Book, enables the study of the thoughts of Xi Jinping, will appeal to Westerners in a context of growing controversies on key topics such as Hong Kong, Tibet, Uyghurs, and the South China Sea.[60]

NOTES

1. Inspired by the model of the Goethe Institute, the Alliance Française, and the British Council, Confucius Institutes are language schools established by Beijing in cooperation with foreign educational partners to promote Chinese culture internationally.
2. Anne-Marie Brady, *Magic Weapons: China's Political Influence Activities under Xi Jinping* (Washington, DC: Wilson Center, 2017); Xingmiu Liao and Wen-Hsuan Tsai, "Clientelistic State Corporatism: The United Front Model of 'Pairing-Up' in the Xi Jinping Era," *China Review* 19, no. 1 (2019): 21–56.

3. Contrary to the Propaganda Department (which was replaced during the 1966–76 Cultural Revolution) and the United Front Work Department, the CPAFFC has continued to exist without interruption since its creation. Initiated by the Chinese People's Committee to Safeguard World Peace in 1949 (in parallel with the Chinese People's Institute of Foreign Affairs), it was formally founded as the Chinese People's Association for Cultural Relations with Foreign Countries on May 1954 before adopting its present name in 1969.

4. The CPAFFC could be compared to the Soviet VOKS (All-Union Society for Cultural Relations with Foreign Countries [1925–58]) and SSOD (Union of Soviet Societies for Friendship and Cultural Relations with Foreign Countries [1958–92]) since its aim was to "influence the non-communist mass and the petty bourgeois intelligentsia." Jean-François Fayet, *VOKS: Le laboratoire helvétique; Histoire de la diplomatie culturelle soviétique durant l'entre-deux-guerres* (Genève: Georg, 2014), 20. Similarly, other instruments of the Chinese propaganda apparatus—such as the press agency Xinhua (New China), Radio Peking, Lüxingshe (the official travel agency), and Beijing Foreign Languages Press—were inspired by the Soviet model. Derek R. Hall, ed., *Tourism and Economic Development in Eastern Europe and the Soviet Union* (London: Belhaven Press, 1991); Deborah A. Kaple, *Dream of a Red Factory: The Legacy of High Stalinism in China* (New York: Oxford University Press, 1994); Cagdas Ungor, "Reaching the Distant Comrade: Chinese Communist Propaganda Abroad (1949–1976)" (PhD diss., State University of New York, 2009); Lucien Bianco, *La récidive: Révolution russe, révolution chinoise* (Paris: Gallimard, 2014).

5. Anne-Marie Brady, *Making the Foreign Serve China: Managing Foreigners in the People's Republic* (Lanham, MD: Rowman & Littlefield, 2003).

6. Alistair Shaw, "Telling the Truth about People's China" (PhD diss., Victoria University of Wellington, 2010); Perry Johansson, *Saluting the Yellow Emperor: A Case of Swedish Sinography* (Leiden: Brill, 2012); Kaixuan Liu, "Le miroir chinois: Les attitudes françaises face à la Chine dans les milieux politique, diplomatique, intellectuel et médiatique, de 1949 au milieu des années 1980" (PhD diss., Sciences Po Paris, 2019); Yuxi Liu, "Les relations transnationales entre le Québec et la Chine populaire (1960–1980): Acteurs, savoirs et representations" (PhD diss., University of Québec and University of Angers, 2019); Cyril Cordoba, *China-Swiss Relations during the Cold War, 1949–89: Between Soft Power and Propaganda* (London: Routledge, 2022).

7. Letter from Han Suyin to Paul-Yves Rio, Howard Gotlieb Archival Research Center, Han Suyin Collection, box 90, 14.6.1979. Sino-Belgian writer Han Suyin was one of China's most famous propagandists in the West and frequently collaborated with friendship associations. (All translations from the French are by the author.) For more about Han Suyin's activities, see Cyril Cordoba, "A Chinese Janus? Han Suyin's Tightrope Walk between East and West (1917–2012)," *Chinese Historical Review* 28, no. 1 (2021): 49–67.

8. Nye repeatedly wrote about China's soft power, emphasizing its attractive traditional culture but noting how far behind the United States' it was, especially in regard to Japan and South Korea. Joseph S. Nye, "The Rise of China's Soft Power," *Wall Street Journal Asia*, December 29, 2005; Joseph S. Nye, "Hard Decisions on Soft Power: Opportunities and Difficulties for Chinese Soft Power," *Harvard International Review* 31, no. 2 (2009): 18–22; Joseph S. Nye, "China and Soft Power," *South African Journal of International Affairs* 19, no. 2 (2012): 151–55.

9. Kingsley Edney, "Soft Power and the Chinese Propaganda System," *Journal of Contemporary China* 27, no. 78 (2012): 899–914.

10. Yiwei Wang, "Public Diplomacy and the Rise of Chinese Soft Power," *Annals of the American Academy of Political and Social Science* 616 (2008): 257–73.

11. Weiying Peng, "China, Film Coproduction and Soft Power Competition" (PhD thesis, Queensland University of Technology, 2015), 21; Maria Repnikova, *Chinese Soft Power* (Cambridge: Cambridge University Press, 2022), 5.

12. Zhongying Pang, "The Evolution of China's Soft-Power Quest from the Late 1980s to the 2010s," in *Soft-Power Internationalism: Competing for Cultural Influence in the 21st Century Global Order*, ed. Burcu Baykurt and Victoria de Grazia (New York: Columbia University Press, 2021), 216.

13. Nye, "China and Soft Power," 152, 203.

14. Utpal Vyas, "Cool, Warm, Soft and Sharp: Paradigms of Cultural Exchange in Japan-China Relations," *International Journal of Cultural Policy* 26, no. 7 (2020): 3.

15. Kingsley Edney, "Soft Power and the Chinese Propaganda System," *Journal of Contemporary China* 27, no. 78 (2012): 908.

16. Peter S. Henne, "What We Talk about When We Talk about Soft Power," *International Studies Perspectives* (2021): 1–18.

17. E.g., the CCP Central Committee Propaganda Department has been renamed "Publicity Department." Thymian Bussemer, *Propaganda: Konzepte und Theorien* (Wiesbaden, Ger.: VS Verlag für Sozialwissenschaften, 2005); Jonathan Auerbach, ed., *The Oxford Handbook of Propaganda Studies* (Oxford: Oxford University Press, 2013); Garth S. Jowett and Victoria O'Donnell, *Propaganda and Persuasion* (Thousand Oaks, CA: Sage, 2015); Jason Stanley, *How Propaganda Works* (Princeton, NJ: Princeton University Press, 2015); Stephen Lovell, "Communist Propaganda and Media in the Era of the Cold War," in *The Cambridge History of Communism*, vol. 3, ed. Juliane Fürst, Silvio Pons, and Mark Selden (Cambridge: Cambridge University Press, 2017), 354–75.

18. In the words of Jacques Ellul, we will, therefore, consider propaganda to be "the set of methods used by an organized group in order to make a targeted public participate actively or passively in its action." Jacques Ellul, *Propagandes* (Paris: Economica, [1962] 1990): 75.

19. Mareike Svea Ohlberg, "Creating a Favorable International Public Opinion Environment: External Propaganda (*Duiwai Xuanchuan*) as a Global Concept with Chinese Characteristics" (PhD diss., Heidelberg University, 2013); Kingsley Edney, *The Globalization of Chinese Propaganda: International Power and Domestic Political Cohesion* (New York: Palgrave Macmillan, 2014).

20. Joseph S. Nye, "Soft Power: The Evolution of a Concept," *Journal of Political Power* 14, no. 1 (2021): 202.

21. As Peter Martin recently put it, "Mao's new regime badly needed to build bridges with the outside world. Establishing ties with capitalist nations would strengthen its claim to be the sole legitimate government of China." *China's Civilian Army: The Inside Story of China's Quest for Global Power* (Oxford: Oxford University Press, 2021): 5–6.

22. Ingrid d'Hooghe, *The Limits of China's Soft Power in Europe: Beijing's Public Diplomacy Puzzle*, Clingeandael Diplomacy Papers no. 25 (The Hague: Netherlands Institute of International Relations, 2010), 1.

23. In that regard, they replied to a preexisting "countertext." Ohlberg, "Creating a Favorable International Public Opinion Environment," 30.

24. Gerry Groot, *Managing Transitions: The Chinese Communist Party, United Front Work, Corporatism and Hegemony* (New York: Routledge, 2004), xiii.

25. Maoist (or Marxist-Leninist) parties' relations with the PRC's International Liaison Department will not be addressed here. It could, however, be noted that after the Sino-Soviet split, the opportunity for a foreign Maoist party to be quoted in the official mouthpiece of the regime (*Peking Review*) by respecting the CCP's watchwords functioned as a particularly gratifying reward for their loyalty.

26. Email from Jan Myrdal to the author, November 10, 2016. See also Johansson, *Saluting the Yellow Emperor*.

27. Minutes of the executive committee meeting, September 19, 1974, Archives of the Association Belgium-China. See also Sarah Windey, "L'Association Belgique-Chine: 1957–1983" (BA diss., Free University of Brussels, 2005).

28. Kaixuan Liu, "Les amis de la Chine? Le cas de l'Association des amitiés franco-chinoises (1952–1981)," in *La Révolution culturelle en Chine et en France*, ed. Miao Chi et al. (Paris: Riveneuve, 2017): 231–45.

29. This political maneuver was launched by Mao to eliminate his adversaries and impose his radical ideas. It plunged China into civil war (1966–69), and it took the People's Liberation Army several months to take control of the situation and put an end to the violent exactions of the Red Guards (a paramilitary movement that Mao officially supported). After the brutal disappearing of his designated successor (Marshal Lin Biao), the Great Helmsman slowly fell into infirmity while his supporters and adversaries engaged in a power struggle (1971–76).

30. Alexander C. Cook, ed., *Mao's Little Red Book: A global history* (Cambridge: Cambridge University Press, 2014); François Hourmant, *Les Années Mao en France: Avant, pendant et après mai 68* (Paris: Odile Jacob, 2018).

31. Cyril Cordoba, "'Le blabla sur l'amitié et la paix m'ennuie': La diplomatie suisse face à la propagande chinoise (1949–1976)," *Relations internationales* 2, no. 186 (2021): 83–96.

32. Report from the Swiss associations after their trip in China, November 1975, Archives Contestataires (hereafter AC), 002-CP-SS115-D029.

33. Transcript of the Swiss friendship associations' meeting with the CPAFFC, July 20, 1977, AC, 002-CP-SS115-D029.

34. Transcript of the national coordination's meeting with the CPAFFC, July 4, 1977. AC, 002-CP-SS115-D029-SD003.

35. In the early 1970s the PRC used table tennis matches to signal its desire for rapprochement with various countries, especially the United States. The slogan of the PRC's "ping-pong diplomacy" campaign was "Friendship First, Competition Second." Guanhua Wang, "'Friendship First': China's Sports Diplomacy during the Cold War," *Journal of American-East Asian Relations* 12, nos. 3–4 (2003): 133–53; Mayumi Itoh, *The Origin of Ping-Pong Diplomacy: The Forgotten Architect of Sino-U.S. Rapprochement* (New York: Palgrave Macmillan, 2011); Amanda Shuman, "Friendship Is Solidarity: The Chinese Ping-Pong Team Visits Africa in 1962," in *Sport and Diplomacy: Games within Games*, ed. J. Simon Rofe (Manchester: Manchester University Press, 2018).

36. In 1979 this clash between two former allies launched to defend Cambodia strongly discredited Beijing's anti-imperialist discourse. John D. Ciorciari, "China and the Pol Pot Regime," *Cold War History* 14, no. 2 (2013): 215–35; Ben Kiernan, "Cambodia: Detonator of Communism's Implosion," in *The Cambridge History of Communism*, vol. 3, ed. Juliane Fürst, Silvio Pons, and Mark Selden (Cambridge: Cambridge University Press, 2017): 121–50.

37. Discussion paper of the USCPFA-Eastern Region Association, May 1983, New York Public Library, manuscript collection 6176, folder 9.6.

38. E.g., Michel Rocard and Maurice Schumann (two high-profile politicians) became honorary presidents of the Association des Amitiés Franco-Chinoises. Kaixuan Liu, "Les amis de la Chine?," 231–45.

39. Daniel F. Vukovich, *China and Orientalism: Western Knowledge Production and the P.R.C.* (London: Routledge, 2012).

40. Jeffrey Gil, *Soft Power and the Worldwide Promotion of Chinese Language Learning: The Confucius Institute Project* (Bristol, UK: Multilingual Matters, 2017).

41. Preston King and Graham M. Smith, ed., "Friendship in Politics," *Critical Review of International Social and Political Philosophy* 10, no. 2 (2007).

42. See in particular Jan C. Behrends, *Die erfundene Freundschaft: Propaganda für die Sowjetunion in Polen und in der DDR* (Köln: Böhlau, 2006).

43. Sonja Grossmann, *Falsche Freunde im Kalten Krieg? Sowjetische Freundschaftsgesellschaften in Westeuropa als Instrumente und Akteure der Cultural Diplomacy* (Berlin: De Gruyter Oldenbourg, 2019).

44. Windey, "L'Association Belgique-Chine"; Utpal Vyas, *Soft Power in Japan-China Relations: State, Sub-State and Non-State Relations* (London: Routledge, 2011).

45. Johansson, *Saluting the Yellow Emperor*; Simon Winchester, *Bomb, Book and Compass: Joseph Needham and the Great Secrets of China* (London: Viking, 2008).

46. Daniel Gaxie, "Rétributions du militantisme et paradoxes de l'action collective," *Swiss Political Science Review* 11, no. 1 (2005): 157–88.

47. Brigitte Studer, *The Transnational World of the Cominternians* (Basingstoke, UK: Palgrave Macmillan, 2015).

48. Gioia Weber Pazmiño, "Klientelismus: Annäherungen an das Konzept" (PhD diss., University of Zürich, 1991); Jean-François Médard, "Clientélisme politique et corruption," *Tiers-Monde* 41, no. 161 (2000): 75–87.

49. Donatella Della Porta, "The Vicious Circles of Corruption in Italy," *Democracy and Corruption in Europe*, ed. Donatella Della Porta and Yves Mény (London: Pinter, 1997): 35–49; Jean-Louis Briquet, "La politique clientélaire: Clientélisme et processus politiques," in *Le clientélisme politique dans les sociétés contemporaines*, ed. Jean-Louis Briquet and Frédéric Sawicki (Paris: PUF, 1998): 7–37.

50. Pierre Bourdieu, "Un acte désintéressé est-il possible?," in *Raisons pratiques: Sur la théorie de l'action* (Paris: Seuil, 1994): 147–67.

51. Jean-Louis Briquet, "Des amitiés paradoxales: Échanges intéressés et morale du désintéressement dans les relations de clientèle," *Politix* 12, no. 45 (1999): 10–11.

52. Kwang-Kuo Hwang, "Face and Favor: The Chinese Power Game," *American Journal of Sociology* 92, no. 4 (1987): 944–74.

53. Martin, *China's Civilian Army*, 78.

54. Raùl Bernal-Meza, "China and Latin America Relations: The Win-Win Rhetoric," *Journal of China and International Relations*, special issue (2016): 27–43; Anastas Vangeli, "Global China and Symbolic Power in the Era of the Belt and Road," in Baykurt and De Grazia *Soft-Power Internationalism*, 224–48.

55. Christopher Walker, Shanthi Kalathil, and Jessica Ludwig, "The Cutting Edge of Sharp Power," *Journal of Democracy* 1, no. 1 (2020): 124–37; Ingrid d'Hooghe, "China's Public Diplomacy Goes Political," *The Hague Journal of Diplomacy* 16 (2021): 299–322.

56. Joseph S. Nye, *Bound to Lead: The Changing Nature of American Power* (New York: Basic Books, 1990), 31.

57. It is worth noting that China disqualified this notion as a "pseudo-academic concept." Christopher Walker, "What Is 'Sharp Power'?," *Journal of Democracy* 29, no. 3 (2018): 12; Jingkai Shao, "Exploring China's 'Sharp Power': Conceptual Deficiencies and Alternatives," *Transcommunication* 6, no. 2 (2019): 129–48.

58. Dean Cheng, "Challenging China's 'Wolf Warrior' Diplomats," Heritage Foundation, July 6, 2020, 1, https://www.heritage.org/asia/report/challenging-chinas-wolf-warrior-diplomats.

59. Paul Charon and Jean-Baptiste Jeangène Vilmer, *Chinese Influence Operations: A Macchiavellian Moment* (Paris: IRSEM, 2022).

60. Jean-Yves Heurtebise and Emmanuel Dubois de Prisque, eds., "La diplomatie publique chinoise et ses limites," *Monde chinois* 4, no. 60 (2019).

CHAPTER 8

Honors and Dishonors

Table Tennis Champions Representing Ghana Abroad

Claire Nicolas

In September 1961 the *Daily Graphic* urged Ghanaian table tennis champions to "win back the 'Azikiwe Cup,'" and the *Ghanaian Times* suggested that the competition would be "most exciting." As the West African table tennis championship began in Accra, one sports editor promised that "fans will have a lot to cheer about."[1] And Emmanuel Quaye, Ghana's most promising player, made a confident and upbeat assertion: "We will not let Ghana down."[2] This championship was one of the many encounters that took place between African table tennis players, and it was no small event in the eyes of the press, the players themselves, and the nation's sports administration. Following independence, international sports competitions were on the rise on the African continent and rapidly became closely intertwined with Pan-African politics.

The centrality of Ghana in Pan-African ideals and alliances was fostered by Kwame Nkrumah, the Ghanaian head of state from 1957 to 1966. Since the late 1940s, he had been a key actor, part of a broader movement seeking to "create a domination-free and egalitarian international order" on the global stage, beyond bilateral metropolitan-colony relations.[3] As Adom Getachew demonstrates, Nkrumah and others were "worldmakers rather than solely nation builders."[4] Nkrumah relentlessly advocated for Pan-Africanism. This durably influenced Ghana's position and self-perception within African diplomacy. After the 1966 military coup, the Ghanaian National Liberation

Council's military leaders sought to "establish, repair and strengthen Ghana's political and economic relations around the world."[5] They valued Western cooperation in lieu of previous socialist alliances and therefore connected with the United States.

Scholars have explored in detail Ghana's endeavors to make political stands in international sports organizations such as the International Olympic Committee (IOC) and the Fédération Internationale de Football Association (FIFA).[6] But sport was also a cultural tool for fostering friendly relationships throughout the Non-Aligned Movement, especially during the Nkrumah era. Amanda Shuman notably highlights the importance of "Ping-Pong diplomacy" as China tried to get closer to African states in the aftermath of various countries achieving independence.[7]

At the domestic level, the leaders of the Convention People's Party (CPP), which followed Nkrumah's ideas, promoted sports to foster the notion of the New African Man, framed by Pan-Africanism and socialism. This new ideal projected a new form of citizenship, crafted at the domestic level as well as cast abroad and entangled within diplomatic relationships. Sportspeople had a special position in this framework. Since the end of World War II, increased global mobility and strengthened international sports organizations had led to dramatic international sports competitions.[8] Elite sportsmen and sportswomen had thus acquired a new prominence through increased film, radio, and press coverage.[9]

This chapter argues that table tennis players, even from a marginal position—far from the state apparatus and the diplomatic sphere—played their part in Ghana's diplomacy by partaking in a minor sport, as they displayed new definitions of citizenship and nationhood at domestic and international levels. They were involved in the government's aim to "exert power in the international arena through attraction and persuasion, rather than force," seeking to exercise soft power.[10] Furthermore, socialist solidarity was a key feature of table tennis diplomacy (in contrast with postimperial events such as the Commonwealth Games, the men's soccer World Cup, and the Olympic Games), which opens up new perspectives when examining Ghana's multifaceted soft power as the country turned its eyes away from Europe. This chapter thus assesses how Ghana's changing diplomatic relationships framed athletes as cultural emissaries, mediators between Ghana's government and its target audiences abroad.[11] Unpacking sports diplomacy from below, this research discusses the role played by table tennis players themselves in their positions as informal ambassadors who were carefully—albeit only partially—monitored by politicians, journalists, and sports administrators.

This chapter integrates archival material collected from the Accra repository of the Public Records and Archives Administration Department (PRAAD), the National Archives (TNA) of the United Kingdom, the IOC's archives, Ghanaian print media (*Daily Graphic, Ghanaian Times*), and video footage (British Pathé's online database). First, I identify the urban and imperial roots of table tennis and the Pan-African and Non-Aligned Movement turn implemented by the Central Organisation of Sports (COS) after independence. Second, I delve into notions of honor and dishonor as they framed table tennis players' training, games, and travel. Finally, I move beyond the 1966 coup to explore how players navigated damaged relationships between Ghana and Nigeria as their mission to sustain "brotherly" connections became strongly contested.

SETTING UP AFRICAN TABLE TENNIS

Nigeria and Ghana were the most prominent African colonies keen on playing table tennis. In both colonies, this sport had its roots in the post-1945 rise of British imperial welfare politics, as the colonial state sought to channel young men's energy away from political activism and rowdyism.[12] In Ghana, table tennis was mainly played in secondary schools and youth clubs in southern cities, such as in Accra's state-funded Youth Centre and in the YMCA center.[13] The YMCA, a Christian youth organization, set up a table tennis school in Accra as early as 1954, which became a key center for young people who wanted to play the sport. Michael Gennaro shows that table tennis in Nigeria was intertwined with the emergence of competing models of masculinity linked to schooling.[14] In Ghana, though, the game was not solely an out-of-school leisure activity for boys: it was also favored by schoolgirls.[15] Unlike soccer and boxing for men or netball and rounders for women, table tennis was not exclusively linked to manhood or womanhood.[16] While it was not an explicitly "feminine" activity, this indoor sport did not require outstanding displays of physical strength or endurance.

Table tennis was formally introduced to international organizations by a wealthy Indian merchant, D. G. Hathiramani, and his fellow African founders of the Gold Coast Table Tennis Association in 1951. Their work resulted in the association being recognized by the International Table Tennis Federation the very same year. This new membership echoed parallel links between national sports associations and a wide range of international sports organizations. These initiatives were taking place against the backdrop of a global rise of nationalist and anticolonial demands throughout the colonies. In 1951 general elections were held for the first time, and these symbolic links were another way of promoting the autonomy of the country. The table tennis association engaged in a series of bilateral intercolonial annual tournaments with Nigeria from 1952 to 1956.[17]

Following independence, Ghana's government took table tennis to the next level. This project was framed by a more general will to promote and recast Ghanaian sports at both domestic and international levels. During the First Republic (1960–66), the sports administration was led by Ohene Djan. This former member of parliament, who was close to Nkrumah, became the pivot of sports politics for six years. He implemented major changes in Ghanaian sports politics and administration, breaking free from the previous sports model that was based on British amateur associations.[18] Highly critical of previous Ghanaian sports leaders (and wary of their interference), he set up a whole new administration at both intermediate and higher levels. In 1960, out of the 126 employees of the state-led COS, only 11 had ever been involved in sports management.[19] In parallel, he tackled the autonomy of sports associations.[20] Thus, in 1961 Djan broke off from most sports leaders and introduced a second major innovation. Drawing explicitly from the Soviet model of sports administration,[21] he encouraged newly formed state-led structures to hire elite sportsmen and sportswomen: the Builders Brigade, the Farmers Council, the Workers Brigade, the Cocoa Marketing Board, and, of course, his very own COS.[22] He also implemented an unusual setup, encouraging male soccer clubs to become multisport, with hockey, athletics, and table tennis teams, and to include women's sports.[23]

For the new Pan-Africanist government led by Kwame Nkrumah, the will to connect Ghana at the continental level was particularly important for fostering friendships between African nations. The government put a lot of effort into creating the West African Table Tennis Federation in 1957 (Ghana, Nigeria, and Sierra Leone), in order to prepare for the World Table Tennis Championship to be held in China in 1961.[24]

The West African Federation was based in Accra, and its general secretary, Elijah Asamoah, was Ghanaian. He also led the Ghana Table Tennis Association. Although the anglophone members of the federation dominated, it soon welcomed Togo and the Republic of Dahomey (now Benin), both former French colonies.[25] The Ghanaian state invested heavily in this *African* organization, which connected territories previously separated by imperialism and reached beyond linguistic divides. This explicitly echoed Nkrumah's Pan-African diplomacy, as underlined by the minister for defense in 1961 when he opened the federation's general assembly in Accra: "While the Politicians and Statesmen of various countries plan and act for the Unity of our continent, we, as sportsmen, must through sports create an atmosphere of understanding and brotherhood throughout the continent."[26]

This public speech echoed those being given all over Ghana at the time to encourage citizens to support Pan-Africanism. Sportswomen, sportsmen, and sports leaders were not to be put to one side during this project; leaders and Ghanaian table tennis champions were to be at the forefront of this "brotherhood" and "understanding." Indeed, Jeffrey S. Ahlman shows that Nkrumah envisioned Ghana as the beacon of Pan-Africanism. Many "looked to the Accra government for guidance on Africa's future" as a "torrent of local and international optimism" reflected an increasingly demanding set of expectations" expressed by the Ghanaian people and fueled by the CPP.[27] Sportswomen and sportsmen were strongly affected by these changes because, according to politicians and public administrators, they became the "natural ambassadors" of the country during international sports meetings.[28]

As part of its largesse toward sports development in general, the government joined Hathiramani in his effort to fund and promote table tennis and train players. The most prominent champions toured Africa and beyond, leaving Ghana for Nigeria, England, China, and the United States to practice or to take part in high-level competitions. Notably, Emmanuel Quaye trained as a coach for several months in London.[29] As highlighted above, he then toured the United States to undertake complimentary training and play in exhibition games.[30] He was not the only table tennis player to get his name in the press. Newspapers regularly highlighted the performances of other players, such as Emmanuel's younger brother, Okine Quaye, and those of women players: Ethel Jacks and two sisters, Theresa and Ernestina Akuetteh.

Table tennis was also sustained by broader South-South international cooperation and connections. In April 1961 Beijing hosted the International Table Tennis Championship.[31] The competition involved over thirty nations, and China won most events.[32] Three women and four men represented Ghana: Ethel Jacks, the Akuetteh sisters, and the Quaye brothers plus E. A. Aryee and S. K. Allotey. For China, the competition was an opportunity to showcase its success as a socialist and anti-imperialist country. Ghanaian players mostly used their participation in the Beijing championship as an opportunity for improvement, as emphasized by Jacks.[33] But the tournament was equally important on a diplomatic level as only the only African nations to take part were Nigeria and Ghana. Nkrumah personally met the team at the airport on their return to commend their achievements.[34]

The event further encouraged the rise of table tennis in the country. First, a national talent-hunt festival was organized in December 1961, and champions publicly called for more attention to be paid to the sport.[35] Second, Ohene Djan asked China for a ping-pong delegation comprising coaches and players (male and female) to go to Ghana to help the national team for the first African table tennis championship to be held by the end of the year in Cairo. This was transformed into an African tour by Chinese trainers and athletes in the spring of 1962, and one Chinese coach, Wang Chuanyao, stayed for three months.[36] Chinese ping-pong specialists visited Egypt, Ghana, Guinea, Mali, and Sudan, sent by their government to demonstrate the camaraderie that existed between the Chinese and African people. As Amanda Shuman suggested, "couched in terms of Afro-Asian solidarity, sports exchanges such as this one thus served as platforms for promoting Chinese socialism at home and abroad."[37] Once again, the Accra airport was a particularly important place to perform politics: Ethel Jacks and Emmanuel Quaye welcomed their guests with a Chinese folk song.[38]

HONORS AND DISHONORS

Ghanaian table tennis rose rapidly at the continental level following the creation of the African Table Tennis Federation in December 1961.[39] Emmanuel Quaye won the African championship in 1962, while Ethel Jacks won in 1964, alongside other successes for their team.[40] Consequently, the players' behaviors and morals were closely scrutinized by the public and politicians.

In 1962 Ghana's parliament reflected on the sportsmen and sportswomen's success, praising their achievements. But members of parliament also took an interest in their behavior, commending the players' dedication to their homeland that interwove nationalism, futurity, and effort:

> On the continent of Africa, Ghana is second to none except the UAR [United Arab Republic]. Last year, Ghana carved a name by winning the annual West Africa International Table Tennis Contest. It is not the totality of the victory that matters. It is the achievement. And since then, Ghana has intensified in coaching, and there is every hope in our players defending Ghana whenever they may be called up to do so. Now with the opportunities being offered for international competition I cannot imagine what our boys and girls will not do in the foreseeable future.[41]

Following this discussion fueled by a heroic lexicon, the champions won in Cairo as exemplary and dutiful Ghanaian citizens.

In parallel with such political praise and encouragement, the champions' sporting achievements abroad were highly praised in the press, notably in articles in the privately owned *Daily Graphic* and the state-oriented *Ghanaian Times*, their photographs appeared in sports columns, and they were shown either in traveling clothes or during games, dressed in white skirts or shorts.[42] Expectations of them were high, particularly as they were viewed as embodying perfect, idealized young Ghanaian citizens. Indeed, both the press and the parliament emphasized values such as discipline, responsibility, honor, and duty. But players did not always meet such expectations.

In 1961 Hathiramani, expressed his disappointment regarding the training that Theresa and Ernestina Akuetteh and Ethel Jacks were doing for the next West African championship, to be held in Lagos, Nigeria, in 1962. He wrote in a letter to Ohene Djan that he was "very much disappointed to say that they are neither regular nor very serious" and asked him to scold the players.[43] Their behavior, as well as their sports skills, was deemed unprofessional.

Although the three women behaved in line with expectations at the 1962 championship, (where Ethel Jacks held on to her title), Okine Quaye was the focus of the authorities' attention. He was then sixteen years old and a student at O'Reilly Secondary School in Accra. Despite his sporting prowess, he had been highly criticized for his scandalous behavior when he assaulted another member of the national table tennis team, E. K. Ekuban, during the West African championship in Lagos in 1961.[44] After a six-month suspension, he returned to the national team but was suspended again in 1963 because of his behavior at the West African championship that took place in Accra. Following his suspension, he made a public statement:

> I . . . humbly and respectfully apologise for my disgraceful behaviour last Saturday night during the International Table-Tennis Championships at the Sports Hall. My behaviour was very bad, I have realised that I have disgraced myself, my father, my Headmaster and Ghana. Because of this I beg you for forgiveness. I promise, from the bottom of my heart, never again in my life to display such foolish conduct anywhere again here or elsewhere. I am now a new boy. I have changed for the better. Whether in private life or in public, I promise to be an honour to God, you, my father, and all. I will always obey my coaches and umpires and accept all their decisions. Kindly pardon me and pray to God for me.[45]

Despite his intense and detailed apologies, Quaye was banned indefinitely. Because of his repeated behavior, he was considered to be a danger to the country's reputation and honor and remained suspended in spite of his excellent sporting performances and the risk of reducing Ghana's chances of victory in upcoming events. His letter, published in the *Daily Graphic*, reveals the importance attached to behavior by the COS, especially when players were attending international competitions. The text asserts the idea of a homeland and emphasizes the respect he owed to his country and to male elders, who embodied family and school authority. Overriding Elijah Asamoah's authority, Ohene Djan finally accepted Quaye's apologies and reinstated him in the national team soon after the letter's publication.[46] The shame he had suffered by making the public apology and being suspended from the team seemed like a proper punishment.

But the young player misbehaved again. Despite Okine Quaye's promises to "never again . . . display such foolish conduct," he provoked yet another scandal during the world championships held in Yugoslavia in May 1965. The *Daily Graphic* reported, "Okine Quaye misconducted himself during the world championships at the competition hall, when he 'openly assaulted Miss Ethel Jacks, a member of the Ghana team, without justification.' The report [by Quaye's evaluation committee further] said Okine Quaye, at the material time was engaged in mixed doubles match with Miss Ernestina Akuetteh. Miss Jacks was sharing a joke with Miss Akuetteh when Okine Quaye left the table unceremoniously and assaulted Miss Jacks."[47]

Following this assault, an evaluation committee was set up to investigate the behavior of the young player, by then eighteen years old. He was banned for life by Ohene Djan. Just like in relation to the previous incident, this had more to do with endangering the country's honor in public than for being violent. Indeed, the archives of both the COS and the press only seem to record such incidents during international competitions, not during domestic events. If Quaye's misbehavior only took place during international competitions, it meant that such international settings mattered—and that it was the image of the country or, rather, its honor that was at stake. According to the evaluation committee's report, Quaye's behavior in 1965 "caused a great stir and embarrassment."[48]

The ban was lifted only in 1968, by the new director of sports who was appointed after Nkrumah and his government were overthrown by a military coup in 1966. Okine Quaye promised again to behave properly or the sports authorities "should never have anything to do with [him] for the rest of [his] life."[49] The same year, Quaye, his older brother Emmanuel Quaye, and Ethel Jacks once again swept up every trophy available to them at the third All-Africa Table Tennis Championship held in Lagos, and Emmanuel and Ethel became African champions. Playing at the University of Lagos in front of a small but enthusiastic crowd as well as local officials, they defeated the Liberian and UAR champions, respectively, before being presented with huge silver trophies.[50]

Okine Quaye's turbulent trajectory and that of more conventional champions, such as Emmanuel Quaye, Ethel Jacks, and the Akuetteh sisters, reflect the high level of interest that the Ghanaian government had in their sporting results, their training, and, most of all, in their behavior; they represented the nation but had to remain subordinate to the nation's expectations. This was neatly summarized by a member of parliament in 1962: "I also congratulate stars like . . . the Quaye brothers . . . and the numerous sportsmen and sportswomen who represent Ghana at national and international games for obeying and accepting the training programmes of the Central Organisation of Sport. And for them to bring fame and glory to Ghana we give them our hearty cheers."[51]

As expectations rose to a high level, sportswomen and sportsmen were increasingly asked to behave in an exemplary manner and to perform their roles as "ambassadors of the Ghana spirit and the Ghana way of life."[52] Their successes were deemed important because they showcased "superior skills, a better understanding of sports, and more important of all, strong spirit of cooperation and goodwill."[53] But their behavior was even more closely monitored when they did not follow the expected path, as seen in the case of Okine Quaye. Tales of apologies and forgiveness thus fueled the press,[54] although they were less about actual individual allegiances and more about the various stories' performative power. As even the most commendable sports stars could be brought to heel, their humility toward the state— illustrated in the *Daily Graphic* and the *Ghanaian Times*—was a lesson for ordinary citizens.

DECLINE OF GHANA'S IMAGE AT INTERNATIONAL COMPETITIONS

Following the 1966 coup, Ghana took a step back from the international and African sports scene. In that year, owing to the coup, Ohene Djan—who was leading the country in most international sports organizations—was sacked.[55] Ghana's National Liberation Council distanced itself from African and global diplomacy at large and notably from Pan-African organizations. Domestic authoritarianism and an economic crisis largely influenced the change implemented in the realm of sports diplomacy as Djan's international actions were rightly understood as stemming from Kwame Nkrumah's

Pan-African politics. Thus, while decisions were being made regarding nominations, the organization of events, and sponsorship at the international level, Ghana's sports administration was about to face a few turbulent years. After Djan's dismissal, different officials came and went, and many letters crossed and remained unanswered owing to this power vacuum.[56]

In 1969 the short-term military-led National Liberation Council let Kofi Abrefa Busia, who headed the Progress Party, run for election, and he became head of state. In a context of deep economic recession and harsh financial restraints, the new sports director, Francis Selormey, was not as keen as his predecessors to be present on the international stage at all costs. Furthermore, Ghana's foreign policy at this time did not target international organizations as aggressively as it used to. Thus, when the chairman of the English Table Tennis Association asked both Nigeria and Ghana to select someone to be the African representative for Commonwealth-related events,[57] Selormey's answer was quite diplomatic and friendly: "I am sure you will agree with me that our two sister countries have everything in common stemming from a very long tradition and that our objects and aspirations are identical. What affects Nigeria therefore affects Ghana as well."[58]

The idea that both countries' aspirations were "identical" marked a break from Ohene Djan's desire to be at the forefront of most events. Adegboyega Efunkoya, chairman of the Nigeria Table Tennis Federation, thus became the African representative on the Commonwealth Table Tennis Organisation.[59] This nomination reflected a broader trend. Various Nigerian officials became members of the IOC's and Commonwealth Games' boards, and Abraham Ordia became the chairman of the Supreme Council for Sport in Africa, famously advocating the boycotting of apartheid countries, as Ohene Djan had done.[60] However, in Ghana not everyone had a position as pragmatic and friendly as that of Selormey when it came to the "sisterly" relationship that could be maintained between Ghana and Nigeria.

Sports journalists, on the contrary, put the rivalry between the two countries to the fore. For example, Nana Addo-Twum, the sports editor of the *Daily Graphic*, compared in an unfavorable light Ghana's decline in international sports organizations with the rise of the Ivory Coast (now Côte d'Ivoire) and Nigeria:

> The decline of Ghana's image in international sports meeting should be the concern of all lovers of sports in the country. At the moment we have M. Abraham Ordia of Nigeria.... Our other neighbour, Ivory Coast, has also a member serving on the International Olympic Committee in the person or Mr Louis Guirandou N'Diaye....

We have no men to fight for our cause in time of crisis. The people at the helm of our sports organisation must buck up and improve upon our image. This weak point stems from the selection of poor type of personalities accompanying our teams to international matches.[61]

Strong criticism of officials accompanying teams abroad became pervasive in the 1970s in the press and within sports institutions.[62] This was also an opportunity to voice a more fundamental (albeit implicit) criticism of the corruption of Ghana's administration and the broader economic hardship that affected Ghanaians at large.[63] Against this backdrop, the specific case of Nigeria took center stage, but this did not occur in the previously mentioned "sisterly" manner.

In November 1969 Ghana's Prime Minister Busia issued the Alien Compliance Order, expelling every foreigner from the country. Targeting the large Nigerian community that had settled in Ghana, this decision stemmed from a rising xenophobia in the late 1960s as Nigerians became the scapegoats for the economic crisis.[64] They were also increasingly targeted for supposedly meddling in national politics.[65] This xenophobia had a longer history. However, it became particularly acute as thousands of Nigerians were expelled from Ghana in November and December 1969.[66]

Only a few months later, in August 1970, the Ghana national table tennis team traveled to Lagos to take part in the West African championship. The competitors were from Ghana, Nigeria, Togo, Mali, Sierra Leone, Niger, Liberia, Dahomey (now Benin), and Upper Volta (now Burkina Faso). Emmanuel Quaye was by this time both team captain and national coach. He flew to Lagos with ten players (five women and five men) and Nat Opinam, the official representative of the Ghana Table Tennis Association.[67]

But everything went wrong for the Ghanaian group. From a sporting perspective, the final games were "all Nigerian affairs, as Ghana, pioneers of the West African Table Tennis, became mere spectators."[68] The description provided by the Ghana Sports Council was severe: Ghana's hopes were "dashed" during this "day of bad luck."

The *Sports Bulletin*, a weekly newsletter published by the Ghana Sports Council, deplored the defeat of the Ghanaians. In no fewer than three long articles, officials wrote emotionally about the disappointment: "And for the first time in the championship series, Ghana did not only lose its leading position but returned home without a single trophy. A strong critic will simply pass this off as an ignoble feat by the Ghanaian team but a true analysis is far more important as a yard-stick for passing judgement than bare-face results."[69]

As Ghana had been dominating the championship for the previous twenty years, this outcome, without a single title, was particularly harsh for the sports authorities, who had expected great results, even in the absence of Ethel Jacks.[70] But, differentiating sports from national honor, they excused the Ghanaian team: "With its usual sense of absolute nationalism, [the team] fought grimly but crumpled against a more skilful, more determined and better prepared side which had also an advantage of home support. It is an undeniable fact that the standard of table tennis in Nigeria has risen beyond expectation."[71]

However, after recognizing the undeniable rise of Nigeria in table tennis, Ghanaian authors quickly moved away from sporting matters, targeting their Nigerian hosts by using extremely harsh words. One said that "in an apparent move to punish the Ghanaians for demanding a decent accommodation, Nigerians have tried hard to break down the Ghanaians physically and morally."[72] The Ghanaians complained of deficient accommodations, lack of training facilities, and below-standard sports equipment and reported their heated objections. The lexicon used in the *Sports Bulletin* to express these accusations echoed broader xenophobic terminology against Nigerians, targeted in Ghana for being "clannish," "thrifty," and "arrogant."[73] Further, paper claimed that

> Nigeria adopted inhuman treatment to the participating teams.... The Nigerian officials played hide and seek with the team.... Quickly the six men and the leader of the team, Mr Nat Opintam, suspected that the Nigerians were once more up to their tricks.... The Nigerians made sure that the Ghanaian did not get the chance to train and got [sic] used to the atmosphere of the hall and the tables which the Ghanaians described as "out of international quality."[74]

Ghanaians were annoyed about what they perceived to be the Nigerians' lack of civility and formulated the view that their hosts should have followed diplomatic conventions, given the significance of such an international sporting event. This report was not meant for Nigerian eyes (even though it found its way into the IOC archives) and did not give any more clues regarding the behavior of the Ghanaian team and whether they themselves upheld the etiquette expected of informal ambassadors.[75]

Furthermore, the poor welcome given to the table tennis players—which was particularly blatant for the female players, who were not even invited to the opening ceremony and struggled to find decent accommodations—was far from being anecdotal as it reflected a particularly difficult political context. Nigeria was facing intense conflicts regarding the allocation of political power and resources stemming successive military coups and the Biafran War as well as the growing unpopularity of Ghana at large.[76]

All in all, the "sisterly" relations between table tennis officials the previous year and the "brotherhood" promoted by the West African Table Tennis Conference in 1961 seemed quite distant when the players and managers were quarreling with their Nigerian hosts at the championship.

CONCLUSION

The anger and disappointment expressed by table tennis officials during the 1970 Lagos championship did not solely relate to the bad relationship between Ghana and Nigeria. Indeed, in contemporary interviews, sportsmen and sportswomen from the 1970s reminisced about the hardship they faced because the country was in a state of constant economic crisis, compared to the largesse of Djan's COS in the early 1960s. This was notably the case for Ethel Jacks, who became an international champion with her first African title in 1964. She was a single mother without a university degree and with limited economic prospects, and because of the government's lack of support, she moved to Nigeria (her parents' home country), even though she said she wanted to "serve my country." She eventually represented Nigeria during the 1976 African championship and became a coach there before returning to Ghana a few years later.[77] Focusing on the trajectories of Ethel Jacks and her teammates—either while they were famous or afterward—allows marginal actors in Ghana's Pan-African diplomacy to be put to the fore. Furthermore, the stress on their behavior, honorable or otherwise, was an integral part of the country's cultural diplomacy, which stemmed from a more general concern with building a new, ideal postcolonial citizenship.

In the end this history of the Ghanaian table tennis champions' travels, defeats, and victories, as well as the negotiations conducted by sports administrators, was part of a larger project to "place Ghana firmly on the map" of international sports diplomacy.[78] It allows an understanding of sports as a soft power with two sides.

On one hand, it was performed and discussed by state actors, such as directors, ministers, and members of parliament, when they endeavored to promote Ghanaian sports or used it to promote Ghana's image abroad. In the introduction of this edited volume, Sylvia Dummer Scheel, Charlotte Faucher, and Camila Gatica Mizala emphasized that countries from the Global South had been exercising intense cultural diplomacy work for a long time.[79] In this sense, Ghana was a true agent of soft power. Far from the country only being a target of Western endeavors, its administrators and politicians followed their own objectives, at regional and global scales. Hence, during the First Republic, table tennis was explicitly used as an instrument for strengthening Pan-African unity and the Non-Aligned Movement.

On the other hand, sportsmen and sportswomen got involved as well as informal representatives. Ghanaian table tennis champions were not as closely monitored as Soviet cultural emissaries (who were carefully selected to perform according to the Soviet model[80]), their roles as representatives of their nation were more imprecise—that is, more loosely defined. However, state control remained pervasive, as highlighted by successive admonishments as well as careful scrutiny of international competitions. As "intermediate agents," table tennis players "responded not only to the interests of the soft power agent, but also to their own motivations and personal perceptions,"[81] and they had room to maneuver, as showcased by Okine Quaye's unruly spirit and Ethel Jacks's move to Nigeria. Thus, even if political actors aimed at presenting a neat image of upstanding and nationalist sportsmen and sportswomen to their "sister" African countries, the athletes did not necessarily comply. From this perspective, if one cannot assume what the consequences of such ambiguous performances abroad were, the quest of political actors for soft power was quite evocative. It engaged a conversation about how Ghana's head of state and politicians wanted to define and present their citizens and for which audience. In this case, the ideal Pan-African citizen was to be perceived by fellow Africans to be strong, healthy, and successful but also dutiful, hardworking, and loyal.

NOTES

I would like to thank Sylvia Dummer Scheel, Charlotte Faucher, and Camila Gatica Mizala for inviting me to circulate this research at the online workshop organized in December 2021, "Soft Power beyond National Allegiances," and for its participants' constructive criticism and advice. I would also like to thank Beverley Sykes and Georgetown University Press's editors for their careful reading and correction of the manuscript.

1. "We Should Win Back the 'Azikiwe Cup,'" *Daily Graphic*, September 9, 1961; "West African Table Tennis Championship Starts Today," *Ghanaian Times*, September 29, 1961.
2. "West African Table Tennis Championship Starts Today."
3. Adom Getachew, *Worldmaking after Empire: The Rise and Fall of Self-Determination* (Princeton, NJ: Princeton University Press, 2019), 2.
4. Getachew, 3.

5. Bianca Murillo, *Market Encounters: Consumer Cultures in Twentieth-Century Ghana* (Athens: Ohio University Press, 2017), 126.

6. Claire Nicolas and Philippe Vonnard, "Ohene Djan: An Ambivalent Position between Pan-Africanism and Internationalism," *Staps* 3, no. 125 (2019): 49–68; Paul Darby, *Africa, Football, and FIFA: Politics, Colonialism, and Resistance* (London: Franck Cass, 2002).

7. Amanda Shuman, "Friendship Is Solidarity: The Chinese Ping Pong Team Visits Africa in 1962," in *Sport and Diplomacy: Games within Games,* ed. Simon J. Rofe (Manchester: Manchester University Press, 2018), 110–29.

8. For recent discussions of sports and diplomacy, see Simon J. Rofe, "Sport and Diplomacy: A Global Diplomacy Framework," *Diplomacy and Statecraft* 27, no. 2 (2016): 212–30, and Patrick Clastres, "Olympisme et guerre froide: Du paradigme réaliste au paradigme culturel," *Guerres mondiales et conflits contemporains* 1, no. 277 (2020): 7–25.

9. Sports and cinema/television histories are closely intertwined. For instance, Flora Losch recently noted that the first live TV program in Senegal broadcasted the 1972 Munich Olympic Games. Flora Losch, "Les pérégrinations de Guy Bernède, acteur et témoin de la coopération télévisuelle post-indépendances: De l'Ocora Télévision à FR3 Dom-Tom (1962–1975)," *Revue d'histoire contemporaine de l'Afrique* 1 (2021): 159–62.

10. Sylvia Dummer Scheel, Charlotte Faucher, and Camila Gatica Mizala, "Introduction," present volume.

11. Dummer Scheel, Faucher, and Gatica Mizala.

12. Laurent Fourchard, *Trier, exclure et policer: Vies urbaines en Afrique du Sud et au Nigeria* (Paris: Presses de Sciences Po, 2018).

13. Invitation by the acting director of the Gold Coast Social Welfare and Housing Department to attend the semifinals of Accra Youth Centre's table tennis competition, December 31, 1946, Public Records and Archives Administration Department (hereafter PRAAD), CSO 25.1.121.

14. Michael J. Gennaro, "'I Was Really Disgusted at Seeing Healthy Young Boys Playing Ping-Pong': Ping-Pong and Masculinity in Post–World War II Nigeria," in *Sports in African History, Politics, and Identity Formation,* ed. Michael J. Gennaro and Saheed Aderinto (Abingdon, UK: Routledge, 2019), 14–26.

15. Future champion Ethel Jacks joined the YMCA training when she was fifteen years old, in 1958. Ethel Jacks, "Exclusive Interview with Africa's Female Table Tennis Legend Ethel Jacks," interview by Samuel Delali Zigah, *YouTube,* December 20, 2019, video, 43:53, https://www.youtube.com/watch?v=9-Ozeoutpil.

16. Reports on physical education by the Education Department officers Catrine Miller and I. B. Boye-Doye, 1955–56, PRAAD, RG 3.5.1570.

17. Kwasi Opoku-Fianko, "The Growth and Development of Physical Education and Sports in Ghana" (PhD diss., Ohio State University, 1985).

18. James A. Mangan, *The Games Ethic and Imperialism: Aspects of the Diffusion of an Ideal* (London: Franck Cass, 1986).

19. Minutes of the Executive Committee of the Ghana Amateur Sports Council, April 7, 1960, PRAAD, RG.9.1.18.

20. Minutes of the Executive Committee of the Ghana Amateur Sports Council, May 26, 1960, PRAAD, RG 9.1.92.

21. Sylvain Dufraisse, *Les héros du sport: Une histoire des champions soviétiques (années 1930–années 1980)* (Ceyzérieu, Fr.: Champ Vallon, 2019).

22. List of employees of the COS, 1963, PRAAD, RG 9.1.37; Letter from S. K. Danko (Great Ashanti Sporting Club) to Nana Fredua Mensah (president of the Ghana Amateur Football Association), August 23, 1966, PRAAD, RG 9.1.21.

23. Letter from Francis Selormey (director of sports) to William Ofori Atta (minister for education), December 15, 1969, PRAAD, RG 9.1.45.

24. D. G. Hathiramani, interview by Kwasi Opoku-Fianko, in Opoku-Fianko, "Physical Education and Sports in Ghana," 171.

25. Letter from Elijah Asamoah (general secretary of the West African Table Tennis Federation) to Blaise Soglo (general secretary of the Fédération Dahoméenne de Tennis de Table), May 2, 1962, PRAAD, RG 9.1.122.

26. Kofi Baako (minister for defense), opening speech, sixth general assembly of the West African Table Tennis Federation, October 28, 1961, PRAAD, RG 9.1.122.

27. Jeffrey S. Ahlman, *Living with Nkrumahism: Nation, State, and Pan-Africanism in Ghana* (Athens: Ohio University Press, 2017), 85–86.

28. Speech by Charles Ebenezer Donkoh (Wenchi West District, Brong-Ahafo Region), September 30, 1964, in Ghana National Assembly, *Parliamentary Debates: Official Report* (Accra: Government Printing Department, 1965), 113.

29. "Scholarship for Coaching Course: Mr E. A. Quaye," August 22, 1960, PRAAD, RG 9.1.107.

30. "'Bring Back New Ideas,'" *Daily Graphic*, November 1, 1961; "Table Tennis Star Quaye to Tour America," *Ghanaian Times*, October 6, 1961.

31. The Ghanaians' visit to Beijing may be connected to a broader trend implemented by the People's Republic of China, as the government invited cultural visitors in the 1960s to admire the "successes" of the country. This was notably the case for Chilean intellectuals and Swiss "friendship associations," as demonstrated by Cyril Cordoba and Maria Montt Strabucchi in this volume.

32. China won the men's team competition, the men's singles, and the women's singles. Japan won the women's team competition, the men's doubles, and the mixed doubles. Romania won the women's doubles. "China's Men and Japan's Women Win Championship," *Peking Review*, April 14, 1961.

33. Jacks, "Exclusive Interview."

34. Hathiramani, interview.

35. E. K. Ekuban, "What about Table Tennis?," *Daily Graphic*, November 15, 1961.

36. Shuman, "Friendship Is Solidarity," 116.

37. Amanda Shuman, "From Soviet Kin to Afro-Asian Leader: The People's Republic of China and International Sport in the Early 1960s," *Comparativ* 23, no. 3 (2013): 85.

38. Shuman, "Friendship Is Solidarity," 117.

39. "Unprecedented Times for Africa," *International Table Tennis Federation*, May 6, 2022, https://www.ittf.com/2022/05/06/unprecedented-times-africa/.

40. Jacks, "Exclusive Interview."

41. Ebenezer Adam (Gulkpego-Nanton District, Northern Region), speech, December 5, 1962, in Ghana National Assembly, *Parliamentary Debates: Official Report* (Accra: Government Printing Department, 1962), 54.

42. "We Should Win Back 'Azikiwe Cup,'" *Daily Graphic*, September 29, 1961.

43. D. G. Hathiramani, "Progress Report on the Training of the International Players for the West African Table Tennis Championship," September 11, 1961, PRAAD, RG 9.1.122.

44. "Ban on Okine Lifted," *Daily Graphic*, June 19, 1968.

45. Letter from Okine Quaye to Elijah Asamoah, October 10, 1963, PRAAD. RG 9.1.122.

46. Handwritten comment by Ohene Djan on Okine Quaye's letter.

47. Okine Quaye's evaluation committee report, in "Ban on Okine Lifted."

48. Okine Quaye's evaluation committee report.

49. Okine Quaye's evaluation committee report.

50. "Nigeria: Third All-Africa Table Tennis Championships Ends 1968," 1968, University of Lagos, video, 02:24, https://www.britishpathe.com/video /VLVA80JI15VXKJBLRLF70HKXL2ODL-NIGERIA-THIRD-ALL-AFRICA -TABLE-TENNIS-CHAMPIONSHIPS-ENDS/query/Ghana+Table+tennis.

51. Ebenezer Adam, speech, December 5, 1962, 56.

52. Christiana Wilmot (second member from the Central and Western Regions), speech, December 5, 1962, in Ghana National Assembly, *Parliamentary Debates: Official Report* (Accra: Government Printing Department, 1962), 60.

53. Wilmot, 61.

54. We might also note Wilberforce Mfum's case. A player on the soccer club Asante Kotoko, he protested against Djan's soccer policies during a game played on African Unity Day in 1963, which was being watched by Nkrumah himself. Similarly, Christiana "Christie" Boateng, in spite of being regularly depicted as a model for other athletes, also had to publicly apologize. "Christie: Sorry; She's Set for the Big Game," *Daily Graphic*, April 2, 1962; "Yesterday's Match," *Daily Graphic*, July 29, 1963.

55. *The Tibo Committee Report on Ghana Sports* (Accra: Government Printing Department, 1967); *Report of the Manyo-Plange (Assets) Commission, Appointed under the Commissions of Enquiry Act, 1964 (Act 250) and N.L.C. (Investigation and Forfeiture of Assets) Decree, 1966 (N.L.C.D. 72) to Enquire into the Assets of Specified Persons* (Accra: Government Printing Department, 1969).

56. Handwritten comments on a letter from Charles Itabor (Nigeria Table Tennis Federation) to Conrad Jashke (English Table Tennis Association), June 10, 1969, PRAAD, RG 1.133.

57. Letter from Conrad Jashke to L. T. Caesar (director of sports) and M. A. Alabi (Nigeria Table Tennis Federation), May 2, 1969, PRAAD, RG 1.133.

58. Letter from Francis Selormey (director of sport) to M. A. Alabi, June 13, 1969, PRAAD, RG 1.133.

59. Letter from Charles Itabor to Conrad Jaschke, June 10, 1969, PRAAD, RG 1.133.

60. Pascal Camara, "A Divided House: The Foundation and Evolution of the Supreme Council for Sport in Africa, 1965–2013," *Sport in History* (2023): 1–23.

61. "Talking Sports with Addo Twum," *Daily Graphic*, August 24, 1970.

62. E.g., the 1975 Men's Hockey World Cup led to strenuous complaints against the team manager and coach, whose behavior shocked both players and officials. As recollected by commissioner Lt.-Col. K. B. Agbo, "His turn out was below the required standard most of the time. As an example, he wore one round neck [shirt] and one torn trousers most of the time in Kuala Lumpur. On one occasion, at a dinner party when he had to bend down to perform a ceremony, most guests at the right places could see the split bottom of his trousers." K. B. Agbo, "Report on the Visit of the National Hockey Team to the Third World Hockey Competition, Kuala Lumpur," April 1975, PRAAD, RG 9.1.46.

63. Albert Adu Boahen, *The Ghanaian Sphinx: Reflections on the Contemporary History of Ghana, 1972–1987* (Accra: Sankofa Educational Publisher, 1992).

64. Samuel Fury Childs Daly, "Ghana Must Go: Nativism and the Politics of Expulsion in West Africa, 1969–1985," *Past and Present* 259, no. 1 (2023): 229–61.

65. Letter from Harold Smedley (British High Commission in Accra) to David Hunt (British High Commission in Lagos), September 30, 1967, National Archives of the United Kingdom (hereafter TNA), DO 153.60.

66. Jonson Olaosebikan Aremu and Adeyinka Theresa Ajayi, "Expulsion of Nigerian Immigrant Community from Ghana in 1969: Causes and Impact," *Developing Country Studies* 4, no. 10 (2014): 176–86; Nana Osei Quashie, "Mass Expulsion as Internal Exclusion: Police Raids and the Imprisonment of West African Immigrants in Ghana, 1969–1974," in *Confinement, Punishment and Prisons in Africa*, ed. Marie Morelle, Frédéric Le Marcis, and Julia Hornberger (London: Routledge, 2021), 194–234.

67. *Sports Bulletin* 1, no. 11 (August 1970), 12, IOC, D-RM01-Ghana.

68. "International," *Sports Bulletin* 1, no. 12 (August 1970), 8, IOC, D-RM01-Ghana.

69. "The West African Table Tennis Championship," *Sports Bulletin* 1, no. 12 (August 1970), 11, IOC, D-RM01-Ghana.

70. Ethel Jacks eventually won the singles title at the 1974 African Table Tennis Championship, the third African title she won while representing Ghana.

71. "West African Table Tennis Championship."

72. "International."

73. Aremu and Ajayi, "Expulsion of Nigerian Immigrant Community from Ghana in 1969."

74. "West African Table Tennis Championship."

75. See Charlotte Faucher's discussion in "Women, Gender and the Professionalisation of French Cultural Diplomacy in Britain, 1900–1940," *English Historical Review* 136, no. 583 (2021): 1516–17.

76. Getachew, *Worldmaking after Empire*, 103; Letter from Douglas Reid (British High Commission in Accra) to G. D. Anderson (British High Commission in Accra), August 25, 1967, TNA, DO 153.60; Telegram from the British High Commissioner in Accra to the Foreign and Commonwealth Office, December 22, 1969, TNA, FCO 65.292.

77. Jacks, "Exclusive Interview."

78. Public speech by Ohene Djan broadcast on national television and radio, October 1964, PRAAD, RG 9.1.7.

79. Dummer Scheel, Faucher, and Gatica Mizala, "Introduction."

80. This mix of different strategies may also be perceived in other African countries in the 1960s. In chapter 10 of the present volume, Coline Desportes underlined that it was the case in Senegal where the president and poet Leopold Sédar Senghor partly drew from French cultural diplomacy to build an artistic Senegalese soft power. See also Sylvain Dufraisse, Sophie Momzikoff, and Rafael Pedemonte, "Les Soviétiques hors d'URSS: Quels voyages pour quelles expériences?" *Les Cahiers Sirice* 2, no. 16 (2016): 11–18.

81. Dummer Scheel, Faucher, and Gatica Mizala, "Introduction."

CHAPTER 9

Nonlinear Cultural Diplomacy

A Latin American Traveler to China during the Cold War

Maria Montt Strabucchi

On December 9, 1970, in Santiago, Chile, at the park Cerro Santa Lucía,[1] the Museo de Arte Popular Americano (MAPA; Museum of American Popular Art) inaugurated an exhibition of Chinese art in homage to Salvador Allende's election as president.[2] Much of MAPA's Chinese art collection was a result of the cultural diplomacy of the People's Republic of China (PRC), most of the collection having been donated to the museum when it was under the direction of Tomás Lago, who had founded the museum in 1944 and led it until 1968. Lago himself was invited to the PRC in 1957 by the Chinese government. A month after the exhibition of Chinese art opened, on January 5, 1971, Chile and the PRC announced publicly that they were establishing diplomatic relations. Until then, Chile had diplomatic relations with the Republic of China (ROC), or Taiwan.

During the 1950s and 1960s, the PRC had tried to get around its international isolation by developing a program that has been described in the literature as "cultural diplomacy." Like the United States and the Soviet Union during the Cold War, the PRC, using different associations both abroad and in China,[3] sent out invitations to various groups of foreign visitors. Through cultural diplomacy, the PRC hoped that these strategies of public diplomacy would shape guests' views during their visits and that, once back home, they would report positively on their visit, thus becoming precious agents of soft power. The diverse results of the invitations contributed to sharing knowledge about the host country.[4] Bypassing traditional diplomatic structures, people-to-people diplomacy became an important way through which the PRC developed links with other countries,[5] including Chile. By the end of 1959, 27,204 people had visited the PRC as part of the country's program of invitations,[6] and yet we still know little about the several hundred Latin American visitors who traveled to China via these invitations. Some of them, we know, published magazines or books. In Argentina, for example, the magazines *Cultura China* and *Capricornio* shared contents on China and Chinese culture.[7] In Chile, Professor Olga Poblete de Espinoza, who also traveled to the PRC, published the books *Hablemos de China nueva* (Let us talk about new China) (1953) and, two years later, *Tres ensayos para una historia cultural de China: Para una mejor comprensión de nuestros vecinos de la ribera occidental del Pacífico* (Three essays for a cultural history of China: For a better understanding of our neighbors on the western coast of the Pacific) (1955). Despite some exceptions,[8] we still understand very little about how audiences in Latin America acknowledged Chinese soft power policies and how they were understood at the local level at the time.

This chapter considers travelers as foreign intermediaries of (Chinese) soft power. It does so by departing from the top-down approach favored by historians of the Cold War, who often think about soft power solely as an instrument of state diplomacy. It also examines how foreign visitors were part of what I call "nonlinear cultural diplomacy," whereby soft power is articulated in alternative ways I shall attempt to describe.

Travelers were central to nonlinear cultural diplomacy, and the present analysis considers that, on one hand, they were on the receiving end of the PRC's soft power and, on the other, they acted as foreign intermediaries and were thus part of the PRC's soft power. As mediators between their country and China, they did not necessarily become a mouthpiece for the PRC. The experience of travel expressed in different ways, such as public talks, columns in newspapers, publications, and even private conversations, contributed to creating knowledge about China mediated by the traveler's own experience.

Focusing on a Latin American visitor, the Chilean Tomás Lago, and using sources available at the Foreign Affairs Archives in Santiago and the Shanghai Municipal Archives, the chapter will address the following questions: What role did foreign visitors play within Chinese soft power toward Latin America? What ideas did they disseminate about the country? Did these align with PRC's expectations? How did audiences in Latin America respond to Chinese soft power strategies, and how were they reworked at the local level? While Lago was one of many travelers invited by China,[9] studying his life permits a broader methodological intervention in studies of soft power because it allows tracing how soft power was disseminated and reworked at a local level. The chapter concludes that travelers produced public knowledge about the PRC that often departed from revolutionary discourses churned out by PRC officials. I argue that travelers were not passive recipients of the PRC's policies. Instead, I suggest that their exercise of agency (and their differences with the host country) contributed to the development of China's soft power—traveler-exercised agency that must be integrated into studies of soft power.

Soft power operated on a national level but was also part of broader global dynamics marked by the Cold War, mediated by persons who were inserted in such dynamics. It is among the latter that we must situate travelers' experiences and writings of their trip to the PRC. By establishing a "dialogue" between Lago's travel account and his professional work and introducing the idea of delayed effect and nonlinear cultural diplomacy, I argue in this chapter that Latin American visitors interrupted public diplomacy objectives formulated by the PRC government, although they still contributed to China's cultural diplomacy and soft power. Because of works such as Lago's, the PRC was presented in more holistic terms and not filtered exclusively for its political and revolutionary aspects. More knowledge about the PRC, produced by Chileans, ultimately allowed for a variation of meanings regarding China in Chile that lasted through political changes.

To understand the dynamics of travel to the PRC, the position of the PRC in the international arena as well as the country's international practices need to be considered. On one level, marked by Cold War dynamics, the global position staked out by the PRC was changing as it opened diplomatic relations with more countries, became part of the United Nations (UN) in 1971, and was visited by US president Richard Nixon in 1972. That Chile opened relations with the PRC can also be seen as leading a series of diplomatic recognitions of the PRC by different countries. In terms of the US-Soviet relationship, this period is characterized by détente, which lasted into the late 1970s, while the PRC-Soviet split led to the division of communist parties worldwide. In the case of Chile, the Maoist faction was limited in comparison to the Soviet-inclined Communist Party. At the time, Latin American Marxism was engaged in complex intercontinental dialogues, mostly with Europe but also with Asia.[10] Regarding the reception of Chinese communism, for which the French reading of Maoism and the impact of the Chinese case on Europe was central to the process,[11] direct exchange between the PRC and Latin American people also played its part. The influence of the PRC in Chile depended on the decision and will of local actors,[12] and as Jian Ren argues, specific figures and their relationship with the PRC through travel and with Chinese diplomats in Chile "enabled Chinese leaders to consider Chile as a reliable diplomatic partner despite dramatic political changes."[13]

On another level, it was the PRC's cultural diplomacy, in addition to official diplomatic advances through their strategies and the establishment of a commercial office in Santiago, that indirectly contributed to the opening of diplomatic relations when Allende was elected president in September 1970. With this act, he was fulfilling a historical wish of the Left to open diplomatic relations with the PRC, notwithstanding the fact that the Chilean Left was closer to the Soviet line and had strong links with Cuba, as well as a well-organized and articulated Communist Party. Allende was a lifelong member of the Socialist Party and won the 1970 election leading the Unidad Popular coalition made up of most of the Chilean Left. Allende had a special relationship with the PRC: he was one of the first members of the Instituto Chileno Chino de Cultura (Chilean Chinese Cultural Institute), founded in 1952. He held positions on the board and as president, and he visited China as a senator in August 1954. When he became president of Chile, he endorsed the PRC's entry PRC into the UN in October 1971.[14]

Within this context, this paper discusses how people-to-people diplomacy relates to Chilean-Chinese relations because the "products" of this exchange contributed to the knowledge of China in Chile in the long term. In this sense, it cannot be described as a linear, clear-cut, cause-and-effect relationship, but rather I show how these products contributed to strengthening the links between Chile and the PRC. This leads to the observation that the timings of soft power may develop at different rhythms and with different results.

Ever since the late 1980s, when Joseph S. Nye coined the term "soft power," the concept has been closely linked to the idea of nation, and it has gained traction in relation to the PRC since the beginning of the twenty-first century. It is, I argue here, a useful term with which to explore the PRC's public diplomacy during the Mao era, especially before its entry into the UN, when it was arguably aiming to position itself as a sovereign nation internationally. Much of soft power literature has focused on the Cold War and the following decades, and most of it has taken a top-down approach focusing on the great powers of the time since soft power was a tool used by governments of the United States, the Soviet Union, and the PRC.

One tool of soft power was invitations to delegations of various countries to sports, cultural, and scientific activities abroad. In the case of the PRC, as mentioned earlier, diverse groups of foreigners were invited during the 1950s and 1960s,[15] among them, intellectuals, artists, poets, politicians, and students as well as Maoist supporters in general, although being a Maoist was not mandatory. Some of them participated in guerrilla training,[16] and many of them returned to give talks or publish books and magazine articles on different topics linked to China.[17] In addition to inviting travelers who toured or worked in China, the PRC also funded political groups abroad and distributed publications in different languages across the world,[18] and it helped fund or collaborate with local Chinese sympathetic organizations abroad, such as the Chilean-Chinese Institute of Cooperation.[19] The latter became central to the PRC's cultural diplomacy, as they became spaces in which preparatory meetings were held and travel experiences were shared with others and where literature could be distributed, cultural activities organized, and PRC anniversaries celebrated. In Chile the Instituto Chileno-Chino de Cultura, as mentioned above, was founded in 1952.[20]

TRAVELERS AS INTERMEDIARIES OF SOFT POWER: THE CASE OF TOMÁS LAGO

Tomás Lago was a journalist and a writer. In 1943 he organized an inter-American exhibition of handicrafts, which led to the establishment of MAPA in 1944. In 1960 he organized an exhibition of Chinese handicrafts and art at the museum. This collection is still there, and its role in the projection of China in Chile will be discussed in this chapter. Lago, accompanied by his wife, traveled to China once, in 1957, publishing *Artesanías Clásicas de China* (1963) after his return.[21] Lago was not, in his own words, a "militant communist."[22] A well-known figure in Chile's cultural scene—he published a poetry book with Nobel Prize winner Pablo Neruda—he had a personal and professional interest in handicrafts that explains his trip to the PRC and the curating of the tour by his Chinese hosts (mentioned in his book).[23]

However, Lago's trip to China was similar to that of others visiting the country, if with a different emphasis.[24] At the time, such trips were mainly by invitation from the Chinese government or through state-sponsored agencies. Trips followed specific formulas, as recounted in many of the real-life or openly fictional accounts of the experience of travel to China during the Cold War. Although undisclosed in his travel account, documentation available at the Shanghai Municipal Archives reveals that the trip was organized by the Chinese government and lasted about a month.[25] In China, Lago visited workshops making traditional Chinese handicrafts as well as traditional tourism sites and museums. He was assigned an interpreter; his Chinese hosts emphasized his interest in handicrafts. Well-planned arrangements were made for him; personnel were regularly present to welcome him and to escort him to places to visit and events to attend; and a budget was assigned to him for food, a car, accommodations, and even the costs of the gifts presented to him following the instructions of the central government.[26] The Shanghai branch of the Chinese People's Association for Cultural Relations with Foreign Countries (CPACRFC)[27] reported his visit to the city of October 20–23, saying that the trip was mostly a success.[28] In a draft report by the CPACRFC's Shanghai branch, he is described as active in the cultural exchange between Chile and China.[29]

Lago's previous connections to China are mostly unknown, although later on, in 1960, he organized the aforementioned traditional Chinese handicrafts exhibition with the Instituto Chileno Chino de Cultura, which his hosts judged as having had a significant role in Chilean-Chinese relations. In addition, he was a friend of the intellectual Luis Oyarzún, who in 1960 was also invited to the PRC, and many of his friends and acquaintances in Chile at the time also traveled to China,[30] all part of the same group of Left-sympathizing intellectuals.[31] As Darío de la Fuente explains, during this period the Instituto Chileno-Chino de Cultura focused on the need to establish diplomatic relations with the PRC and that conversations took place with CPACRFC and to whom members of the Instituto Chileno-Chino de Cultura proposed "that they invite personalities whose knowledge of the truth about China was of high interest."[32]

The role of the Chinese state as central to the development of the industry of handicrafts is made explicit in the catalogue that accompanied the 1960 exhibition mounted in Chile. Lago wrote in it, "Old artisans who, in a moment of crisis, would have had to change over to other activities, even abandoning the cities to work the land, have been rediscovered and have returned to the workshops, currently organized in cooperatives or joint ventures."[33] As I shall show later, when coming to advertise the revolutionary process itself, Lago was less explicitly enthusiastic.

Handicrafts and art were at the center of Lago's intellectual preoccupations.[34] That the PRC's government was playing a role for the continuity of such activities was thus a positive outcome of the Chinese Revolution. In this sense, although there was no open endorsement of the revolution on the part of Lago, he did endorse its results, shedding a positive light on the PRC and thus enhancing its soft power. The widening of discussion about the PRC from a political to an artistic framing thus gave complexity to the knowledge of China in Chile. *Artesanías Clásicas Chinas*, Lago's book, was published at a moment of growing sensibility to the fact that the "largest,"

China, was being left out of the UN. In it, he focuses on Chinese handicrafts, narrating his visits to various workshops, museums, and local institutions.

Lago's report after his trip to China suggests that his visit was mostly aligned with PRC's expectations: he toured places showed to him by his Chinese hosts, and when back in Chile he published a book that overall can be described as positive regarding the PRC's revolutionary process and the role of the CCP. He describes his trip in apparently chronological order, first flying over the Gobi Desert and then arriving in Beijing. Impressed by the city, in his first chapter he mentions the busy streets and the traditional historical and touristic landmarks, among them the Summer Palace, the Forbidden City, and Tiananmen Avenue. The following chapters are about various workshops, such as one on cloisonné, a cooperative making silk flowers and animals; an ivory cooperative; painters in Nanjing; and the creation of paper cuttings, silk embroidery, jade carvings, and lacquer art. In other chapters he describes specific places, such as the Museum of Shanghai and the School of Fine Arts and Handicrafts. In some chapters he is more analytical, as when discussing the planning of artisanal production in China, the development of Western-style painting in China, and what he calls the "unknown aspects of Chinese reality."

In his book, Lago describes tradition as an "essential" part of China, implying that historical Chinese culture can be separated out from the revolutionary process. This "separation" appears to leave room in which to value the positive changes of revolution, and so, without upsetting his hosts, Lago conveys images of "revolutionary" and "essentialist" China, while simultaneously challenging stereotypes. Elements central to the book are the notions of difference and distance, to which a binary understanding of East and West is at the center, as can be seen in the following quote: "In the first pages of this publication we have already noted the reactions that the strange and disconcerting life of the Orient produces in a Western person, felt in the immediate circumstances. A background of very old history—visible just by looking out into the street—presides over this experience."[35]

These ideas of difference are presented in relation to what Lago considers China to be (and what is perceived by him as China or Chinese). Lago is honest in his acknowledgment of prejudice (blamed on the geographical distance) but also opens to a realization of the sameness of humanity, challenging the idea of difference.[36] While the notion of difference is presented by the author as a result of distinct tradition but also because of the revolutionary changes, which impress him, it leads to a reflection on the automation of artistic processes. Indeed, he shows a preoccupation with the subject, his own life being devoted to handicrafts. He states that "local industries tend to disappear as industrialization increases. How to avoid it?"[37] And he continues: "At this point I once again expressed my concerns about the future of Chinese trades and techniques, within the process of mechanization of industry sponsored by the new State."[38] "Didn't [crafts, art] run the risk of losing their own characteristics, intimately linked to work with one's hands? Was it not considered in the government's plans to defend the formal tradition of Chinese culture?"[39]

The notion of distance is present in the form of the trip itself. He reflects on its strict organization by his hosts: "The reception was formulaic everywhere. We are received by a responsible teacher of rather mature age, who offers us a seat in the room, at a table. . . . And there is the green tea that someone silently serves while presentations are made and then, in an adjoining room, a sample of the products of those workshops."[40]

There is distance also in the fact that the trip itself is a government-organized tour, and moreover all communication is mediated by a translator, keeping the artisan at two removes. While Lago shows how the revolution brings positive changes in terms of better living conditions for the Chinese people, there is distance in the impossibility of a nonmediated—by the tour organizers—view of China. This mediation is also a result of language; an interpreter is inevitable to this traveling experience. Significantly, a photo of this companion is included at the end of the book, where he is presented as "Juanito,"[41] with no reference to his actual Chinese name.

As can be seen through the previous quotes, there is clearly a reaction to China, with emotions including surprise. This is not necessarily positive. There is an underlying skepticism regarding handicrafts and arts in the light of industrialization. And yet if we consider the idea of nonlinear cultural diplomacy, the written account of the "reaction" ultimately helps shorten the gap and feeling of difference between cultures and countries.

In its foreword, the book is presented as a medium that responds to the lack of knowledge and mutual understanding between two cultures. Luis Oyarzún, also a traveler to China, says there that the author explicitly states that the objective of the book is to be a goodwill guide.

The author himself tells us that he does not intend this book to be anything but a goodwill guide through the living museum of people's occupations. We are in great need, by the way, of companions with such a broad and rich perspective, more urgent than ever in a time like ours, in which misunderstanding and lack of mutual knowledge between cultures contrast with the increasingly urgent need to reconcile traditions and systems only apparently hostile to each other, in a harmonious universal synthesis.[42]

The texts of different travelers to the PRC, including Lago's, report their own personal impressions of a traditional China and of the advances and development of the Chinese Revolution. Nuances are observed in such accounts, which are suggestive of a complexity that escapes the bipolar interpretations of the Cold War and indicate the relevance of the agency and subjectivity of the protagonists. Lago's book presents the reader with contradictions regarding the industrial advances of the Chinese revolution.

In Lago's text, there are also noteworthy "silences" suggesting a certain distance and even skepticism with the revolutionary process itself. Such is the case when he does not comment on or discuss the data that is given to him. For example, when he visits a cloisonné cooperative, he includes information on the target production for that year is but does not comment further.[43] This "silence" can also be observed when he mentions but does not discuss the mechanization he observes in handicrafts.[44] For Lago, as someone who values handicrafts, mechanization is indeed problematic, and yet it is only discussed partially. Lago presents his vision explicitly: "The native industries have to disappear as industrialization increases. How to avoid it?"[45] And he continues: "At this point I again expressed my concerns about the future of Chinese trades and techniques, within the process of mechanization of industry sponsored by the new state."[46] This, perhaps explains the silences we noticed when mentioning the data. They seem to reaffirm his concern, made explicit in his observation of the mechanization of industry: "Did it not run the risk of losing its own character, intimately linked to handmade work? Was it not considered in the government's plans to defend the formal tradition of Chinese culture?"[47] In terms of the message China gives, Lago acknowledges the revolution ("the most impressive of our time"[48]) but does not spare expressing his doubts about the process and Chinese creativity and art. For Lago, as we noted at the beginning, the value of China's crafts is based on tradition and artisanal craft; mechanization is instead referred to with skepticism. These reactions go against the expectations of cultural diplomacy. As Cyril Cordoba says in his chapter in this book, the PRC judged it was important for the "friends of China" to talk about politics but also to celebrate them. Similar to Oyarzún in his travel diary where he continuously states his admiration and disagreement when he visits the PRC,[49] Lago is not blinded by what he sees.

And yet this was not necessarily how Lago's book was reviewed by some readers. In a 1963 review in *Revista Ercilla*, an undisclosed author states, "More than an essay on an artistic or technical topic about such an important aspect of Chinese culture, it is rather an attempt to conciliate the current political-economic system with the modus operandi of men who dedicate themselves to handicrafts."[50]

Thus, it is possible to think again of the delayed effect mentioned above in that the revolution is not immediately celebrated, but it remains in the long term. Industrialization, as shall be seen below, will be part of the argument through which PRC representatives in Chile show Chilean officials that relations with China were positive for the Latin American country.

It has not been possible to find more information on the circulation of the book, whether there were readings, or even if there was a book launch. And yet it remains as a material object in time, now available online for free and part of the construction of a narrative of a specific Chilean-Chinese relation that emphasized the long-term duration of such relations. In this sense, Lago's book appears not only to have contributed to the PRC's soft power during the Cold War but also today, as it adds to knowledge on China in Spanish in Chile.

Once back in Chile, Lago continued his relationship with China.[51] According to Darío de la Fuente, in 1958 the Instituto Chileno Chino de Cultura inaugurated on September 29 a Chinese Engraving Exhibition and on September 30 an Exhibition on Chinese Handicrafts and Popular Art at MAPA, "with explanations from the director of the museum, writer Tomás Lago."[52] And in October 1960 the aforementioned exhibition Artesanías Tradicional y Arte Popular Chino was held at MAPA with the collaboration of the Instituto Chileno-Chino de Cultura. This exhibition included the museum's own collection and one provided by the Asociación de Amistad Chino-Latinoamericana.[53] Different traditional handicrafts, including ivory objects, cloisonné, lacquer, silk, brocade, and painting reproductions were displayed, a total of 197 objects.[54] These exhibitions indeed, directly or indirectly, contributed to reinforcing the knowledge of China in Chile, with impressions reinterpreted by Lago.

The exhibition organized by Lago in 1960 as well as the publication of his book in 1963 show the ways in which the PRC was increasing its influence in the country. This was accompanied by the establishment in 1961 of the Oficina de Informaciones Comerciales de la República Popular China, directed by Li Yen-nien (or Li Yannian), who had arrived in Chile as head of a commercial mission early that year.[55] The ROC embassy in Santiago actively objected to communist activists in Chile in the early 1960s and Li's arrival as well as complained about the distribution of books and journals from the PRC,[56] and yet there is no mention (to my knowledge) in the archives of the Ministry of Foreign Affairs about the publication of Lago's book (or those of other travelers to the PRC during this period). From May 16 to June 7, 1964, the Oficina de Informaciones Comerciales de la República Popular China held an exhibition, Exposición Económica y Comercial de la República Popular China, that, according to Li, was visited by half a million people and at which, he said, contracts for the sale of twenty thousand tons of saltpeter and five thousand tons of copper bars were signed.[57] In a letter to President Eduardo Frei Montalva, Li is emphatic in showing the economic power of the PRC:

> Regarding the acquisition of saltpeter, the Chinese representatives requested 200,000 tons from the Corporación de Ventas de Salitre y Yodo (COVENSA), the institution that signed the agreement, but unfortunately COVENSA only had the aforementioned 20,000 tons. The operation with saltpeter has already been finalized and canceled.
>
> In relation to the purchase of 5,000 tons of copper ingots that was formalized with the Empresa Nacional de Minería (ENAMI), the Chinese representatives expressed their desire to acquire 20,000 tons, including 10,000 tons of copper wire. ENAMI was only able to offer 5,000 tons of copper ingots for delivery next year. I allow myself to inform H. E. that the People's Republic of China wishes to acquire from Chile saltpeter, copper, wool, cellulose for paper, etc. and in return can offer Chile 20,000 kinds of products.[58]

Li also sent a letter to the minister of foreign affairs, Gabriel Valdés, in which he mentions the importance of establishing and organizing an *effective* commercial office of the PRC in Chile, with more staff, including interpreters.[59] As these documents show, together with a cultural diplomacy program, the PRC was also taking an economic approach to convince Chile to recognize the PRC instead of the ROC.

During this time, ROC representatives in Chile were actively explaining why diplomatic relations should be maintained with them, also using culture and art as a means.[60] As an example, we find the exhibition *3.000 Años de Arte Chino* at the prestigious Museo Nacional de Bellas Artes in Santiago, supported by the Ministry of Education of Chile, in September 1968. Regardless of their efforts, however, with the election in 1970 of Chile's first socialist president, Salvador Allende, the ROC representation in Chile, and diplomatic relations, came to an end.

Indeed, the PRC deployed a strategy to gain influence in Chile that worked. When Allende was elected president as the candidate of a leftist coalition (which had seen its Maoist faction excised in the early 1960s), the Chilean government soon established diplomatic relations with the PRC, with an agreement was signed in Paris on December 15, 1970.[61] In this way, Chile shifted recognition from the ROC to the PRC.

CONCLUSION

Since the 1970s, Chilean-Chinese relations have grown notably in complexity, with economics at their center, as the PRC gradually became Chile's primary trading partner.[62] Accompanying economic and growing political exchange, there is a PRC-Chilean shared discourse of the "four firsts" (to which other "firsts" have been added) or "narrative of the firsts," which refers to a "special and unique relationship" of Chile with the PRC within Latin America. This discourse is based on the facts that Chile was the first South American country to establish diplomatic relations with the PRC, to support its entry into the UN, to sign a bilateral agreement with the PRC on its entry into the World Trade Organization, to recognize the PRC's full market-economy status, and to launch bilateral free-trade agreement negotiations.[63]

From this perspective, considering the role of foreign visitors to the PRC in the 1960s and reflecting on the potential of their publications and dissemination of ideas in their home countries shed new light on the ways in which soft power works at a local level. Whether the results of such travels were in line with the PRC's expectations thus becomes a question that needs to be asked at different points in time. In other words, the question really is whether the results of such travels were in line with the PRC's expectations in the 1970s. Lago's book permitted easier access to knowledge of the PRC, contributing nonlinearly to narrow the gap between Chile and the PRC. Whether Lago's work mirrored the PRC's expectations is beyond the scope of this text and, at least for now, not available through primary sources. And yet Lago's agency, exercised in the publication of his book, in which one can find nuanced visions of the PRC's revolutionary process, shows that he was more than a propagandist.

Today, more than five decades after the Chinese art exhibition at MAPA and the subsequent establishment of diplomatic relations between Chile and the PRC, nonlinear cultural diplomacy reveals the way in which nonlinearity and eventual delay and silences (or omissions) play out. Both Chilean and Chinese authorities refer to the "four firsts" to describe the relationship between the countries, highlighting those first contacts. In this sense, I do not mean that Tomás Lago or visitors to China like him are to be celebrated as central to Chilean-Chinese relations, but rather I want to argue that there is something to be learned by focusing on the people and policies that tend to be considered passive recipients. The agency of such actors must be integrated in studies of soft power, as these seemingly passive actors allow access to the complexities and nuances that cultural diplomacy entails. Whether the PRC was targeting people like Lago, a nonfervent sympathizer of the revolutionary process, to downplay the revolutionary aspect of the PRC is an interesting question to be explored further, perhaps strengthening the argument that the PRC at the time was aiming for legitimacy in the international sphere in different ways.[64]

In their study of European countries, Luigi Zingales, Paola Sapienza, Luigi Guiso, and others have found that "cultural relationships affect trust and are an important omitted factor in international trade and investments,"[65] an idea that can be extrapolated to diplomatic exchange. As Jian Ren has shown, specific actors can be key in the continuity of bilateral relations.[66] Lago's experience echoes other case studies of the period: as Kazushi Minami argues, for example, in the 1960s and 1970s women reshaped US relations with the PRC.[67] Like Minami, I do not argue that travelers such as Lago made direct contributions to the relations between countries (which, in the case of the United States,[68] Minami argues was the primary product of the countries' shared security interests[69]). However, the promotion of a discourse where the PRC becomes more familiar and less a "communist autocracy," helped broaden knowledge of China in Chile—a case of nonlinear cultural diplomacy. Furthermore, Lago's book, available in digital form, and the art collection he added to MAPA can still be studied today in light of their contributions to the PRC's long-term soft power.

NOTES

This chapter is part of ANID Fondecyt Iniciación no. 11200151, "Viajeros de la Guerra Fría: Diplomacia cultural y redes transnacionales entre Chile y la República Popular China (1949–1979)" (IR Maria Montt Strabucchi), and was funded by ANID Millennium Science Initiative Program NCS2022_053. I would also like to thank Felipe Quijada and Paula Cabrera from the Museo de Arte Popular Americano Tomás Lago.

1. Cerro Santa Lucía, also known as Cerro Huelén, is a park that uses up the space of a small hill in the center of Santiago. It is a city landmark.
2. This was the second of a series of exhibits, the first being on Romania.
3. For more information on associations linked to the PRC, see Cyril Cordoba and Liu Kaixuan, "Unconditional Followers of the PRC? Friendship Associations with China in France and Switzerland, 1950s–1980s," in *Europe and China in the Cold War: Exchanges beyond the Bloc Logic and the Sino-Soviet Split*, ed. Janick Marina Schaufelbuehl, Marco

Wyss, and Valeria Zanier (Leiden: Brill, 2019), 85–107, https://doi.org/10.1163/9789004388123_006.

4. Rafael Pedemonte, *Guerra por as ideas en América Latina* (Santiago: Universidad Alberto Hurtado, 2020).

5. Cyril Cordoba, *China-Swiss Relations during the Cold War, 1949–1989: Between Soft Power and Propaganda* (London: Routledge, 2022).

6. Zhixiang Zhang, "Lessons Learned from Ten Years of Foreign Cultural Work, Future Tasks and Guidelines," trans. David Cowhig, History and Public Policy Program Digital Archive, PRC FMA 102-00015-03, Wilson Center, July 1, 1960, https://digitalarchive.wilsoncenter.org/document/zhang-zhiziang-lessons-learned-ten-years-foreign-cultural-work-future-tasks-and-guidelines.

7. Jorge J. Locane and Maria Montt Strabucchi, "Cultura china y Capricornio: Dos proyectos pioneros para el comercio simbólico (y material) entre América Latina y China," *Revista Izquierdas* 49 (2020): 2521–44.

8. Megan M. Ferry, "China as Utopia: Visions of the Chinese Cultural Revolution in Latin America," *Modern Chinese Literature and Culture* 12, no. 2 (2000): 236–69; Matthew Rothwell, *Transpacific Revolutionaries: The Chinese Revolution in Latin America* (New York: Routledge, 2013).

9. See, among others, Mónica Ahumada, "Viajeros a la República Popular China: José Venturelli, los intelectuales, políticos y parlamentarios chilenos en los años cincuenta y sesenta," *Transmodernity: Journal of Peripheral Cultural Production of the Luso-Hispanic World* 9, no. 3 (2020): 6–33; Maria Montt Strabucchi, "The PRC's Cultural Diplomacy towards Latin America in the 1950s and 1960s," *International Journal of Current Chinese Studies* 1 (2010): 58–83; Maria Montt Strabucchi, "'Writing about China': Latin American Travelogues during the Cold War; Bernardo Kordon's '600 millones y uno' (1958), and Luis Oyarzún's 'Diario de Oriente, Unión Soviética, China e India' (1960)," *Caminhos da História* 21, no. 1 (2016): 93–124; José Miguel Vidal Kunstmann, "Entre lo local y lo global: Pablo de Rokha y el proyecto maoísta," *Transmodernity: Journal of Peripheral Cultural Production of the Luso-Hispanic World* 9, no. 3 (2020): 161–94.

10. Andrés Estefane and Luis Thielemann, "Latin American Marxism and the Atlantic," Oxford Research Encyclopedia of Latin American History, February 26, 2018, https://doi.org/10.1093/acrefore/9780199366439.013.402.

11. Estefane and Thielemann.

12. Marjorie Rojas, "La Formación del Partido Comunista Revolucionario," unpublished seminar paper, 2007, Pontificia Universidad Católica de Chile.

13. Jian Ren, "Repensar la diplomacia cultural desde la perspectiva china: Guillermo del Pedregal y la imagen del liderazgo chino sobre Chile (1959–1975)," *Intus: Legere Historia* 15, no. 1 (2021): 171, https://doi.org/10.15691/%x.

14. For the session, Chile was represented by its minister of foreign affairs, Clodomiro Almeyda; Almeyda also traveled to the PRC later in 1973. "Clodomiro Almeyda Medina: Reseñas biográficas parlamentarias," Biblioteca del Congreso Nacional de Chile, 2020, https://www.bcn.cl/historiapolitica/resenas_parlamentarias/wiki/Clodomiro_Almeyda_Medina.

15. For the experience of travel, soft power, and cultural diplomacy, there is a broad and growing literature. See, among others, Michael David-Fox, *Showcasing the Great Experiment: Cultural Diplomacy and Western Visitors to the Soviet Union, 1921–1941* (Oxford: Oxford University Press, 2011); Paul Hollander, *Political Pilgrims: Travels of Western*

Intellectuals to the Soviet Union, China, and Cuba, 1928–1978 (New York: Oxford University Press, 1981); Guido Samarani, Carla Meneguzzi Rostagni, and Sofia Graziani, eds., *Roads to Reconciliation People's Republic of China, Western Europe and Italy During the Cold War Period (1949–1971)* (Venecia: Edizioni Ca' Foscari, 2018); Ariane Knüsel, *China's European Headquarters: Switzerland and China during the Cold War*, Cambridge Studies in the History of the People's Republic of China (Cambridge: Cambridge University Press, 2022), https://doi.org/10.1017/9781009169486.

16. Rothwell, *Transpacific Revolutionaries*.

17. It is still unclear how many people from Latin America visited the PRC and how many of those published books or shared with others their experience. This paper aims to contribute to this topic of study.

18. The ROC also had a cultural diplomacy program that aimed to oppose the advances of the PRC. An interesting case study is explored by Chinfang Kuo and Hsienwei Kuo, who show how the ROC's table tennis coaches to Latin America during the Cold War promoted understanding of "Free China" to prevent the penetration of communist ideas. They set up channels of trust communication through coaches and with different interest groups, and they developed diplomatic support for the ROC (2021). Chinfang Kuo and Hsienwei Kuo, "Sport Diplomacy and Survival: Republic of China Table Tennis Coaches in Latin America during the Cold War," *International Journal of the History of Sport* 37, no. 14 (2020), 1479–99, https://doi.org/10.1080/09523367.2020.1860943.

19. Cordoba, *China-Swiss Relations during the Cold War*.

20. We found other organizations beyond the Institutes of Cooperation that were also central to the exchange and ways of soft power, facilitating the development of networks and allowing for links to be developed. In China, these were the Chinese People's Association for Cultural Relations with Foreign Countries (CPACRFC) and the Asociación de Amistad Sino-Latinoamericana. For a detailed analysis of them, see Cordoba.

21. A register of his trip is held at the Shanghai Municipal Archives.

22. Tomás Lago, *Ojos y oídos cerca de Neruda* (Santiago: LOM Ediciones, 1999), 5.

23. By the time of his China trip, Lago was no longer on friendly terms with Neruda, to whom he had been very close. This was because Neruda had left his wife, Delia del Carril, for Matilde Urrutia. The men's falling-out is relevant to this paper because during this period and that of the Sino-Soviet split Neruda was openly critical of the PRC.

24. Guided tours in the PRC all had similar programs, with shifts regarding the specialization of the person or group touring. For example, one can notice the focus on legal aspects in a trip of twenty Chilean lawyers to China in 1963. See, e.g., Miguel Saidel, *China rompe la historia* (Santiago: Arancibia Hnos., 1963).

25. The exact duration of his trip is, to date, unknown. It is surely a methodological issue to write about Lago's trip with limited access to archives both in Chile and in China due to the COVID-19 pandemic.

26. Shanghai Municipal Archives, October 18, 1957.

27. Still active, the association describes itself as "a national people's organization engaged in people-to-people diplomacy of the People's Republic of China. The aims of the Association are to enhance people's friendship, further international cooperation, safeguard world peace and promote common development." "Chinese People's Association for Friendship with Foreign Countries," CPAFFC, 2021, https://cpaffc.org.cn/index/xiehui/xiehui_list/cate/12/lang/2.html.

28. Shanghai Municipal Archives, October 24, 1957.

29. Shanghai Municipal Archives, October 18, 1957.

30. Among them were the Chileans Francisco Coloane, Pablo de Rokha, José Venturelli, Olga Poblete, and Pablo Neruda and the Argentine Maria Rosa Oliver (Lago, *Ojos y oídos cerca de Neruda*). On how guests were overall selected to be invited, see Cordoba, *China-Swiss Relations during the Cold War*. See also Matthew Rothwell, "Agente secreto para el maoísmo internacional: José Venturelli, la diplomacia informal china y el maoísmo latinoamericano," *Revista Asia América Latina* 1, no. 4 (2017): 1–14.

31. In Lago's memoir of 1954, he mentions, regarding the choice of Pablo Neruda's cover for his book *Las uvas y el viento* (1954): "He wanted a cheerful cover corresponding to his current interest. He emphasized the paper cutout figure, Chinese, of which some boxes have come from the People's Republic recently, brought by political travelers going to the East or sent as propaganda." (Lago, *Ojos y oídos cerca de Neruda*, 192; my translation). It is interesting to note that Lago refers to them as "political travelers"; later he would be one of the travelers himself.

32. Darío de la Fuente, *Instituto Chileno-Chino de Cultura: Cuarenta años* (Santiago: Instituto Chileno-Chino de Cultura, 1992), 38.

33. Museo de Arte Popular, Universidad de Chile and Instituto Chileno Chino de Cultura, *Artesanías tradicionales y arte popular chino* (Santiago: Editorial Universitaria, 1960).

34. Olaya Sanfuentes, "Latin American Popular Art in a Museum: How Things Become Art," *Artium Quaestiones*, no. 29 (May 7, 2019): 63–89, https://doi.org/10.14746/aq.2018.29.3.

35. Tomás Lago, *Artesanías clásicas chinas* (Santiago: Facultad de Bellas Artes, Universidad de Chile, 1963), 89.

36. Lago, 89.

37. Lago, 155.

38. Lago, 155.

39. Lago, 155.

40. Lago, 50.

41. In Chile, "Juanito" is often used as a generic name, similar to the way "Joe" is in American English.

42. Oyarzún in Lago, *Artesanías Clásicas Chinas*, 9.

43. Lago, 26.

44. Lago, 132.

45. Lago, 155.

46. Lago, 157.

47. Lago, 157.

48. Lago, 168.

49. Luis Oyarzún, *Diario de Oriente: Unión Soviética, China e India* (Santiago: Editorial Universitaria, 1960).

50. "Por China tomando te verde," *Revista Ercilla*, May 1, 1963.

51. It has been impossible, to date, to trace his links to China beyond the institute or sources used here. I do not know if he maintained links with officials or people in China, if he organized these exhibits on his own initiative or because they were suggested by others, or if there was anyone he met in China or acquaintances in Chile who were involved in the creation of such exhibitions.

52. De la Fuente, *Instituto Chileno-Chino de Cultura*, 37.

53. Probably the same as the Asociación de Amistad del Pueblo Chino con el Extranjero (CPACRFC) mentioned above.

54. Museo de Arte Popular, *Artesanías tradicionales y arte popular chino*.

55. Archivo Histórico, Ministerio de Relaciones Exteriores de Chile, August 24, 1961.

56. Archivo Histórico, Ministerio de Relaciones Exteriores de Chile, January 24, 1964.

57. Archivo Histórico, Ministerio de Relaciones Exteriores de Chile, November 4, 1964.

58. Archivo Histórico, Ministerio de Relaciones Exteriores de Chile, November 4, 1964.

59. Archivo Histórico, Ministerio de Relaciones Exteriores de Chile, November 18, 1964.

60. Ministerio de Educación de Chile and Embajada de la República de China, *3.000 años de arte chino* (Santiago: Museo Nacional de Bellas Artes, 1968).

61. In Paris, Ambassador Enrique Bernstein of the former government of Eduardo Frei was asked to open relations with the PRC. Bernstein says in his memoir that because Pablo Neruda, a member of the Communist Party, was probably to be the ambassador, the agreement was rapidly signed. Enrique Bernstein, *Recuerdos de un diplomático: De la Unidad Popular al gobierno militar* (Santiago: Andrés Bello, 1984).

62. Carol Wise, *Dragonomics: How Latin America Is Maximizing (or Missing Out on) China's International Development Strategy* (New Haven, CT: Yale University Press, 2020).

63. Claudia Labarca and Maria Montt Strabucchi, "Discurso como representación de sentido en las relaciones internacionales: El caso sino-chileno," *Estudios Políticos*, no. 47 (2019): 163–84, http://dx.doi.org/10.22201/fcpys.24484903e.2019.47.69504.

64. Maria Montt Strabucchi, "Una lógica triangulada: Hitos de la relación sino-chilena desde una perspectiva internacional 1949–1978," *Notas de Investigación / Research Notes*, no. 2 (2019): 46–52.

65. Luigi Zingales, Paola Sapienza, and Luigi Guiso, *Cultural Biases in Economic Exchange?*, SSRN Scholarly Papers (Rochester, NY: Social Science Research Network, 2008), 3, https://doi.org/10.2139/ssrn.634210.

66. Ren, "Repensar la diplomacia cultural."

67. Kazushi Minami, "'How Could I Not Love You?': Transnational Feminism and US-Chinese Relations during the Cold War," *Journal of Women's History* 31, no. 4 (2019): 12–36, https://doi.org/10.1353/jowh.2019.0036.

68. For US-China relations during the Cold War, see also Meredith Oyen, *The Diplomacy of Migration: Transnational Lives and the Making of U.S.-Chinese Relations in the Cold War* (Ithaca, NY: Cornell University Press, 2015).

69. For the United States, Minami argues that women "promoted a new discourse on Chinese socialism and feminism characterized by what the historian Judy Tzu-Chu Wu calls 'radical orientalism'—a mentality among activists in the 'long 1960s' that 'idealized the East and denigrated the West.' It portrayed China as 'a source of alternative values' and 'new political possibilities' for America, not as a communist autocracy threatening US national security." Minami, "'How Could I Not Love You?,'" 14.

CHAPTER 10

The Construction of a Senegalese Soft Power under Senghor

Art, *Métissage*, and Decentering

Coline Desportes

On April 1, 2022, the exhibition *Picasso à Dakar, 1972–2022* opened at the Musée des Civilisations Noires in Dakar. The artist's works had returned to Senegal fifty years after the exhibition *Picasso* that had taken place at the Musée Dynamique in the same city, resurfacing the memories of that event. While most of the actors in the Senegalese art world remembered the earlier Picasso exhibition almost like a myth, French agents had, until recently, forgotten it. Its organization was a tour de force of the then Senegalese president, Léopold Sédar Senghor, and his government, which received minimal support from France. It is difficult to assess the impact on Franco-Senegalese relationships that this exhibition had at the time, but it seems to have had a delayed effect. If in 1972 the French government did not want to be involved in the project, today, as French cultural diplomacy toward Africa is reconfiguring, the 2022 Picasso exhibition contributed to strengthening Senegal's soft power, as well as that of France, by celebrating the collaboration between French and Senegalese museums. This so-called exemplary partnership was recently underlined by French president Emmanuel Macron and Senegalese president Macky Sall and by the four curators, reactivating, according to Sall, an "exceptional experience of encounter, dialogue and expression of diversity in a world space that has become global."[1] This description seems to neglect the struggle of the former Senegalese government to allow the first exhibition to take place. This current international celebration of the 1972

Picasso erases—by ignorance of its promoters or on purpose because their cultural diplomacy is shifting—the efforts that the Senegalese government had to engage in as it tried to put in place a strategy of cultural influence abroad. This shared silence minimizes the imbalance that remained between the two countries in those years.

The stories of the exhibitions must be situated in 1960 Senegal's global strategy for soft power, which Senghor, the first Senegalese president (1960–80), developed in the 1970s and that included organization of art exhibitions both in Senegal and abroad. The 1972 *Picasso* exhibition was a project initiated by Senghor and was preceded by a *Chagall* exhibition in 1971 and followed by a *Soulages* exhibition in 1974 and *Manessier* in 1976.[2] Together, these painters are linked to the School of Paris, and their Dakar exhibitions formed what the Senegalese government called "the cycle of the great masters."[3] These Dakar exhibitions of artists from the School of Paris were accompanied by a major exhibition in the spring of 1974 in Paris of the School of Dakar,[4] a term referring to young Senegalese artists.

This article follows a dynamic trend of research. Building upon Elizabeth Harney's pioneering study of the exceptional artistic patronage of President Senghor, who gave enormous support to some of his country's artists, several researchers have explored the political dimensions of this backing. In particular, they have traced how Senghor assumed several key roles in the art world: critic, patron, and collector. Until recently, these studies have mainly explored the local and national dimensions of such patronage, which may have obscured trans- and international artistic circulations.[5] Moreover, a growing body of literature has shown how states sought to develop or consolidate their influence in West Africa through the first World Festival of Negro Arts in 1966, which was organized by Senegal in the context of the Cold War and decolonization.[6] For Senghor's Senegal, the benefits of organizing such an event were significant because it consolidated the country's political role in the subregion. However, studies on the festival take a narrow chronological approach. On the contrary, this article considers a longer-term period and the international significance of Senegal's cultural policies. I try to show how the exhibitions organized after the 1966 festival were conceived by the Senegalese government as the main axis of its soft power toward France. In a context where Senegal remained dependent on funding from the French government, it is striking that the Senegalese government succeeded in imposing a cultural strategy nourished by the theories of its president, in particular those of *métissage*.[7] And freed itself from what France envisioned for its former colonies. Senghor's project was elitist and demanding, whereas France favored exhibition projects intended for vast audiences that were dictated by a stated concern for development.[8] The reception of Senghor's project in France by the 1970s revealed conceptions still impregnated in the colonial paradigm.

The argument and research for this chapter are based on a study of rare catalogs published for the exhibitions, unpublished archives from the diplomatic post in Dakar, the French ministries of foreign affairs and culture, and interviews conducted in France and Senegal. Documents that would allow researchers to know more about the debates taking place among Senegalese actors remain inaccessible.

BYPASSING FRENCH PROJECTS TO DEVELOP A SENEGALESE SOFT POWER

Tracing the history of the exhibitions held in the Senegalese capital in the first decade of the country's independence involves uncovering the economic and political conditions in which they were organized. The founding of institutions, both French and Senegalese, allows us to understand what the city's creative and dissemination centers were, what messages they helped circulating, and by whom they were controlled. Until 1966 the only exhibition spaces in Dakar were those of foreign cultural centers, some of which opened before independence. One of them was the French Cultural Center, which still exists today. Its centrality provoked mixed feelings of attraction, distancing, and repulsion among the different actors of the Senegalese art world. In 1964 the center was renamed the Centre d'Échanges Culturels de Langue Française, a shift that stressed the desire to untie, at least in appearance, its action from that of the French government. The foreign cultural centers were kept at a distance by Senghor, who did not want them to be located near the presidential palace. At the same time, the centers had exhibition spaces that hosted events often inaugurated by Senegalese officials themselves. In 1968 (the year a Soviet center was created) Senghor himself inaugurated the new exhibition hall of the French center in the company of Jacques Foccart, secretary-general for African and Malagasy affairs at the Élysée Palace (1960–74).[9]

The context for the creation of foreign centers reflects the competitive atmosphere between nations at a time when France wanted to maintain Senegal in its zone of influence. For example, the French Cultural Center was founded following the opening of the American Cultural Center in 1958, as the French government feared that it would "be outdistanced by American cultural outreach services."[10] The regular reports written by the French ambassador in Dakar to the Ministry of Foreign Affairs point to the French government's attention to the cultural relations of Senegal and Western countries and in particular to the cultural initiatives of the British (1967), Soviet (1968), and American centers. However, given that these institutions focused their policies on language teaching, the French ambassador rapidly judged them to be unthreatening to France's field of action. This was also the case for the French center, which, in the aftermath of independence, set up a strong book and French language–teaching policy, notably through a generous lending library.

This strategy of cultural influence was very different from the one that France reserved for the West. In West Africa, art exhibitions were far from being the instrument favored by the French government. From 1957 to 1967 the leading French agency of cultural diplomacy (founded in 1922), the Association Française d'Action Artistique (AFAA), organized 581 exhibitions throughout the world, thirty-six of which were in Africa (6 percent).[11] Of these thirty-six exhibitions, only one was in French-speaking sub-Saharan Africa.[12] All the others were sent to English-speaking Africa, the Maghreb, and Egypt. In 1965 the AFAA organized a tour of exhibitions of reproductions of large paintings in East and Southern Africa.[13] This operation in anglophone Africa can be seen as a desire to extend its cultural influence outside the French sphere of influence and in areas where its influence was being restricted. It is interesting to note, however, that the art exhibitions sent to East and Southern Africa by the AFAA were not designed on the model of large international exhibitions either, and most often consisted of showcasing reproductions. This predilection for reproductions obviously made it possible to send images of French art around the world at low cost, but it also showed that the AFAA considered its target audiences populations to be educated rather than art lovers. As the anthropologist Sally Price points out in her book *Primitive Art in Civilized Places*, "much of the conceptualization of the quality of things that we of the Western World tend to take for granted posits a relationship between 'originals' and their 'copies' in which the former has a greater legitimacy and value."[14] These exhibitions of reproductions had mixed success with local audiences, and some ambassadors felt that it would be better to send originals.

Locally, however, the French Cultural Center organized exhibitions, which were not coordinated by the AFAA. Their forms, themes, and objects were very different from those of the AFAA. They were didactic and explicitly chosen for their relevance to the supposed interests of the local general public. Most of the exhibitions organized at the French Cultural Center in Dakar at the beginning of the 1960s were not devoted to art objects or the visual arts but rather to general and educational themes, such as theater, the press, or literature, with the threefold aim of interesting the public, educating it, and contributing to the influence of France.[15] For example, in 1964 the ambassador, Lucien Paye, coordinated several exhibitions on the occasion of "French Week." He chose several themes, including *ferronerie d'art* (ironwork) and emphasized that this craft was chosen because it was in keeping with local society. This choice was welcomed by the curator of the Louvre to whom he was speaking. He also selected an exhibition on *tapisserie française* (French tapestry), for which he benefited from the help of the Association d'Entraide des Français du Sénégal, founded a year earlier, and from private members living for the most part in Dakar. Although the local African public was the main target of the exhibitions, the ambition of this association was threefold, as its director explained to the French minister of cultural affairs, André Malraux: to give greater coherence to the French community, to make it aware of the role it had to play in the future of the young Senegalese state, and to make it known that France would cooperate with the young African nations in order to increase their standard of living and to insert themselves more easily into the major currents of modern life.[16] To get this message across, the association chose tapestry, a medium that was also widely disseminated abroad by the AFAA, as a symbol of France's postwar artistic revival and of a French *art de vivre* synonymous with luxury and modernity. Often accompanied by explanatory booklets and conferences, the French Cultural Center's exhibitions responded to a desire for development and were intended for the society living in Dakar in its Senegalese, French, and postcolonial complexity.

Senghor's inauguration of the Musée Dynamique, which took place on the occasion of the 1966 World Festival of Negro Arts, marked a turning point in the history of exhibitions in Dakar. Beyond its symbolism as the first modern museum on the continent, its creation, which met international standards in terms of conservation, allowed Senegal to organize its own projects. However, they remained largely dependent on credits granted by France, a situation that allowed the French government to constrain the scope of action of Senegalese cultural policy. For example, after the success of the first World Festival of Negro Arts, Senegal tried to organize several exhibitions. The French government intervened as soon as the project took a direction that deviated from the one it had dictated. It was mainly the agents of the Ministry of Cultural Affairs, foremost among them André Malraux, who stepped in. While in public Malraux took every opportunity to spread the image of a generous and humanistic France,[17] numerous letters show, on the contrary, his belief that Senegal owed a debt to France because of the financial aid it provided.[18]

The first three exhibitions presented after 1966 at the Musée Dynamique were *Témoins des temps passés* (December 1966–67) (Witnesses to past),[19] *Préhistoire de l'Ouest africain* (1967) (West African prehistory), and *Art rupestre du Sahara: Les peintures et gravures pariétales du Tassili N-Ajjer* (1969) (Saharan rock art: Cave paintings and engravings of Tassili N- Ajjer).[20] They followed on from *L'Art nègre: Sources, evolution, expansion,* the exhibition of classic African art that inaugurated the festival in the spring of 1966. In these three exhibitions, certain aspects of the continent's history were developed. *Art rupestre du Sahara* aimed to place Senegal in a thousand-year-old history on the scale of the continent and to show the antiquity of "black and African culture," including in the north of Africa, Tassili being a region located in Algeria. They presented an opportunity for Senegal, through its minister of culture, Assane Seck,[21] to deploy a unifying identity discourse, both on the scale of the continent and of the nation. Faced with suggestions from Senegal, the agents of French museums engaged in multiple negotiations, to which the Senegalese government was obliged to give in. In particular, the French museums refused the loan of El Hadj Omar Tall's sword, which had been requested by Salif Diop, the Senegalese curator in charge of organizing the exhibition *Témoins des temps passés.* The exhibition in its first version, conceived by Diop, showcased African resistance to colonization. Malraux felt that such a project was not likely to foster friendship between France and Senegal. Similarly, the Senegalese government renounced its wish to extend the exhibition of the Tassili frescoes to the entire Sahara. With such plans, it had wished to affirm the thousand-year-old presence of Blacks in the Sahara and to confirm a Pan-Africanist and Afrocentric vision providing evidence of the unity and long history of "Black civilization," aiming to decenter history of civilizations.[22] Caught in such an unbalanced situation, Senegal thus benefited from significant aid from France but remained explicitly subject to the conditions laid down by the former colonizer. At the end of the 1960s, the country reached the end of its first decade of independence under restrictive conditions of artistic cooperation that left little room for maneuver in the construction of a cultural strategy of influence. It was in this context that the Senegalese government began to implement the idea of a cycle of exhibitions of artists from the School of Paris to Dakar.

Today Western European countries no longer view the ability of African museums to conserve objects with such suspicion.[23] However, even with hindsight, the 1970s cycle of the great masters appears to be a tour de force: an African museum had succeeded in exhibiting original works of the great masters. The exhibitions, both in Dakar and in Paris, received little support from the French government. Without committing itself scientifically—through the action of its curators or the loan of important works[24]—the French government nevertheless offered a subsidy each time, financed the printing of the catalogs and the transport of the works by military aircraft. French personalities also shared the high patronage of the exhibition, thus offering marginal but real material and symbolic support.

Mostly the exhibitions were made possible by the mobilization of a network of various actors, which points to the multiplicity of agents of cultural diplomacy in postcolonial Senegal. If the idea of the Dakar exhibitions was first put forward in 1967, their realization was probably greatly facilitated by Gérard Bosio, a young French development worker who came from the political milieu of Nice and benefited from a network of politicians and artists in the south of France. Paid by the French government, Bosio had a foot in both Africa and Europe. Hired in 1968, he worked as cultural adviser for Senghor for nearly ten years, getting involved in projects and spreading the president's thoughts through a film and later exhibitions in France.[25] Part of Senegal's cultural strategy abroad was thus in part put in place by French agents working for Senegal. The special status of *cooperants*, French agents seconded to countries in the field, led to a tension between the national interest and the interest of the country in which they were working, especially in the case of positions as advisers or state clerks close to the government. It is difficult to disentangle the exact influence they had on Senegalese projects, but it is certain that their actions facilitated them. This special status sometimes led to a form of mistrust toward them, as shown by the notes about Bosio kept in the French archives.[26]

With the help of Bosio, Senegal turned to nongovernmental actors. They solicited artists, galleries, and collectors directly—including Bosio himself. The Louise Leiris Gallery and Galerie de France lent several paintings. This appeal to the generosity of artists enabled Senegal to bypass the lack of commitment of the French authorities. As early as 1962, Senghor declared his intention to solicit French artists, as evidenced by a letter to the painter and tapestry artist Jean Lurçat, in which he stated, "Senegal intends to pursue its economic development and its cultural development at the same time. . . . In this work of cultural development, we count on the help of France, especially on the help of its greatest artists like you."[27] At the same time as the cycle of the great masters, Senegal was setting up its tapestry factory.[28]

From 1967 to 1971, the Senegalese ministers of culture, Assane Seck and Alioune Sene, repeatedly asked the French government to send an exhibition of modern French artists. The ministers did not specify any particular names, indicating that the idea was to invite modern art from France to Dakar. On at least one occasion, Senghor himself wrote to Prime Minister

Jacques Chaban-Delmas to this effect and discussed the matter with President of the Republic Georges Pompidou. Thus, the project truly emanated from the highest levels of the Senegalese government. It appears from the letters that the model for the exhibitions that they wanted to host was the opposite of the one that was presented in Dakar in French Cultural Centers during the first decade following independence. The Senegalese government instead wanted exhibitions modeled on those organized by the AFAA in Western countries since the aftermath of World War II, which mainly showed modern art from the beginning of the twentieth century.[29] Chagall, Picasso, Soulages, and Manessier, the artists selected by Senghor, did not have a common style, nor did they belong to the same movement. They were brought together by their status as artists who were particularly supported by the French state and promoted abroad under the name of the School of Paris. Several authors have shown the versatility of this term, which acts as a label and sometimes has opposing definitions depending on the commentators and their ideological and political affiliations.[30] Senghor also gave a personal version of it, in line with the discourse he wished to deploy in the context of his soft power.

The cycle of the great masters was not conceived by Senghor as an isolated "coup." In a letter to the Pompidou, he indicated that for the next ten years French painters would occupy the first place in the Senegalese exhibition program.[31] He also unsuccessfully asked that such exhibitions be included in the cooperation program. The Senegalese project was initially misunderstood by French government and museum officials, such as Robert Boyer, head of the exhibition department at the Ministry of Culture. Based on what he imagined to be the demands of the local public, Boyer thought that inexpensive exhibitions on the model of those of the French Cultural Center would be more appropriate. In his eyes, masterpieces from the great French museums had no special appeal for the Senegalese public.[32] In reality, the idea of Senghor and his ministers was that of large monographic exhibitions, on the model of the great international exhibitions, which would be distinguished, for example, from the exhibitions of reproductions received at the Musée Dynamique from the United Nations Educational, Scientific and Cultural Organization.[33] After gaining a better understanding of the Senegalese project, the French government was finally reluctant. As an anonymous note in 1972, preserved in the archives of the Ministry of Culture, pointed out, "these projects, while they testify to the special interest that Senegal has always shown in French art, all presuppose a financial contribution from France."[34] Moreover, French agents judged that they were unlikely to reach a large public, which would reduce their effectiveness in France's outreach strategy. Finally, these exhibitions of French art, organized by Senegal, could have annoyed French president Charles de Gaulle, who believed that only the French government and its agents were entitled to promote French culture.[35]

By requesting major exhibitions in Dakar of artists from the School of Paris, based on the model of those reserved for developed countries, Senghor wanted to project abroad the image of a modern country, capable of digesting and appropriating the modernist discourse. Regarding the impact on the international audience in the context of building Senegalese soft power, this attempt was not a total success. It was initially marked by a relative failure in the sense that the few reports that were published at the time, such as the internal comments of foreign observers, questioned the impact of these events outside the restricted circle of the Dakar elite.[36] In 1971 the Chagall exhibition had a limited reach, and the reports from the French Embassy attest to the disinterest with which the project was received on the French side. But the success of the Picasso exhibition, the most famous living artist in the world, organized largely without French institutional support, constituted a landmark. This was of course most noticeable in France, first in the daily press. The major national dailies *Le Monde* and *Le Figaro* reported on the event, with *Le Figaro* headlining, "The Picasso Exhibition in Dakar: A Turning Point in Afro-European History," explaining that "an exhibition in Dakar . . . can be a milestone in the history of cultural relations between Europe and Africa."[37] Indeed, in a sign of an exceptional event, Jacques Duhamel, then French minister of culture, was present for the inauguration. The change in tone was evident in the French diplomatic representation in Dakar and led French cultural agents to take a different view of the Senegalese proposals for an exhibition in Paris. If it had relatively neglected the Chagall exhibition, the French government saw the advantages of this diplomatic event that it had previously kept at a distance. In the brochure published by the Ministry of Foreign Affairs, *News Briefs from France*, dated May 20, 1972, the section "Cultural Exchanges" showed a photograph of Duhamel and Senghor in front of Picasso's *Le déjeuner sur l'herbe*. Duhamel recalled in the preface he wrote for the catalog that Picasso had chosen "France as the place of his destiny and his fulfillment." The eight o'clock news of French television devoted a few minutes to the exhibition, in which it was clear that the exhibition allowed Senegal to enter the modernity (as defined through French eyes) to which independence had opened the door. Alternating between views of the exhibition and picturesque Senegalese life, with traditional songs and percussion, the report concluded with a voice-over: "Dakar is a big city. It is obvious that in the villages of the bush, the name Picasso does not evoke anything. However, the Africa of today is not the Africa of yesterday, and tomorrow, who knows?"[38] For Duhamel too, the Picasso exhibition was a sign of an Africa "in communion with the most reliable values of the contemporary artistic movement." One must see in these reactions the impact of Senegalese soft power. The mythical aura of Picasso, a star and sacred monster of contemporary art in France, is reflected in Dakar, and his exhibition gives a new image of Senegal, relayed by the French media, which does not hesitate to contrast the "Africa" embodied by this Picasso exhibition in Dakar with the "Africa of yesterday," implicitly designating a colonized Africa.

THE CYCLE OF THE GREAT MASTERS: THE CHOICE OF ARTISTS FROM THE ÉCOLE DE PARIS AS AMBASSADORS OF MÉTISSAGE

This attraction for French painters, whose exhibitions he wanted to see associated with a "Senegalese artists show" in a broader "Dakar season,"[39] is best understood in the light of Senghor's political and philosophical ideas and his overall soft power. The artists chosen were not all French (only Soulages and Manessier were born in France), but they all belonged to the School of Paris, promoted by the French government in the creation of its own soft power. By choosing artists Senghor defined as *métis*, he sought to demonstrate that the path to modernity was a two-step operation: on one hand a "rooting" in one's own culture (Jewish in the case of Chagall, Andalusian in the case of Picasso, Celtic in the case of Soulages, from northern France in the case of Manessier, or African) and on the other an "openness to the fertile contributions of the foreigner."[40] The métissage theorized here by Senghor was not racial but cultural. At the end of the 1950s, Senghor had to abandon his aforementioned project of a confederation that would have linked the former African colonies, themselves organized in federations, and the French metropolis.[41] Such a policy aimed to avoid what he called the "balkanization" of Africa but was also guided by the conviction that the French and "Negro-African" civilizations were complementary. Indeed, Senghor wished to see the emergence of what he called a "Civilization of the Universal" for the twenty-first century through cultural crossbreeding. While he sought to project the image of a modern country abroad, and particularly in France, the exhibition of the most famous artists of the School of Paris was accompanied by a highly intellectualized discourse in which he chose to highlight the characteristics that underpinned his ideas. Senghor's cultural diplomacy thus aimed to decenter the world of the arts, organized around the West, by showing that each culture has its own traits capable of enriching a universal civilization. By multiplying his speeches and interviews, the president himself took on the responsibility of reconfiguring the conceptual tools applied to globalized artistic creation, such as influence, copying, and originality. At the time, the works of subaltern artists, especially those from the former colonial worlds, were still analyzed by art critics and agents through concepts forged in the colonial paradigm. Thus, art critics and commentators questioned the originality of subaltern artists and considered them imitators when they were inspired by Western artists or techniques. Conversely, Senghor underlined the aesthetic and philosophical shock of the discovery of the so-called Negro arts at the beginning of the twentieth century by the artists of the School of Paris and in the first place by Picasso. By insisting on this episode, which has been well documented by art historians,[42] he sought to demonstrate that African artists were imitators of the School of Paris, since the artists of the School of Paris themselves drew their inspiration from African artists. This essentialization of African artists, which included those who produced the objects in the early twentieth century as well as those who worked in Dakar and elsewhere in the 1960s and 1970s, was consistent with his definition of *Négritude*. However, with regard to Picasso and his link to the arts of Africa, Senghor failed to mention that the painter never ceased to demystify the African inspiration in his work, refusing to be reduced to it.

Finally, this discourse of decentering, while deployed in the context of art and culture, was part of a more general discourse of Senghor on the place given to Africa by France. The choice of artists working in France and the many proposals for Senegalese exhibitions in Paris lead one to believe that France, its government, its artists, and, to a lesser extent, its population were the primary targets of this discourse. The holding of an international colloquium on the subject of Picasso and Negro arts, bringing together French and African specialists and an accumulation of references to philosophers and anthropologists such as Pierre Teilhard de Chardin and Leo Frobenius, show that this discourse was primarily aimed at the intellectual elites of Senegal and abroad. Indeed, in 1971 the French embassy estimated that in Senegal only 10 percent of men and just 0.9 percent of women had a working knowledge of French.[43] This audience is in contradiction with the discourse that he deployed elsewhere on art and culture. Conceived as the condition and objective of the country's development, culture was presented by Senghor as one of the strong points of his policy. As part of his doctrine of African socialism, Senghor stated that art had to be made a bathing place for the Senegalese people, repeating that Senegal devoted a quarter of its budget to culture. Even though the state's support for certain Senegalese artists was exceptional, scholars have greatly reduced that amount.[44]

While the soft power policy developed by Senghor's government accommodated the constraints mentioned above, it took little account of the demands of political activists and came up against their occasionally violent protests. If the exhibitions were only attended by a small part of the population, the French presence in Dakar was a source of tension, and culture a symbolic target. While the government undertook a heavy cleanup of the streets of Dakar to welcome President Pompidou in January 1971, the French Cultural Center, a symbol for Senghor's opponents of the French presence in Senegal and his pro-French policy, was the target of an arson attack by a group that included two brothers of prominent student activist Omar Blondin Diop. The brothers were Senegalese political activists in the opposition and denounced the neocolonialist and conservative nature of the culture that was being shown there at the center.[45] The mid-1970s saw the birth of a politicized art collective that challenged Senghor's cultural policy, the Laboratoire Agit'Art, rejecting the elitist inspirations advocated by the Senegalese president.[46] Moreover, the artists of the School of Paris who were shown at the Musée Dynamique offered a consensual and not particularly politicized vision of art at a time when both French and Senegalese society were undergoing profound questioning linked in particular to the events of May 1968.

THE SCHOOL OF DAKAR IN PARIS: THE ESTABLISHMENT OF A SENEGALESE ARTISTIC CANON AS A KEY ELEMENT OF SENEGALESE SOFT POWER

For Senegalese artists, the Dakar exhibitions did have consequences. In his inaugural speeches, Senghor presented the exhibitions of the great masters as lessons for Senegalese artists. Despite the president's undoubted interest in his country's artists, one cannot imagine that this was the reason for these exhibitions. Although few artists visited all the exhibitions, some, like Ibou Diouf, were marked by their discovery of these works.[47] The generous behavior of Soulages and Manessier, who came to open their exhibitions, distinguished the event. They gave advice to the artists and toured the country.[48] However, the absence of Senegalese artists in the Musée Dynamique, which nonetheless celebrated Western artists, is striking. Although the museum hosted the Salon des Artistes Sénégalais on several occasions, exhibitions at the end of which the state regularly made purchases intended to enrich the "private collection of the State," they did not receive the publicity given by the Senegalese and French press to the exhibitions of the School of Paris. The only Senegalese artist who had the honor of a monographic exhibition in 1977 during Senghor's presidency was Iba Ndiaye, a famous painter who was called by Senghor to take over the direction of one of the sections of the Senegalese national school of fine art but who finally left the establishment and Senegal at the end of the 1960s to return to live in France. In response to this minimal investment, it is important to note that during the 1970s, the French Cultural Center began to exhibit more and more local artists, to the point where it is still today one of the nerve centers for artists in the capital.

The Picasso exhibition in Dakar was reported to be exceptional. In reality, it was in Paris that the miracle occurred. According to Senghor's French adviser, Gérard Bosio, the Dakar exhibition cycle was part of a strategy to force Senegalese art into the world of the whites and the French public institutions.[49] From this point of view it was a success. Elizabeth Harney notes that despite the stated intention to place art at the heart of Senegalese life and as a basis for social and economic development, the infrastructure put in place remained essentially export-oriented in order to promote the image of the nation and its aesthetic abroad.[50] The term "School of Dakar" referred to, and helped to spread, the image of a coherent Senegalese national art movement. In 1960, when his country gained independence, Senghor had to present the image of a coherent nation that drew on characteristics such as a national art "school." In support of this political project, he developed a soft power intended to disseminate abroad "a new art for a new nation." Indeed, the Senegalese government's efforts to promote its young artists focused on the organization of an exhibition, first in Paris, then internationally.

The joint study of the context and the archives allows us to understand the tour de force that a Parisian exhibition constituted at a time when African artists were not exhibited in France. The exhibition *Art sénégalais d'aujourd'hui* took place from April 26 to June 24, 1974, in the national galleries of the Grand Palais in Paris, thanks to the success of the Picasso exhibition and the diplomatic aspect of such a project. (It would have been difficult for the French government to say no to Senghor.) A first project was proposed by Bosio in 1971 and refused by French officials. The initial discussions of French museum officials in the same year showed the difficulty of appreciating this contemporary art from Africa. They imagined the project at the Musée des Arts d'Afrique et d'Océanie, but it was eventually planned for the Grand Palais. This was a venue favored by Malraux for major exhibitions during his term of office, but given that the Grand Palais hosted only temporary exhibitions and did not have curators of its own, it meant that French museum staff were less involved technically in the Senegalese project. By moving from an ethnographic museum to the Grand Palais, France was nonetheless accrediting contemporary Senegalese creation. Similarly, Jacques Lassaigne, curator of the Musée d'Art Moderne de la Ville de Paris, wrote the preface to the catalog. However, the quality of the works raised many concerns, as contemporary art was generally neglected by the French public, and French museums sent experts on site to select the works.[51]

The archival documents include numerous, notes, letters, and reports that testify to the difficulty French curators and politicians had understanding the art of Senegal, being equally puzzled about the accompanying descriptions, which had been phrased by a Senegalese curator. The absence of the words "Negro" and "Négritude" in the catalog seems surprising in retrospect, even though Senghor made them a leitmotif of his speeches from the beginning of his presidency, and the terms appeared in the press release. Although there is no document that sheds light on this disappearance, it is obvious that the emblematic "Research in Negro Plastic Arts" section of the Senegalese National School of Fine Arts is transformed in the catalog into the "Research in Plastic Arts" section. The 1970s was a time when this word was gradually abandoned in France, and the discourse here is adapted to fit French discourse, even if it does not reflect the cultural policies implemented in Senegal.

Senegal, through the action of the exhibition curator Souleymane Sidibé but also through Senghor's speeches on television, tried to present the group as coherent. The exhibition presented 143 works for the thirty-three artists, and despite the diversity of styles and mediums (painting, sculpture, tapestry), the selected works contributed to the establishment of an artistic canon. The artists presented were mostly very young and male (with the exception of the painter Younousse Sèye), and most of them had been trained at the Dakar School of Arts. For many of them, this was their very first exhibition. These artists worked in different mediums, formats, and in sometimes very different styles and dealt with equally diverse subjects. Through the press release signed by Souleymane Sidibé,[52] Senegal presented itself as the champion of the "black race"—the first nation to have formed a "true school whose homogeneity is obvious." The curator draws up a certain number of formal and thematic points in common, such as "strength, rhythm and stylization, in the line or approach to volume, the brilliance and sense of contrast in the color and the dominant themes: man and the gods."[53] This discourse is readily taken up by Jacques Lassaigne, who contributes to presenting Senegalese artists as a homogeneous group by taking up elements of

Souleymane Sidibé's statement in his preface.[54] The critical reception shows that this attempt was not a complete success. Raoul-Jean Moulin, a communist journalist and art critic specializing in Africa, published an article in *L'Humanité* titled "Artistes sénégalais d'aujourd'hui," in which he stated that there was no "Senegalese art" in the Grand Palais—only artists. However, several articles in major newspapers such as *Le Monde* gave the event a very positive echo. The media impact was also measured by the television broadcast of a report, during which President Senghor was interviewed.[55] Finally, as a sign of the great resources allocated to the promotion of the event, the poster of the exhibition was displayed in the metro.

Beyond the media echo of the exhibition, this event contributed to extending the friendly and professional network of Senegalese artists in France. These artists, who benefited from Senghor's artistic patronage in the form of grants and scholarships, contributed to the influence of Senegal abroad, in particular by seeing their image associated with those of prestigious international artists. At the same time as the Grand Palais's exhibitions, the artist Amadou Seck exhibited several Chinese inks in a Parisian gallery, La Tortue, in the prestigious and arty Saint-Germain des Près district. He remembers receiving visits from distinguished guests from the Senegalese government, such as Senegalese minister of culture Alioune Sène, former French prime minister Jacques Chaban-Delmas, and Senegalese ambassador to France André Guillabert as well as Pierre Soulages, whose exhibition in Dakar would open a few months later.[56] The success of the Paris exhibition led Senegal to make it the first stage of a ten-year tour. A special curatorial office for traveling exhibitions was created in Senegal, and the exhibition *Art sénégalais d'aujourd'hui*, soon renamed *Contemporary Art of Senegal*, made stops in Rome, Bonn, Mexico City, several cities in the United States, Brazil, and Japan, helping to make Senegalese artists known throughout the world. By presenting the artists as a cohesive national group around the world, this tour was an important part of Senegal's soft power strategy.[57]

CONCLUSION

Studied in the light of Senghor's recommendations, the exhibitions under review in this chapter formed a coherent program. On a discursive level, by systematically highlighting the métisse nature of the work of Western artists, his discourse constituted an attempt to subvert the main narrative of artistic modernity, to make it a métisse modernity. In 1989, looking back on the exhibition *Art sénégalais d'aujourd'hui*, Senghor felt that the exhibition marked the beginning of an outreach program that would make Senegalese artists ambassadors for their country.[58] The history of these exhibitions shows that the president also attributed this role to foreign artists, who allowed and authorized these events outside the framework of Franco-Senegalese cooperation. Finally, Senghor also took on the role of ambassador, challenging concepts forged in the colonial paradigm, such as influence, copy, and imitation, in order to serve the symbolic construction of his nation but also the rehabilitation of Black and African people and the hope of a shared universal world. Exhibitions were one of the main tools in the development of Senegalese soft power. The exhibitions of the World Festival of Negro Arts were added to those of the cycle of the great masters and finally the one in the Grand Palais. Senghor used French artists as champions of métissage and Senegalese artists as ambassadors of a new national art. Even today, Senegal's soft power is closely related to the country's ability to organize large-scale events, first and foremost the Dakar Biennial, an event dedicated to the continent's visual arts founded in 1990, whose success, aura, and resonance continue to grow.

NOTES

1. Guillaume de Sardes, Hélène Joubert, El Hadj Malick Ndiaye, and Ousseynou Wade, *Picasso à Dakar 1972–2022* (Paris: Louison, 2022).

2. Coline Desportes, "Les expositions Chagall, Picasso et Soulages au Musée Dynamique de Dakar" (MA thesis, Paris 1 Panthéon Sorbonne, 2018).

3. This expression was used in 1973 when the exhibition *Manessier* was not yet officially scheduled. It is, however, a continuation of the first three and can be included in the study.

4. There is substantial literature on the School of Dakar, with authors disagreeing on its definition. See Ima Ebong, "Negritude: Between Mask and Flag; Senegalese Cultural Ideology and the École de Dakar," in Susan Vogel, ed., *Africa Explores: 20th Century African Art* (New York: Center of African Art / Munich: Prestel-Verlag, 1991), 198–209; Elizabeth Harney, *In Senghor's Shadow: Art, Politics, and the Avant-garde in Senegal, 1960–1995* (Durham, NC: Duke University Press, 2004); Joanna Grabski, "Painting Fictions / Painting History: Modernist Pioneers at Senegal's Ecole des Arts," *African Arts* 39, no. 1 (spring 2006): 38–94; Abdou Sylla, *L'esthétique de Senghor et l'École de Dakar: Essai* (Dakar: Éditions Feu de Brousse, 2006); Joshua I. Cohen, "Locating Senghor's École de Dakar: International and Transnational Dimensions to Senegalese Modern Art, c. 1959–1980," *African Arts* 51, no. 3 (August 2018): 10–25.

5. The aforementioned article by Joshua I. Cohen marks an important turning point by highlighting the international and transnational aspects of the training and career of artists in Dakar. See also Coline Desportes, "L'exposition itinérante 'Art sénégalais d'aujourd'hui': Le regard de la France sur l'école de Dakar" (MA thesis, Paris 1 Panthéon Sorbonne, 2016); Desportes, "Les expositions Chagall, Picasso et Soulages"; Coline

Desportes, "Négociations et 'influence' sur le terrain des arts: Un échange d'objets entre la France et le Sénégal dans les années 1960," *Politique Africaine* 165, no. 1 (May 2022): 95–115, https://doi.org/10.3917/polaf.165.0095; and Alexandre Girard-Muscagorry, "La modernité en cadeau? Regards des acteurs étatiques africains sur les arts visuels nationaux," in *Avant que la 'magie' n'opère: Modernités artistiques en Afrique*, ed. Nora Greani and Maureen Murphy, published online 2017, https://hicsa.pantheonsorbonne.fr/sites/default/files/2023-09/livre_modernites_africaines.pdf.

6. Jody Blake, "Cold War Diplomacy and Civil Rights Activism at the First World Festival of Negro Arts," *Studies in the History of Art* 71 (2011): 43–58; David Murphy, *The First World Festival of Negro Arts, Dakar 1966: Contexts and Legacies* (Liverpool: Liverpool University Press, 2016); Cinquantenaire du Premier Festival des Arts Nègres et al., ed., *Le 1er festival mondial des arts nègres: Mémoire et actualité; Actes du colloque du cinquantenaire du 1er festival des arts nègres organisé à Dakar du 8 au 10 novembre 2016* (Paris: L'Harmattan, 2020); Éloi Ficquet and Lorraine Gallimardet, "On ne peut nier longtemps l'art nègre," *Gradhiva* 10, no. 2 (November 2009): 134–55.

7. Métissage can be translated as both "mixed blood" and "hybrid." We keep the term in French so as not to privilege one meaning over the other, as Senghor understood it in both its cultural and biological aspects.

8. Set up at the time of independence, development aid was granted by France to former French colonies in Africa to encourage their economic and social progress. Recent publications have shown how this public aid for development was conceived from the beginning by France as a political tool of influence. See Philippe Marchesin, *La politique française de coopération: Je t'aide, moi non plus* (Paris: L'Harmattan, 2021).

9. Archives Diplomatiques de la Courneuve (hereafter ADC), 349QO/99, Relations culturelles avec la France, dossier "Sénégal, affaires culturelles, centres culturels français Dakar, St Louis."

10. ADC, 239QO/622, Sénégal, dossier "Enseignement 62," letter from Jacques Mouradian, chargé de mission at the Dakar embassy, to the French minister for cooperation, July 21, 1962.

11. ADC, 555INVA/42, Répertoire des expositions françaises à l'étranger et étrangères en France organisées par l'AFAA (1957–69). These figures are based on a single directory and would need to be clarified by a more in-depth study.

12. This is an exhibition of reproductions in Elisabethville, Belgian Congo.

13. Archives diplomatiques de la Courneuve, 554INVA/1119, file "expositions de reproductions."

14. Sally Price, *Primitive Art in Civilized Places* (Chicago: University of Chicago Press, 1989), 93–94.

15. ADC, 349QO/98, "Vie culturelle. Arts and sports," subfile "exhibitions, September 62–May 72," letter from Jean de Lagarde Raymond Triboulet, minister delegate for cooperation, November 25, 1964, about the exhibition's "transports and transmissions." The ambassador describes a successful exhibition according to him: "As I have already had occasion to point out, what is didactic and intelligently popularized, what can contribute to the promotion of this country meets with a privileged audience in all its forms. . . . All the more so, when the theme, as was the case this time, responds to the curiosity and concerns of the greatest number." All quotes are translated from French by the author.

16. Centre des Archives Diplomatiques de Nantes (hereafter CADN), 184PO/1/407 Cote 9, dossier "VIII," letter from Paul Bonifay to André Malraux, January 20, 1964.

17. The French minister of cultural affairs stated during the press conference for the festival, "France can provide scientific aid, the aid of French scientists has never been political. . . . French aid and cooperation are not political, [and] the only friendly dialogue is the dialogue of the mind." Interview, *Journal Télévisé*, Channel 1, April 1, 1966, INAthèque, Paris.

18. ADC, 349QO/100, dossier "Europe Occidentale," courrier de Jean de Lagarde, Dakar, June 22, 1965. The French ambassador wrote, for example, about the signing of a cultural agreement with Spain in 1965, that "France cannot spend its time reminding the Senegalese how much they owe it."

19. The exhibition consisted of seven sections titled "Sources," "Prehistory," "Proto-history," "Senegal in the Context of the Great Empires," "Time of the Monarchs," "People of the Sea," and "Preludes to Modern Times."

20. This exhibition is almost always referred to as *Fresques du Tassili*, including in official documents and by historians such as Ousmane Sow Huchard. See Ousmane Sow Huchard, *La culture, ses objets-témoins et l'action muséologique: Sémiotique et témoignage d'un objet-témoin; Le masque Kanaga des Dogons de Sanga* (Dakar: Nègre International Éditions, 2010). I therefore use this title for the sake of clarity.

21. Assane Seck (1919–2012) was an academic who served as a minister of various portfolios from 1966 to 1983. From 1966 until 1968, he was Senegal's first minister of culture. He also served as minister of foreign affairs from 1973 to 1978.

22. CADN, 186/PO/834.

23. At first, requests for the repatriation were met with this kind of argument in the general discussion, but countries such as Benin and Senegal have demonstrated that they are perfectly capable of conserving their objects according to international standards. Such arguments seem to have disappeared fairly quickly from government dialogues.

24. French museums did lend a few smaller works, such as two tapestries from the Mobilier National. See the *Picasso* 1972 exhibition catalog.

25. *Le Poète et les Peintres*, an exhibition at the Bibliothèque Historique de la Ville de Paris, 2006. In 2021 G. Bosio donated part of his archives to the Musée du Quai Branly–Jacques Chirac.

26. See Desportes, "L'exposition itinérante 'Art sénégalais d'aujourd'hui,'" and AN, 20150160/208, file "L'art sénégalais d'aujourd'hui," subfile "Correspondance Gérard Bosio."

27. Archives of the Jean and Simone Lurçat Foundation, Paris, Senegal file, letter from Senghor to Jean Lurçat, Dakar, May 7, 1962.

28. Desportes, "Négociations et 'influence' sur le terrain des arts."

29. See Kathryn Boyer, "Association Française d'Action Artistique and the School of Paris," *Konsthistorisk Tidskrift / Journal of Art History* 70, no. 3 (September 2001): 157–70. Chagall and Picasso were shown in no fewer than forty exhibitions organized by the AFAA from 1949 to 1965.

30. See the work of Laurence Bertrand-Dorléac and Natalie Adamson, *Painting, Politics and the Struggle for the École de Paris, 1944–1964* (London: Routledge, 2016).

31. CADN, 184PO/1/844, dossier ACT. IV.4, subfile "Picasso exhibition," letter from Senghor to Georges Pompidou, March 8, 1972.

32. AN, 19890127/40, "Senegal" file, subfile "L'histoire du Sénégal Dakar décembre 1966," note by Robert Boyer, July 24, 1967.

33. E.g., *2000 Years of Painting in China, French Art from 1900 to 1925,* and *Leonardo da Vinci.*

34. AN, 20000137/28, dossier "Expositions," note of April 26, 1972: "These projects, while they bear witness to the special interest Senegal has always shown in French art, all presuppose a financial contribution from France."

35. CADN 184PO/1/403 1.1, note titled "Grandes lignes de l'action culturelle et perspectives d'avenir," n.d. De Gaulle is said to have exclaimed, "Is French culture not the heritage of France, which alone is entitled to make it known, to develop it and to defend it?"

36. ADC, 349QO/14, dossier "Synthèses 4 janvier–29 mars 1967," comment by the chargé d'affaires on the speeches made by Senghor: "From the presidential trip, which is coming to an end [in Egypt and in the UAE], we can only pick up the echoes in Dakar on the airwaves of Radio-Sénégal, which transmitted over and over again, from Cairo and Algeria, the series of toasts, speeches, and conferences given by President Senghor during his various trips. No doubt the Senegalese, great admirers of the art of oratory, are proud to have a president whose talent in this field shines brightly whenever the opportunity is provided. But how many will have been able to follow the new doctor honoris causa of Al-Azhar University in the meanders of his thought through the numerous quotations, the mark of great erudition, going from Greek and Latin authors, passing by Averroes, Saint Augustine, Frobenius, Ibn Khaldoun, and up to Teilhard de Chardin, to quote only the main ones."

37. "L'exposition Picasso à Dakar: Un tournant de l'histoire afro-européenne" *Le Figaro*, April 20, 1972.

38. *Journal Télévisé de Vingt Heures* (news program) on the chanel Première Chaîne de l'ORTF," April 29, 1972.

39. These two quotations are taken from the letter cited in note 30.

40. See the analysis of Ebong, "Negritude."

41. See Sébastien Heiniger, *Décolonisation, fédéralisme et poésie chez Léopold Sédar Senghor* (Paris: Classiques Garnier, 2022). See also Cohen, "Locating Senghor's École de Dakar."

42. The literature on this subject is extensive and begins soon after Picasso's discovery of the arts of Africa in the first decade of the twentieth century.

43. ADC, 349QO/3, dossier "compte-rendu annuel de l'ambassade, 1971." The majority of the population spoke only Wolof.

44. Notably by Joshua I. Cohen.

45. In 1971 Georges Pompidou went on an official tour of four African countries and stopped in Dakar. On this occasion, the streets were emptied of those considered undesirable and major works were undertaken. On January 15, 1971, the French Cultural Center was burned down. A leaflet described the French Cultural Center as "an instrument of propaganda and intoxication in the service of French imperialism." See CADN, 184PO/1/845, dossier ACT. IV. 5: "The French Cultural Center is an instrument of propaganda and intoxication in the service of French imperialism. The books found there, the films seen there, and all the activities that take place there are a systematic diffusion of reactionary French culture. This propaganda aims to 'assimilate' Senegalese youth, that is, to make them accept the myths of the inferiority of the BLACK and the superiority of the WHITE, so that we love everything but ourselves." The Marxist-Leninist brothers Blondin Diop were arrested. Omar Blondin Diop, who planned to get them released, was charged and died in prison, in murky circumstances that did not allow us to rule out the hypothesis of an assassination ordered by Jean Collin, the Senegalese minister of the interior.

46. See Harney, *In Senghor's Shadow*, 109–12, and Ebong, "Negritude."

47. See El Hadji Malick Ndiaye, "Présence de Picasso à Dakar: 1966–2022," in de Sardes, Joubert, Ndiaye, and Wade, *Picasso à Dakar 1972–2022*.

48. Interview by the author with Amadou Seck, Dakar, December 2021.

49. Interviews by the author with Gérard Bosio, Paris, February 2018 and September and October 2021.

50. Harney, *In Senghor's Shadow*, 78–79.

51. Desportes, "L'exposition itinérante 'Art sénégalais d'aujourd'hui.'" See also Maureen Murphy, "L'exposition 'L'art sénégalais d'aujourd'hui,' Paris, 1974," in *Déborder la négritude: Les arts à Dakar à partir des années 1960*, ed. Maureen Murphy and Mamadou Diouf (Dijon: Les Presses du Réel, 2020), 202.

52. The role of the latter is not clear, as the archived documents only rarely mention his name. AN, 20150160/208, file "L'art sénégalais d'aujourd'hui," subfile "Presse," unsigned press release.

53. AN, 20150160/208, file "l'Art sénégalais d'aujourd'hui."

54. Exhibition catalog, Galeries Nationales du Grand Palais, *Art sénégalais d'aujourd'hui*, 1974.

55. On French television shows: *Forum des Arts* show, May 26, 1974, ORTF; *24 Heures d'Actualités*, broadcast April 26, 1974; and *Journal Télévisé*, ORTF; JT 13H 07/06/1974, ORTF. See http://www.ina.fr/video/CAF91064746. The newspapers *Le Figaro* and *Le Monde* also devoted articles to the exhibition.

56. Interview by the author with Amadou Seck, Dakar, December 2021.

57. In the absence of a systematic catalog, it is difficult to trace all the stages of the exhibition. The Senegalese historian Abdou Sylla notes that it traveled on three continents to fourteen countries: France, Finland, Austria, Italy, Sweden, Norway, Mexico, the United States, Canada, Brazil, Japan, North Korea, South Korea, and China. Sylla, *L'esthétique de Senghor et l'École de Dakar*.

58. Friedrich Axt and Moussa Babacar Sy, eds., *Bildende Kunst der Gegenwart in Senegal* (Frankfurt am Main: Museum für Völkerkunde, 1989). See also Cohen, "Locating Senghor's École de Dakar."

Soft Power in History

Thoughts and Concepts for Future Research

*Sylvia Dummer Scheel, Charlotte Faucher,
and Camila Gatica Mizala*

The new framework to understand soft power that has been provided in *Soft Power beyond the Nation* built upon three thematic axes: first, the circulation of soft power models across national borders; second, the transnational collaboration undertaken by intermediate actors located between soft power sponsors and the target audience but whose interests and objectives did not necessarily align with those of the nation-state; and third, the role of nonnational identities, such as gender, race, and politics, which, on one hand shaped the soft power strategies of nonnational groups and on the other were instrumentalized by governments to enhance their "national" soft power. Here, we studied soft power from a historical perspective and drew upon transnational and pericentric approaches. In addition, the ten chapters that make up this volume allowed us to broaden the typical temporal and geographic understanding of soft power. Central to our approach was an effort to move forward the chronology of soft power, considering practices that took place well before the Cold War, and to decenter the discussion away from world powers. In doing so, we outlined a longer and more complex genealogy of soft power.

In the introduction we discussed how each of the chapters engages with and contributes to the book's three axes. In this conclusion, we deliberately move away from the book's tripartite conceptual framework to examine how each of the chapters approached the concept of soft power in their own distinct ways. Our aim is to signpost exciting questions that have promising relevance for the field of soft power. To do so, we offer below a succinct glossary of terms and arguments present in the chapters to show how the authors contributed to expanding the recent scholarship. Certainly, the terms that we highlight for each of the chapters were not all initially coined by the volume's contributors, yet they play a key role in the ways we can open up the concept of soft power.

Michael L. Krenn offered an early example of **science diplomacy** by exploring how the circulation of (pseudo) scientific knowledge shaped the development of ideas about race in the nineteenth and early-twentieth centuries. Focusing on a group of transnational white male scientists mostly based in North America and Western Europe, Krenn demonstrated how science served as a tool in international relations: ideas about race circulated not only in scholarly publications but also in letters exchanged among scientists as well as at academic conferences. The science diplomacy studied by Krenn facilitated international cooperation, strengthened the supposed superiority of Caucasians, and shaped Western countries' policies toward people of color both at home and abroad. Krenn not only approached science diplomacy in terms of networks, alliances, and knowledge transfer in transnational terms but also showed that the idea or pretense of "scientific knowledge" was a tool that shaped racial and social hierarchies and, by doing so, generated soft power.

Rui Kohiyama focused on the concept of *omotenashi*, meaning a Japanese-style hospitality or thoughtful attentiveness and care given to guests, which include traditional practices such as the tea ceremony. Kohiyama understands this term as part of the industry of tourism, which, she shows, has played a key role in Japan's soft power, in particular from the 1880s to the outbreak of World War II. Kohiyama's chapter encouraged us to think about the **bodily and sensory experience** of soft power: omotenashi was a unique aspect of the experience of attending the resorts she studies, and Japan was able to tap into this culture to attract foreigners to visit the country and live a particular experience of entertainment and pleasure.

Looking at the convergence of the soft power strategies between the USSR and African American groups, Meredith L. Roman introduced the significance of focusing on **activism** when it comes to soft power. In order to advance Black liberation, a group of African Americans saw in Soviet soft power strategies a way to further their antiracist agenda. At the same time, the USSR saw the opportunity to persuade what they considered the most oppressed group within US society to support the communist revolution, giving the Soviets the chance to get their ideas inside a country that seemed unapproachable. In this sense, the idea of revolution and a world beyond Jim Crow and its everyday violence could lead to a wider transformation of the West without the use of hard power. In short, both African Americans and the USSR actively sought to carry out their agendas, which, although aimed at different targets, found themselves in a virtuous circle. Roman's work highlighted both the power of precariousness, opportunity, and strategy when it comes to soft power.

In her chapter, Sylvia Dummer Scheel analyzed the complex **relationship between soft power and domestic propaganda**. She considers diasporas as an in-between audience where the traditional boundaries between these two forms of propaganda are blurred, generating a series of tensions. The chapter studied the public diplomacy that the government of Lazaro Cardenas directed toward the Mexican diasporic communities in the United States in the 1930s, while at the same time directing soft power toward US public opinion. Dummer Scheel particularly notes how difficult it is for governments to keep domestic and foreign propaganda arguments separate when addressing emigrants. In this case, given that the two messages went in opposite directions, propaganda for the diaspora went so far as to jeopardize Mexico's soft power in the United States.

When discussing the concept of soft power, the idea of attractiveness is often the first that appears. However, how does this attractiveness manifest? Drew Flanagan focused on the way local **aesthetic taste and cultural norms** were used by the French author and propagandist Robert Boutet in two of the places where he worked before and after World War II: Morocco and Germany. In both locations, Boutet's soft power efforts were based on studying the cultural codes of the populations he wanted to convince—in this case, the content and format of their folk legends—and then using them as a vehicle to introduce French "civilizing" ideas. Flanagan reminded us that scholars ought to study the "attractiveness" of soft power by considering local aesthetics *as well as* foreign cultural products.

Kelly R. Colvin explored the **absence of agency** on the part of the very individuals who came to be depicted as national symbols of soft power. By offering an original and transnational reading of the story of how, in 1969, French actress Brigitte Bardot became the face of Marianne, "the visual embodiment of the republic," she shows how Bardot actually had very little input in the process. Rather, a multitude of (often male) individuals—French government agents, French unofficial diplomats, and American journalists—worked hard to build Bardot into a French icon, capitalizing on femininity as an international commodity both for the economy and the reputation of the nation.

Cyril Cordoba highlighted the tensions behind the rhetoric of friendship as soft power built by the People's Republic of China (PRC) by comparing it to a **clientelist system**, where the title of "friend" is given in exchange for loyalty. Through this exercise, the asymmetrical relationship of the friendship associations becomes apparent, showing how an intricate network was built. The hierarchical nature of being a "friend of the PRC" translated into resources (both material and symbolic), working almost like a validation stamp that had a direct impact on their connection with China, which was equally beneficial for both the PRC and the associations. This mutual benefit also meant that, as Cordoba highlighted in his chapter, the clientelist aspect did not change the motivation toward friendship of the protagonists involved.

In her chapter, Claire Nicolas discussed the uses of **sports diplomacy** and how table tennis could take an active part in a country's diplomacy in the context of African nations gaining independence. What was at stake were not only games but also an image of the nation, making sportsmen and sportswomen key in the display of new definitions of citizenship and nationhood, both at home and at international level. In short, athletes became national envoys and agents of soft power who did not always participate willingly in the nation-building process.

In her chapter, Maria Montt Strabucchi approached the role of **materiality** in soft power from two angles. On one hand, she studied the role of crafts as a meeting point between the PRC and the interests of the Chilean intellectual Tomás Lago, invited to visit by the Chinese government in 1957. Lago subsequently disseminated "traditional" Chinese crafts in Chile through exhibitions and a book. These handicrafts and the explanations that accompanied them expressed traditional China but at the same time carried political connotations in relation to the PRC. On the other hand, Montt Strabucchi problematized the role of the book written by Lago as an object that had an afterlife of its own. It fulfilled a mediating and disseminating role of Chinese culture in Chile not only at the time it was written but continues to do so to this day.

Finally, by looking at **patronage**, Coline Desportes explored the political dimensions of backing art from a national perspective. By looking at Senegal's former president and poet Léopold Sédar Senghor and how he assumed key roles in the art world as critic, patron, collector, and policymaker, Desportes was able to draw transnational and international artistic circulations between Senegal and Europe (mainly France). Through patronage and indeed being associated with internationally acknowledged artists, Senghor was not only able to consolidate Senegal's political influence but his own international reputation too.

These chapters explored, stretched, and went beyond recent scholarly understandings of soft power. They offered new ways of thinking about how different actors have approached tools of soft power throughout the world and during the modern period. We hope that this edited volume will encourage scholars to continue thinking about soft power through transnational and pericentered approaches. Historical analyses still have much to say about this concept, and as new questions and perspectives emerge in the field of history of international relations, they will also feed into the scholarship on soft power.

As we complete this years-long book project, we would like to outline three promising areas for future research. First, there remains much to be said about the material aspect of soft power in history. This dimension is being discussed in relation to current digital technologies,[1] but it is also relevant to ask about their past manifestations. Thus, following actor-network theories that invite us to consider the agency of the material,[2] it is possible to ask about the role that various technologies, artifacts, and media have historically played in shaping the scope of soft power as well as in constraining its possibilities. The material is often an economic resource that amplifies the potential of soft power, given the control of certain nation-states over physical infrastructures (e.g., ports, railways, steamship lines, and aviation) and information and communication technologies (e.g., radio stations and cable and telegraph networks). This has led several authors to recognize that the success of soft power can be directly linked to hard power.[3] However, the material dimension of soft power is not limited to its means of dissemination but also to the material expressions developed to display national symbolism and ideas—such as in architecture and design[4]—and the way these are experienced by their recipients. As noted above, Montt Strabucchi's chapter in this book addressed these issues. One might also look into the role of material culture for soft power, building on ongoing research on fashion, international relations, and influence. This relatively new strand of research speaks to questions of gender and "nation brand" and reflects on how and why some governments considered fashion a field worthy of receiving state funding.[5]

Second, in the debate over impact and reception of soft power policies, historians ought to recognize the agency of those on the receiving end at different levels. Studying how local audiences interpret and create their own meanings based on their own cultural contexts therefore matters. It is also important to examine the extent to which local actors and institutions replicate the messages received by making decisions based on them. In addition, as Desportes reminded us when evoking the diverging attitudes of the French government over the 1972 Picasso exhibition in Dakar when it first opened and when it was commemorated in 2022, the reception of soft power policy has a chronology of its own and must be understood both in the short and long term. Certainly, the methodological issues on reception that preoccupies those who study soft power today are even more challenging for historians.[6] Essentially, it is often difficult to measure reception in part because historians cannot conduct surveys or focus groups retrospectively, making reception of soft power a thorny issue that continues to pose methodological problems. For example, the reports produced by government officials on the efficiency of soft power tend to highlight success rather than failure, in part because there were elements such as career progression or funding requests at stake. But as some scholars have pointed out, other sources and methods can be explored to suggest a causality between campaigns and outcomes, such as local media coverage of foreign public diplomacy messages;[7] public opinion polls carried out during the period under study;[8] and the opinions and imaginaries about other nations captured in chronicles, literature, and illustrations.[9] Some chapters in this book touched on reception tangentially. These include Montt Strabucchi's chapter on the travelers' reinterpretation of the Chinese reality and the knowledge of China in Chile in the long term and Dummer Scheel's chapter on the negative reaction of American authorities to Mexican propaganda in the United States.

Third, intersectionality is a method that historians of soft power might want to turn to in order to appreciate the overlapping and interdependent cultural and social dynamics at play in the making of soft power. As we highlighted in the introduction, some of the chapters in this volume that touched on or focused on gender also contributed to thinking about race (in particular the texts by Colvin and Kohiyama). Other scholars have thought about how upper-class white women were able to draw on their looks as well as socioeconomic and cultural capital to raise themselves to the position of unofficial cultural diplomats.[10] Krenn's chapter also explored a masculine world (academic science in the nineteenth and early twentieth century) to make a broader argument on race. Intersectionality is also fruitful to debunk the often narrow definitions of who a diplomat was. As this volume showed, in the context of soft power official diplomats were not the only ones to produce and implement policies of soft power. Intersectionality helps to open up the masculine, often white, world of diplomacy to appreciate that there were individuals (including people who were long forbidden to or prevented from working for their country's foreign offices owing to their gender, religion, or race) who operated as agents of soft power.

To conclude, material culture, reception, and intersectionality are but three elements of soft power that we hope will continue to fuel discussion among historians and scholars from other disciplines.

NOTES

1. Craig Hayden, "Technologies of Influence: The Materiality of Soft Power in Public Diplomacy (Section Overview)," in *The Routledge Handbook of Soft Power*, ed. Naren Chitty et al. (London: Routledge, 2016).

2. Bruno Latour, *Reassembling the Social: An Introduction to Actor-Network Theory* (Oxford: Oxford University Press, 2007).

3. Ludovic Tournès, *Américanisation: Une histoire mondiale, XVIIIe–XXIe siècle* (Paris: Fayard, 2020), 210.

4. Melissa Nisbett, "Who Holds the Power in Soft Power?," *Arts and International Affairs* 1, no. 1 (2016): 11, https://doi.org/10.18278/aia.1.1.7; Ivan Filipović, and Dragana Tomić, "Japanska soft power arhitektura: (Ne)namerno i neočekivano u politici kulturne razmene" [Japanese soft power architecture: (Un)intentional and incidental in culture relations policies], *Arhitektura i urbanizam* 49 (2019): 18–31, https://doi.org/10.5937/a-u0-24483; Louise Hardiman, *Courtly Gifts and Cultural Diplomacy: Art, Material Culture and British-Russian Relations* (Paderborn, Ger.: Brill Schöningh, 2023).

5. Sophie Kurkdjian, *Géopolitique de la mode: Vers de nouveaux modèles?* (Paris: Le Cavalier Bleu, 2021); Vincent Dubé-Senécal, "Fashion's Diplomatic Role: An Instrument of French Prestige-Based Commercial Diplomacy, 1960s–1970s," *International Relations*, published online 2022, https://doi.org/10.1177/00471178221123506; Susan E. Hiner, "Fashion's Soft Power in Nineteenth-Century France: Introduction," *Dix-Neuf* 26, no. 4 (2022): 187–91, https://doi.org10.1080/14787318.2023.2166860.

6. David Clarke, "Theorising the Role of Cultural Products in Cultural Diplomacy from a Cultural Studies Perspective," *International Journal of Cultural Policy* 22, no. 2 (March 14, 2016): 147–63, https://doi.org/10.1080/10286632.2014.958481.

7. E.g., Charlotte Faucher uses press articles about foreign cultural events and institutions in twentieth-century Britain not in an empirical way but as indicators of the success of cultural diplomacy: the fact that newspapers agreed to reproduce verbatim a press release issued by a foreign cultural institution or even the propaganda office signals that the efforts of diplomats to reach foreign audiences were successful. See Charlotte Faucher, *Propaganda, Gender, and Cultural Power: Projections and Perceptions of France in Britain c. 1880–1944* (Oxford: Oxford University Press, 2022), 18–19.

8. Kornel Chang, "Muted Reception: U.S. Propaganda and the Construction of Mexican Popular Opinion during the Second World War," *Diplomatic History* 38, no. 3 (June 2014): 569–98, https://doi.org/10.1093/dh/dht107; David Welch, *The Third Reich: Politics and Propaganda* (London: Routledge, 2002).

9. Maria Montt Strabucchi, *Representations of China in Contemporary Latin American Literature (1987–2016)* (Liverpool: Liverpool University Press, 2023).

10. Charlotte Faucher, "Restoring the Image of France in Britain, 1944–1947," *Historical Journal* 64, no. 5 (December 2021): 1428–48, doi:10.1017/S0018246X21000017; Robert Huesca, "The Mexican Oil Expropriation," ed. Institute of Latin American Studies, University of Texas at Austin, *Texas Papers on Latin America* 88, no. 4 (1988).

CONTRIBUTORS

Kelly R. Colvin is an assistant professor of history at the University of Massachusetts Boston, where she specializes in modern French gender and cultural history. She is the author of two books on those subjects, *Gender and French Identity after the Second World War, 1944–1954: Engendering Frenchness*, about gender and postwar recovery, and *Charm Offensive: Commodifying Femininity in Postwar France*, about the development and spread of idealized French femininity, as well as several peer-reviewed articles. She is currently working on a project about conceptions of food and identity in late twentieth-century France.

Cyril Cordoba is a postdoctoral researcher teaching contemporary history at the University of Fribourg and UniDistance (Switzerland). His first book, *China-Swiss Relations during the Cold War*, was published in both French and English. He has contributed essays to volumes such as *Europe and China in the Cold War* and *Transnational History of Switzerland* and coedited a special issue of the historical journal *Traverse* about Switzerland and East Asia. His second book deals with the political history of the Locarno International Film Festival (1946–83), a hub for "emerging cinema."

Coline Desportes is a PhD candidate at the École des Hautes Études en Sciences Sociales and the Institut National d'Histoire de l'Art. Her dissertation focuses on the history of tapestry in Senegal and the cultural diplomacy of Léopold Sédar Senghor. She published her first works in journals such as *Politique Africaine, Critique d'Art,* and *Perspective*. She is a member of the Groupe Senghor International (formed by the École Normale Supérieure, the Centre National de la Recherche Scientifique, and the Université Cheikh Anta Diop) and teaches African art history at the École du Louvre.

Sylvia Dummer Scheel is a historian specializing in the cultural and transnational history of Latin America in the twentieth century. Her work has focused on public diplomacy and the representation of national imaginaries in Chile and Mexico. She obtained her PhD from the Freie Universität Berlin with a thesis on the foreign propaganda of the Mexican government of Lázaro Cárdenas. Her postdoctoral project, funded by Fondecyt-ANID and held at the Pontificia Universidad Católica de Chile, focused on Chile's public diplomacy from 1920 to 1970. She is the author of *Sin tropicalismos ni exageraciones: La construcción de la imagen de Chile para la Exposición Iberoamericana de Sevilla en 1929* [No tropicalisms or exaggerations: The construction of Chile's image for the Ibero-American Exposition of Seville in 1929] and several academic articles on the public diplomacy of Mexico and Chile in the first half of the twentieth century. She is currently a lecturer at the Instituto de Historia and Escuela de Diseño at the Pontificia Universidad Católica de Chile.

Charlotte FAUCHER is a lecturer in modern French history at the University of Bristol. Her research has been supported by Horizon 2020 and the British Academy. She previously conducted research at Paris 3 Sorbonne Nouvelle and the University of Manchester. Her first monograph was *Propaganda, Gender, and Cultural Power: Projections and Perceptions of France in Britain c. 1880–1944*. She has written several articles on women in diplomacy, including one on gender and French soft power during the liberation of France, for the *Historical Journal* (2021), and "Women, Gender and the Professionalisation of French Cultural Diplomacy in Britain, 1900–1940," for the *English Historical Review*. Other pieces have appeared in the *Journal of Contemporary History* and the *European Review of History*, and she is currently coediting a book on French cultural diplomacy. Her next book-length project is a transnational history of European cultural diplomacy from 1870 to 1940.

Drew FLANAGAN is a historian of modern France and Germany, with a research focus on transnational and borderlands history and the impact of European colonial projects on European politics and societies. He is currently an assistant professor of international and global history at the University of Pittsburgh at Bradford. His current book project focuses on the French occupation of southwestern Germany after World War II. It considers France's efforts at remaking German culture and society in its zone of occupation, with an emphasis on the application of "civilizing" methods developed in France's overseas colonies to a European population.

Camila GATICA MIZALA is an assistant professor at Universidad de Chile's Departamento de Ciencias Históricas. Her research has been funded by Fondecyt-ANID and the Institute of Latin American Studies (now CLACS,

School of Advanced Studies, University of London). Her first monograph was *Modernity at the Movies: Cinema-Going in Buenos Aires and Santiago, 1915–1945*. She has published articles on the Americanization of Chilean society and cultural diplomacy in Argentina and Chile. Other pieces have appeared in different books on Latin American cinema. She is currently working on an edited volume on the concept of resilience.

Chandrika KAUL is a professor of modern history at the University of St Andrews. She received her doctorate from the University of Oxford and is a historian of modern Britain, imperialism, and the media. She was awarded the prestigious Leverhulme Major Research Fellowship for a project on the BBC's soft power in India, to be published as a book. Her areas of interest and publications include modern communications, British media and politics, the British monarchy, imperial propaganda, and modern South Asia, especially India. She is author, editor, or coeditor of several books, including *Communications, Media and the Imperial Experience: Britain and India in the Twentieth Century*; *Reporting the Raj: The British Press and India c. 1880–1922*; *Media and the British Empire*; and *International Communications and Global News Networks: Historical Perspectives*. She is the founding coeditor of the major book series Palgrave Studies in the History of the Media.

Rui KOHIYAMA is the president of Ferris University and was formerly a professor of American and gender studies at Tokyo Woman's Christian University in Japan. Some of her books and articles include *Amerika Fujin Senkyoshi: Rainichi no Haikei to Sono Eikyo* (American women missionaries: Their backgrounds and influences), which received Aoyama Nao Award for distinguished book on women's history; *Teikoku no Fukuin: Lucy Peabody to Amerika no Kaigai Dendo* (The gospel of empire: Lucy Peabody and the American foreign mission enterprise), which received Nakahara Nobuyuki Award for distinguished book in American studies; and "The 1927 Exchange of Friendship Dolls: U.S.-Japan Cultural Diplomacy in the Inter-War Years," *Diplomatic History* 43, no. 2 (April 2019).

Michael L. KRENN is a professor of history at Appalachian State University. He received his PhD from Rutgers University, where he studied with Lloyd Gardner. His books include *The Color of Empire: Race and American Foreign Relations*; *Fall-out Shelters for the Human Spirit: American Art and the Cold War*; and *The History of U.S. Cultural Diplomacy: From 1770 to the Present Day*. His book *Black Diplomacy: African Americans and the State Department, 1945–1969* helped to inspire the documentary *The American Diplomat*, which premiered on the PBS series *American Experience* in 2022.

Maria Montt Strabucchi is an associate professor at the Institute of History and a member of the Asian Studies Center at the Pontificia Universidad Católica de Chile. She is also an alternate director of the Millenium Nucleus on the Impacts of China in LAC. She holds a PhD in Latin American cultural studies from the University of Manchester and an MA in Chinese studies from the School of Oriental and African Studies of the University of London and is licentiate in history from the Pontificia Universidad Católica de Chile. Her research interests are the representations of China in Latin America, travel to China since the Cold War, and the overall cultural and political relationship between China and Latin America.

Claire Nicolas is a historian with a strong focus on transnational and transimperial history. She holds a PhD from Lausanne University and Sciences Po Paris. Since 2020 she has been a research fellow at the Swiss National Science Foundation. Her research interests center on gender and leisure in West Africa, with a forthcoming monograph to be titled *Une si longue course: Sport, genre et citoyenneté au Ghana et en Côte d'Ivoire (années 1900–1970)* [So long a race: Sports, gender, and citizenship in Ghana and Côte d'Ivoire (1900–1970)]. She has also published in academic journals such as *Monde(s)* and *Politique Africaine*. In parallel, she taught global history at the University of Lausanne and the School of Oriental and African Studies.

Meredith L. Roman is an associate professor of history at the State University of New York Brockport, an alumna of the Comparative Black History Program at Michigan State University, and the author of *Opposing Jim Crow: African Americans and the Soviet Indictment of U.S. Racism, 1928–1937*. Her research has appeared in several academic journals, including the *Journal of Communist Studies and Transition Politics, Race and Class, Cold War History,* the *Journal of Russian American Studies,* and *Women, Gender, and Families of Color.* Her current book project compares human rights activism and political repression in the Soviet Union and United States during the Cold War.